DROP TOO MANY

The Stackpole Military History Series

THE AMERICAN CIVIL WAR
Cavalry Raids of the Civil War
Ghost, Thunderbolt, and Wizard
Pickett's Charge
Witness to Gettysburg

WORLD WAR II
Armor Battles of the Waffen-SS, 1943–45
Army of the West
Australian Commandos
The B-24 in China
Backwater War
The Battle of Sicily
Beyond the Beachhead
The Brandenburger Commandos
The Brigade
Bringing the Thunder
Coast Watching in World War II
Colossal Cracks
A Dangerous Assignment
D-Day to Berlin
Dive Bomber!
A Drop Too Many
Eagles of the Third Reich
Exit Rommel
Fist from the Sky
Flying American Combat Aircraft of World War II
Forging the Thunderbolt
Fortress France
The German Defeat in the East, 1944–45
German Order of Battle, Vol. 1
German Order of Battle, Vol. 2
German Order of Battle, Vol. 3
The Germans in Normandy
Germany's Panzer Arm in World War II
GI Ingenuity
The Great Ships
Grenadiers
Infantry Aces
Iron Arm
Iron Knights
Kampfgruppe Peiper at the Battle of the Bulge
Kursk
Luftwaffe Aces
Massacre at Tobruk

Mechanized Juggernaut or Military Anachronism?
Messerschmitts over Sicily
Michael Wittmann, Vol. 1
Michael Wittmann, Vol. 2
Mountain Warriors
The Nazi Rocketeers
On the Canal
Operation Mercury
Packs On!
Panzer Aces
Panzer Aces II
Panzer Commanders of the Western Front
The Panzer Legions
Panzers in Winter
The Path to Blitzkrieg
Retreat to the Reich
Rommel's Desert Commanders
Rommel's Desert War
The Savage Sky
A Soldier in the Cockpit
Soviet Blitzkrieg
Stalin's Keys to Victory
Surviving Bataan and Beyond
T-34 in Action
Tigers in the Mud
The 12th SS, Vol. 1
The 12th SS, Vol. 2
The War against Rommel's Supply Lines
War in the Aegean

THE COLD WAR / VIETNAM
Cyclops in the Jungle
Flying American Combat Aircraft: The Cold War
Here There Are Tigers
Land with No Sun
Street without Joy
Through the Valley

WARS OF THE MIDDLE EAST
Never-Ending Conflict

GENERAL MILITARY HISTORY
Carriers in Combat
Desert Battles
Guerrilla Warfare

A DROP TOO MANY

A Paratrooper at Arnhem

John Frost

STACKPOLE
BOOKS

Copyright © 1994, 2002 the Executors of the late Major-General J.D. Frost

Published in paperback in 2008 by
STACKPOLE BOOKS
5067 Ritter Road
Mechanicsburg, PA 17055
www.stackpolebooks.com

A DROP TOO MANY: A PARATROOPER IN ARNHEM by John Frost was origi-
nally published in hardcover by Leo Cooper, an imprint of Pen & Sword Ltd.,
South Yorkshire, England. Copyright © 1994, 2002 the Executors of the late Major-
General J.D. Frost. Paperback edition by arrangement with Pen & Sword Ltd.

Cover design by Tracy Patterson

Printed in the United States of America

10 9 8 7 6 5 4 3 2 1

ISBN 0-8117-3486-2 (Stackpole paperback)
ISBN 978-0-8117-3486-8 (Stackpole paperback)

The Library of Congress cataloging-in-publication data:
Frost, John, 1912–
  A drop too many : a paratrooper at Arnhem / John Frost.
     p. cm.
  Originally published: London : Leo Cooper, 2002.
  Includes index.
  ISBN-13: 978-0-8117-3486-8
  ISBN-10: 0-8117-3486-2
  1. Frost, John, 1912– 2. Great Britain. Army. Parachute Regiment. Battalion, 2nd.
  3. Arnhem, Battle of, Arnhem, Netherlands, 1944—Personal narratives, British. 4.
  World War, 1939–1945—Prisoners and prisons, German. 5. Great Britain. Army—
  Biography. 6. Generals—Great Britain—Biography. I. Title.
  D759.63.F76 2008
    940.54'1241092—dc22
    [B]
                          2008041387

To every man in the Second Battalion of the
Parachute Regiment:
past, present, and in the future

PARACHUTE BATTALION

Platoon by platoon in formation proudly,
Plane upon plane from the valley's mouth,
Piercing, with their black-winged squadrons
In powerful flight, the dark hill.

To the wild pipe's bidding
Last night they danced reel and jig,
Glad for the light in each other's eyes;
To the wild pipe's bidding
They have sprung at the unknown shadows of the North

In what lowering mountain range
Will they make their stand and fight
And which strange-named stream shall be their bed,
Lying quietly together, strong in death?

To-day some silent valley of Tunisia
Shall tremble at their stroke from sky unsheathed,
And, with the night, perhaps some God looking down
With dull, cold eyes, by the near stars, will see
One lonely, grim battalion cut its way
Through agony and death to fame's high crown,
And wonderingly watch the friendless strength
Of little men, who die that the great Truths shall live.

Richard Spender

Contents

Illustrations and Maps

following page 176

The Officers of the 2nd Battalion the Parachute Regiment
Emplanement*
Men dropping on to their D.Z.s eight miles from Arnhem*
Tough-looking S.S. Panzer Grenadiers*
Arnhem bridge on the first day, taken by a Spitfire pilot*
Lieut-General Willi Bittrich, G.O.C. of the 2nd S.S.
    Panzer Corps
Field Marshal Walter Model, C.-in-C. of the German
    Armies in the West
The ruins of the building from which H.Q. of the 1st
    Parachute Brigade operated (*Ministry of Defence,
    Crown Copyright*)
Lieut-Col. John Frost addressing the people of Arnhem in
    1945*
The bridge at Deventer used to represent Arnhem Bridge
    in the film *A Bridge Too Far* (*By courtesy of* United
    Artists and the National Film Archive)

**Imperial War Museum* photographs

Maps

Preface

I began to write this book while I was a prisoner-of-war and the memory of the battle of Arnhem was fresh in my mind. I kept the original draft under my bedclothes when we were visited by the Gestapo, so I feel that it must have some authentic value. I made several attempts to finish it, but so much intervened that I was discouraged from going further. However, since the publication of *A Bridge Too Far* by Cornelius Ryan, and the production of the film of the same title, I have been urged by so many people to tell my own story that I have now succumbed. With the active encouragement of my wife, Jeannie, I have written an account of my war service which will, I hope, interest and amuse people and yet provide some lessons for my peers and happy recollections for our old soldiers.

The story starts with my service with the Iraq Levies, when I commanded No. 2 Assyrian Company, a body of men whose watchword was 'Perfection'. They set a standard which I have never seen exceeded. Whether they could have withstood the hard pounding that British troops habitually do I cannot say, but they were the direct descendants of the Assyrians of old whose 'cohorts were gleaming in purple and gold', and as such I shall always remember them.

After a short sojourn with my old regiment, the Cameronians (Scottish Rifles), always outstanding for dour, dogged slogging matches in every campaign and whose soldiers were as hardy and enduring as any in the world, I ventured into something quite new – the Airborne Forces.

I hope that I have said enough in the following chapters to convey just what stuff the paratroops were made of. They were men of whom you could never ask too much. Wherever there was a Red Beret, there was a way.

Although some of the actions have been described before, especially Arnhem, Bruneval and Sicily, I am so glad to be able to narrate the part played by the 1st Parachute Brigade when, after completing their initial airborne operations in the Tunisian compaign, they remained to fight as infantry almost to the end. We were not meant to be so employed (indeed, Winston Churchill was adamant that we should not), but the generals on the spot were so hard-pressed that we had to be. The snag was that both the Prime Minister and the public at home had to be hoodwinked, and so the Press were debarred from our part of the front and all our fighting was attributed to other units and formations. We did not know of this at the time for we seldom saw newspapers from home, but it did hurt when letters from relatives implied that we must be having a nice easy life lying about under the Mediterranean sun. When one had been swopping punches with the German Parachute Regiment, Sturmregiment Koch, the Witzig Regiment and the 10th Panzer, one felt entitled to credit for having opposed crack German army units.

Much has been said and written about the battle of Arnhem, that great venture which could have changed the course of history had it been pursued with the vigour it deserved, but as I am so often asked: 'What went wrong at Arnhem?' it is perhaps appropriate that I should take this opportunity of saying what I think.

The unwillingness of the air forces to fly more than one sortie in the day was one of the chief factors that militated against success. The transport aircraft could have been loaded before dawn on D-day, taken off at dawn, completed their mission and returned in time to have embarked their second lifts by noon. This would have allowed the bulk of the first lifts to make straight for the main objectives and dispensed with the time-consuming commitment to secure the D.Z.s for lifts on following days, when the weather might, and did, cause further delay.

Then again, the air force planners who insisted that the

farmland between the rivers was unsuitable for landing gliders and that the enemy flak was too formidable to allow D.Z.s near the objectives, exerted a fatal handicap on the airborne troops. The exact locations of all the guns had been made known by the Dutch underground, and with the degree of air superiority available, it is unduly pessimistic to maintain that these could not have been destroyed or neutralized.

The presence north of Arnhem of 2nd S.S. Panzer Corps was known to H.Q.s Army Group, Army and Airborne Corps, yet this vital information was withheld from H.Q.s XXX Corps and 1st British Airborne Division. Perhaps it was feared that the troops involved would jib at going if they knew, but it had the effect of making the leading brigade of 1st Airborne adopt the wrong plan and deprived it of the opportunity of increasing its anti-tank capability. The 1st Parachute Brigade advanced on a broad front, which is quickest when the opposition is thought to be light, but the worst course to take when it is otherwise. Thus, when one of the battalions succeeded in reaching the bridge, the others had become too involved to be readily switched on to the going route.

Failure by both the Army and the Air Force to make full use of the Dutch underground meant that a most effective means of producing and confirming information was discarded. It was known that the underground had been partially penetrated, but it was still highly organized and consisted of people of great courage and integrity. Perhaps it was wise not to give warning of the impending operation, but once the landing had taken place, every chance should have been taken of using their services, for they had much to give.

However, by far the worst mistake was the lack of priority given to the capture of Nijmegen Bridge. The whole essence of the plan was to lay an airborne carpet across the obstacles in southern Holland so that the Army could motor through, yet the capture of this, perhaps the biggest and most vital bridge in that its destruction would have sounded the death-knell of the troops committed at Arnhem, was not accorded priority. The capture of this bridge would have been a walk-over on D-day, yet the

American 82nd Airborne Division could spare only one battalion as they must at all costs secure a feature called the Groesbeek Heights, where, incidentally, the H.Q. of Airborne Corps was to be sited. It was thought that the retention of this feature would prevent the debouchment of German armour from the Reichwald in Germany. This armour was there by courtesy of rumour only and its presence was not confirmed by the underground. In fact, as a feature it is by no means dominating and its retention or otherwise had absolutely no bearing on what happened at Nijmegen Bridge.

The very presence of the Airborne Corps H.Q. was nothing more than a nuisance. Airlift that could have been used to fly in another combat unit was squandered and the commander would have been far more effective if he had remained with the air commander in the U.K., whence he could have directed resupply and the movement of reinforcements and reserves. The failure of communications at all levels within the Airborne Corps was phenomenal, but a commander with all the resources of the Air Forces in the U.K., near at hand, would have had many options open. Incidentally, whereas the communications within the infantry and signals were so abysmal, the Royal Artillery net was excellent throughout.

Finally, when it was decided that Nijmegen Bridge ought to be taken, the Germans had been able to strengthen their hold to such an extent that the American parachute troops had to paddle across the river in British canvas assault boats, with which they were totally unfamiliar. This most unpleasant task was carried out in daylight in the teeth of well-established opposition and really must rank as one of the bravest feats of all time. This Division was inspired by General James Gavin, and it was a pity that so little credit was given to it by the allies, either then or since. At the time censorship within the British chain of command precluded the appearance of accounts in the Press.

The German generalship was vigorous and inspired. Field Marshal Model, the German C.-in-C., who had his Sunday lunch party rudely interrupted by the arrival of British troops in Oosterbeek, near Arnhem, drove around the German positions like a devil possessed. He was able to telephone direct to Hitler's H.Q. asking for reinforcements and to galvanize his subordinates with formidable threats. On the right flank of the advancing British Army was the highly experienced old parachutist, General Student. Considerably helped by the capture of a map which showed in detail all his opponents' plans and strengths, he continually urged his men to break through the thin British corridor leading past him northwards, and this greatly inhibited our own efforts to reach the objectives. On our left flank, German troops were moved across water obstacles in broad daylight, apparently unimpeded by our air forces, and these were brought to bear against the westerly positions of our beleaguered Airborne in due course.

At the time, the Prime Minister and the C.I.G.S. were away in Canada at the Quebec Conference, so perhaps all concerned on our side breathed a little easier and tended to take things a bit more quietly. Whether this is the case or not, there does seem to have been a lack of drive all the way through the British chain of command. In Field Marshal Montgomery's memoirs there is no mention of his visiting and urging anyone to greater exertions. General Horrocks, XXX Corps Commander, was not once visited by General Dempsey, the 2nd Army Commander, during the whole nine days of battle. Indeed, on one occasion, Horrocks, this most gallant of all generals, had to turn part of his spearhead about so as to open the corridor behind him. General O'Connor, XIII Corps Commander on the right flank, was not even told about the operation until the day before it was due and then his orders were merely to sidestep and take over the XXX Corps front. Yet this was the Corps which would have been able to fend off all the efforts of General Student to cut the XXX Corps corridor.

So maybe some of our generals were having an off-day, or several off-days for that matter. Certainly there seemed to be a lack of urgency. Even after the Nijmegen Bridge had been captured undamaged on Wednesday the 20th, and while we of the 1st Airborne Division were still holding out by the skin of our teeth at Arnhem Bridge, it was several hours before a very tentative effort was made by the Guards Armoured Division to reach us, and after four tanks had been knocked out the whole thing came to a grinding halt. Several more hours were to elapse before a thoroughly plodding infantry formation was produced to continue on another axis.

Perhaps the casualty lists speak for themselves. During the nine days, while the British 1st Airborne Division was virtually written off with over eight thousand casualties, the two American Airborne Divisions suffered three thousand five hundred, but the British 2nd Army, consisting of nine divisions, suffered to the tune of three thousand seven hundred only. These figures hardly suggest resolute, continuous, determined fighting, by day and night, to achieve an Olympian victory. This was not the time to count the cost: the Germans had practically no reserves left and most of the population would have then welcomed the end of the war. The Russian armies were still back in Poland. All this was before the dreadful conference at Yalta that conceded so much. If we had won, Europe and the world would be very different today.

On 17 December 1977, those fine Dutch people who suffered so much with us during and after the battle did us the most signal honour by renaming their famous old bridge:

JOHN FROSTBRUG

J.D.F
Northend Farm, 1980, 1982

Preface to the Second Edition

After the publication of the first edition of *A Drop Too Many*, in October 1980, several people intimated that my ending was too abrupt, and suggested that I add further information about what happened to me thereafter. So, besides some necessary revisions, I have added three more chapters.

JOHN FROST

June 1982

CHAPTER 1

Iraq

I was in the Syrian Desert when the war began. I had been seconded from my regiment, The Cameronians, to the Iraq Levies, a force of Assyrian, Kurdish and Arab tribesmen, organized into infantry rifle companies, with a small support weapons and signals element. The main base was the R.A.F. Station at Habbaniya, some eighty miles northwest of Baghdad on the river Euphrates. The Levies' role was to guard the R.A.F. airfields and installations and, in emergency, keep open the lines of communication with Jordan.

When it was considered that our bases in Egypt might be threatened, the training establishment located there was to be moved to Iraq and the operational bomber squadrons in Iraq moved to Egypt, and now, in September 1939, preliminary arrangements had been made and I was proudly commanding Landing Ground Number 5. My garrison comprised one half-platoon of Assyrians, one section of R.A.F. Armoured Cars, some signals and thirty Arab labourers. Several hundred gallons of petrol had been dumped and large water tanks erected so that the ground convoys could fill up on their way. Already most of the bomber echelons had passed through and the arrival of the training parties from Egypt was imminent. Our task would have been quite straightforward had it not been for the breakdowns en route which caused haphazard arrival times and considerable anxiety for the safety of the crews of the stranded vehicles, or being towed or limping in.

There was not much to be feared from potential

enemies. The local tribes were peaceable enough, though never above filching or looting if given a chance. But an old Palestinian enemy, Fawzi el din Kawawjki, had been reported to be in my area. He had led the first rebellion there and it was expected that he would take any opportunity offered to stir up trouble. Moreover the desert could be very unkind to the inexperienced who took chances. There were always several tracks going in roughly the same direction, but some of these could lead the unwary straggler a long way off his course, and untrained men can last only a few hours without water in the great heat. However, no serious casualties came from the various mishaps.

The convoys going east or west looked formidable when approaching or leaving, surrounded by great clouds of dust. Every man was armed and R.A.F. armoured cars provided escort, so that they were considered to be pretty safe. The Landing Ground was hardly ever used as such, and though we had very occasional visits from senior officers, most aircraft passed far overhead. We were just below the Imperial Airways and K.L.M. routes; the great ponderous British flying boats staged at Lake Habbaniya near the R.A.F. base, but passengers in a hurry preferred the twin-engined Dutchman using Baghdad.

I was more worried by the long and complex enciphered messages that I had to unravel than by anything else. These could come at any time, day or night, and often those which bore the most imposing classification turned out to be about the most unimportant things. One series was all about the Arab coolies' pay. As I had no money or means of paying them, nor they anything to spend money on, it was annoying and apt to make one feel naughty about accepting messages at all.

I can still clearly remember the exact text of one message. 'War has broken out with Germany only.'

The first person I told was an R.A.S.C. Captain who leaped for joy, saying: 'Marvellous, marvellous! I was terrified that old Chamberbottom would settle up once again.'

However, most other people heard the news rather solemnly. My foremost thought was that it might perhaps mean promotion.

The Syrian Desert is similar to the Libyan, much of the

surface being gravel, with hard, sandy pans here and there. Hillocks and low ranges of hills, some sloping gently and some more harshly, and dry water courses which can restrict vehicle movement in places, though their banks can give cover and even shade from the sun. Some of the hillocks have been carved into weird shapes by the wind and these can be useful as landmarks. There always seems to be some sort of feature on the horizon, beckoning, tempting one on. Dried grass and camelthorn cover part of the gravel and all the vegetation is transformed in and after rain. But now, after the summer everything above ground was dry and prickly and the loose sand on the surface moved easily with the wind which blew once the sun was up.

The nights were usually quiet, still and cool, with all sounds travelling far to give early warning of any moving vehicle, but in the daytime any wheels put up clouds of dust which you could see from several miles away.

My little garrison was fortified and practised for any emergency that we could think of. Once the last of the main convoys had passed through, we were more or less left to our own devices and I, as any regular officer should, set about making the whole thing immaculate and devising ways and means of keeping all concerned trained, fit and happy. The biggest problem was varying our diet, for we were basically on bully beef and biscuits. Compo rations had not yet been thought of. There were a number of small herds of gazelle nearby and some of us became adept at picking them off with a rifle from the back of our pick-up truck – no easy feat when the vehicle was bucketing, swerving and braking to avoid rocky outcrops and nullahs, with the animals going at full gallop. However, they usually couldn't resist trying to race the vehicle and pass in front as if to show their superiority and it was then that they gave a reasonable chance. I particularly liked their liver for breakfast.

We also managed to shoot bustard flying and wheeling well above the range of any shotgun and these were quite delicious. Some of the smaller plover-type birds were also quite good. Kinneas Khoshaba, my Assyrian bearer, looked after me and always managed to ring the changes.

All the drinks that one would have liked to be cold were tepid. It was only at night that the water in the canvas containers had a chance of cooling.

Each evening, Rab Khamsi (Lieutenant) Beijo Rahana, my Assyrian officer, came to my tent for a talk and a drink and it was then that we planned the things for the day ahead. Luckily for us – the British officers of the Levies – our Assyrians were fine linguists and nearly all of them spoke English. We all had to pass an exam in colloquial Arabic which got us by in our daily dealings with most of the local inhabitants, but Assyrian was beyond us. These Assyrians were the direct descendants of those who 'swept down like a wolf on the fold' in Biblical times, and bore the old names like Nimrod, Sennacherib and Tiglath-Pileser, natural soldiers, having many of the Gurkha soldiers' characteristics, taking great pride in their marksmanship and mountaineering capabilities. We who commanded them grew to love them dearly and to this day I feel that I never had the privilege of leading better men.

Punishments for infringements could almost be restricted to verbal condemnation. It was only necessary to say: 'And what would your father have thought?'

Then an explanation of the need for the regulation that had been contravened and the possible dire consequences to his comrades and himself on active service that such contravention would bring, after a short silence, and perhaps a struggle to restrain tears:

'It is all too much shame on me and my family.' And then condolence rather than reprimand often ensured that the offender offended not again.

Now at the close of each day, Beijo and I would recapitulate, criticize and reconsider. I must confess that there was nothing else to do.

Some hundred and fifty miles further to the west, near an Iraq Oil Company pumping station, was another staging post commanded by Alastair Graham. He lived alongside all kinds of comforts and facilities, including the wives of some of the British employees. Alastair was irrepressible and debonair to a degree and one quiet afternoon bursts of machine-gun fire cracking in the air above our heads had us

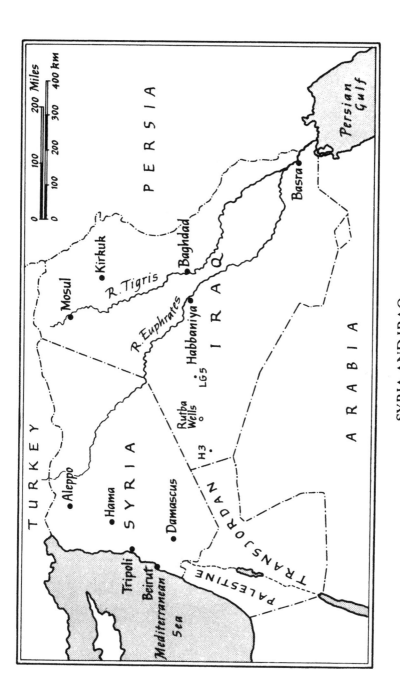

SYRIA AND IRAQ

diving to our defence positions. Then we recognized Alastair standing in the back of his truck with a Lewis gun mounted over the cab. It was great to see his cheerful face, and we had a lot to talk about. Apart from comparing notes on desert staging posts, I was the master and he the first whip of a pack of hounds called the Royal Exodus, which were kennelled at Habbaniya, and we were worried that the authorities might order their destruction as part of the war effort. There were the usual antis in the high places and it was ominous in a way that both Alastair and I had been selected for the desert. However, we knew that there were others who would offer their dead bodies in the cause. I decided to escort him back part of the way as far as Rutba Wells. This was an old Turkish fort and the hub of that part of the desert. There was a rest house and restaurant there presided over by a great personality known as Abu George.

It was here that the huge air-conditioned multi-wheeled buses travelling between Baghdad and Damascus used to stop for an hour or two. Up to the start of the war, most people came to Iraq via Suez by sea, then took the train to Damascus and finally came across the Syrian desert by Nairn Transport. Anyway, Abu George was able to cater for all tastes and now Alastair and I set about his champagne, resplendent in wine coolers, with gusto. We were on our way back to the posts long before dawn.

It was with quite mixed feelings that I got orders to pack up and move back to Habbaniya. Our time in the desert after the last convoy had gone could have seemed wasted and boring and yet a feeling of peace and contentment settled on us. It is said that all Englishmen love a desert and I found that this one certainly fascinated me. Quite a few of the British R.A.F. Armoured Car men, who flitted about between their various tasks, seemed to be delighted to spend as much time as possible with us. L.G.5 had become a home from home. In next to no time what was left of our petrol dump was loaded and the water tanks dismantled, tents struck, barbed wire rolled up and trenches filled in. Leaving the desert nice and tidy was a 'must'. We carefully buried all our rubbish, though we knew that the Bedou would come soon after to dig it up to go through it all.

Before and after this dismemberment, I drove out to a high point to look back on my domain, not without a sense of pride, and while there, I turned my back on it so as to gaze on the wilderness which I knew I would never forget.

Back in Habbaniya we were soon settled down to a very routine existence. Our main task was to guard the perimeter round the R.A.F. station. Block-houses had been built every so often and there was a quite formidable permanent fence to discourage marauders. There was a large so-called native cantonment within the perimeter, and as some of the inhabitants of this were considered unreliable, all vital installations had to be guarded also. This meant that about one quarter of our Levies were on guard each night and what with continual work on improving the defensive measures, there was little time for anything else. However, the phoney war phase in Europe allowed us to have easy consciences about enjoying ourselves as well as we were able while we could, and so we did.

We found hounds in good shape. Pat Uniacke and Conger Ross had managed things very well. Gordon Arthur of the R.A.F., who was P.A. to the Air Vice Marshal, had been enlisted as a whipper-in. It was well to have friends in high places and luckily for us Mrs Air Vice Marshal and her daughter were two of our most enthusiastic members. That winter we enjoyed as good a season as the Royal Exodus Hunt had ever had. We hunted jackal that lived in the tamarisk coverts along the river banks or among the wadis leading up to the plateau which rose above the airfield. 'Jack' that had gorged themselves the night before were easy meat and we sometimes killed three or four in a morning, but a big dog jack could take us up to ten miles, first across the irrigated land by the river where there were very tricky built-up water-courses to jump and then on to hard pounding across the plateau where our own dog hounds were required to pull him down, for those jack were capable of seeing the bitches off.

At Christmas time we took hounds to Baghdad where our meets became great social events. H.R.H. The Amir Abdulilla, who was then the Regent of Iraq, would turn out with several officers of the Bodyguard. Ambassadors and

Ministers entertained us and all the gaiety and beauty of the city would be there. Until the start of the war, one of our staunchest supporters had been the German Minister, Herr Doctor Grobba. When, because of a rabies scare, we were unable to send our trophies back to England to be mounted, Doctor Grobba elected to send them to Berlin. When I thanked him for thus rescuing us in our predicament and suggested reimbursement, he said: 'Do not worry about that, my friend, I will put it down to propaganda.'

We held three point-to-points in the spring – hurdle races really – and these attracted huge crowds. Polo scurries were interspersed with the more serious events and we made enough money to keep hounds going for the year. The pack was reinforced by drafts from the U.K. from time to time. I was lucky during my mastership, for Bryce Knox of Ayrshire was an old friend and he sent me ten couple of the best that ever set foot in the Land of Two Rivers. We bred some of our own, but despite all our efforts, it always turned out that the best dog covered the worst bitch and the best bitch would have nothing to do with any but the least attractive hound. It was a job to get bone into our local-bred animals and at the end of the war, when no fresh blood had been put in in four years, the pack were very light and racy – in fact beginning to look more like long dogs and not so keen to work out a line.

We had an excellent old kennelman called Aziz. We all thought that he had come to look like a hound himself but certainly he was skilful and perceptive. He could pick out any hound that might be sickening for something far quicker than any of us. When he said: 'Warrior, I theenk he have seek face,' we knew that Warrior needed attention, for it was not easy to keep hounds fit during the long hot summer with the temperature up to 120° in the shade. We used to take them down to the river each evening where they wallowed and paddled to their hearts' content. On our way, the local pi-dogs would bark and sometimes make threatening advances which our gentlemen would feign to ignore. Every now and then, a saluki would appear. Evidently these were Anglophile for they would turn furiously upon the pi-dogs and then stand with dignity while our hounds trotted by. The Arabs, while despising the ordinary dogs, called the salukis 'Hassil', which could be translated as 'Noble'. We always tried to persuade them that our hounds were also 'Hassil', but I fear they were doubtful. However, it would seem their salukis accepted them as such.

The hunt horses and chargers all had to take their turn on the polo ground most of the year except in the rainy season, when the mud ground became unplayable. I had a somewhat cantankerous, obstinate, yet dedicated head groom called Nashmi. He was good with hounds, but having a mind of his own it was sometimes hard to get him to obey orders. Every morning when I saw him at the stables, I told him which horses I wanted for either polo or hound exercise and quite often I found he had gone off on exercise with the horses I wanted for polo and sent others for me. He was quite unmoved when I remonstrated, saying that he knew best. On more than one occasion, exasperated, I yelled in Arabic: 'You're sacked. Leave the stable. Get out.'

'I won't be sacked. I stay. These are my horses.'

'You are sacked. You will get no more pay. I have got another groom.'

'I don't want money. If another man touches my horses I will kill him. I no go.'

Unfortunately I couldn't really get rid of Nashmi because he was so useful with the hounds and it was difficult to find Moslems willing to handle them. So we reached a *modus vivendi* whereby he never went too far and I was expected to curse and damn him for all to hear at least once a week. It is said that when Habbaniya was under siege long after I had left, Nashmi was seen to be sharpening one of the hog spears that I had left him. When asked why, he said: 'When the Iraqi Army comes I am going to settle with Captain Frost's Inglezi friends who did not support me when he troubled me.'

I hate to think this to be true for when we had parted it was with genuine tears.

I think that our relationships with other people in Iraq were on the whole praiseworthy. Certainly we were very close to our own Assyrian officers, so much so that some of us spent our leaves with them in the mountains in Kurdistan. From a small base camp we would wander with mule-borne baggage from village to village attending weddings and other parties, trying for bear or ibex, climbing, singing, even swimming in the ice-cold waters of the Zab and always talking while drinking wine well into the night till it was time to shoot the tops off the surrounding trees and tumble into a rooftop bed. Everyone went about armed to the teeth. There were no roads or police or any trappings of civilisation.

Assyrian and Kurdish villages were often close together and on the whole Christian and Moslem lived amicably, but it was considered unwise ever to be without a weapon close to hand. For want of anything nicer, I always took mine to bed with me.

The difference in behaviour between the tribes down in the plains and desert was marked. Round Habbaniya, the Dulaimi had a reputation for treachery and they could be unpleasant when we were shooting black partridge through the tamarisk coverts in their tribal area. Nearby the Beni Lam had delightful manners and always joined us to help beat, retrieve and then share the hot-pot stew we brewed at the end of the day. Like all townsmen in the Middle East, the local Baghdadees were unpredictable. Anti-this or anti-that riots could start in a twinkling, but Baghdad could be enormous fun in those days. We knew people from every nation there. Charmaine, the Turkish Ambassador's daughter, was our toast for beauty. There were wonderful dinner parties, sitting in the open beside the Tigris, with champagne and caviare ad lib. Then dancing at cabarets or the Alwiya Club, ending with a dive into the pool, fully clothed, for changing into bathing dress would have taken valuable time.

Our own seniors were a little band of retired officers, re-employed on contract, who had been in Iraq for several years. They were very fixed in their ideas, the main one of which was to live as quiet a life as possible and to keep on the best possible terms with our real masters, the R.A.F. Iraq had been one of those countries within the pre-war nominal jurisdiction of Britain, where the experiment of pacification from the air had been tried. Like all such measures foisted on them through unwillingness of Government to assert accepted responsibilities, it had merely resulted in Britain being despised for trying a cheap way out. Whenever there was real trouble the soldiers had to be sent for, but the R.A.F. had remained in overall operational command. Not unnaturally, the R.A.F. enjoyed being the top dog. Some of the senior air staff officers made a ruling that we, the regular army officers of the R.A.F. Iraq Levies, should be subject to R.A.F. discipline which included some irksome restrictions quite out of keeping with the traditional customs of officers brought up in the old regiments of the army. These were to do with life in the officers' quarters and messes. In the R.A.F. officers below the rank of squadron leader were debarred from entertaining in their quarters and had to limit their mess wine bills to £5 per month. An army captain ranked below a squadron leader and was therefore similarly checked. Most of us were captains though as old as the average squadron leader and usually with more service. We much wanted to entertain in our quarters because we all had special interests which were unsuitable for general discussion in the mess and we had subordinate native officers with whom it was important to be able to meet during off-duty hours. Spirits were very cheap and it was possible for a man who stuck to gin to drink himself silly within the £5 limit, but if you liked good wine and enjoyed asking people to dine occasionally, you could be over the legal limit within the first week of the month. This was a continual bone of contention, but we usually found ways of circumventing the regulations or else ignored them.

So, there was friction at times, and then our own seniors were inclined to take the R.A.F. standpoint. This tended to strain our loyalty and bring wildness every now and then. Only a few R.A.F. officers joined us for polo or hunting though we went out of our way to encourage them. For many, just being able to fly was sufficient and this I could well understand. I had many happy hours flying with them in their old Audaxes or dual-control Moths and secretly envied the pilots of the Blenheims, these then being the most modern bomber the U.K. had.

Despite a feeling that we were not exactly appreciated, we never ceased trying the achieve the highest possible

standards with our soldiers. It was difficult to find fault with
our drill or turnout on any occasion, even when mounting a
guard of a hundred men. Our barracks and stores were
spotless. It was almost unheard of for any item of equipment to be missing. After commanding the same company
for two years and more, on handing over we found that one
stop pawl spring of a Lewis gun was deficient. Nearly eighty
per cent of some of the companies were marksmen, while
the weapon handling of both the Lewis and Vickers guns I
have never seen approached. However, the men were not
so good at marching on the flat though they claimed that
they could beat a Gurkha on a mountain. The idea of being
late on parade was too terrible to contemplate and rather
that this should happen to me, Kinneas, my bearer, kept a
sponge in my ice box, and having gingerly raised the mos-
quito net, he would splosh this on my face. This had me
bounding out of bed roaring wide-awake and thus punctual
for whatever might be.

Meanwhile the phoney war in Europe became the real
thing. My two-year contract with the Levies was up in June
1940 and I applied to return to my regiment. This was
refused on the grounds that as I spoke Arabic and had local
knowledge, I would be much more useful to my country by
staying in Iraq. This I found I really could not stomach.
Stories about Dunkirk percolated back. I felt that our army
hadn't done so very well and yearned to get back to help
them take revenge. I was told that there would be grave
threats to Iraq, but I did not want to fight for Iraq. I felt
trapped and had visions of being stuck irretrievably. There
were numbers of British officer types within the oil and
trading companies in Iraq who, I felt, could take my place.
All the previous joy from our blessings turned sour for me
and I found that I could only hope and scheme and pray to
be relieved.

One morning while I was sitting in my office Mr Sethi,
my Indian Company Clerk, came in and put before me a
paper concerning the proposed establishment of a parachute battalion. I perused it slowly while Mr Sethi grinned.

'What on earth made you think that I would be
interested in this?' said I. 'You don't suppose I would ever
want to get mixed up with that kind of thing, do you? All I

want to do is to get back to the Cameronians.'

Mr Sethi paused. 'You might be surprised, Captain Sahib. You never know all that is to come.'

The Battle of Britain began, and with the great stories of the feats of the airmen, it seemed to me that the R.A.F. became almost unbearably cocky. Perhaps I was unduly sensitive, but morose and brooding, I began to feel like a second-class citizen, and my attitude may have unwittingly engineered my salvation, for even my friends began to put pressure on authority, until at last a request was made for me to be relieved. I was able to slip away quietly with only one small farewell party at which the Hunt Committee presented me with a copper hunting-horn duly inscribed. This was to be one of the best presents I ever had.

CHAPTER 2

Home Again

I sailed down the Persian Gulf on a little British India Line boat. It had a cargo of dried fish, a permanent list to starboard and the decks filled with passengers cooking and sleeping where they lay. We called at all the small ports on both sides of the Gulf and had time for a swim in a cove at Muscat. Among the first-class passengers was Houston-Boswall who had been Chief Counsellor at the Embassy in Baghdad. He told me much about the intrigue and latent unrest that was prevalent throughout Iraq and predicted a serious anti-British uprising in the fairly near future.

Sure enough, this came in the spring of 1941, and among other things it resulted in the investment of Habbaniya by the Iraq Army. The airfield and ancillary buildings had been sited and built without consideration for external defence and the whole conglomeration with the road approaches to it was overlooked by a plateau from which a hostile force could dominate it and prevent movement in or out. The Euphrates River, some two hundred yards wide, flowed round the other three sides, so the base was well and truly sealed in. The Iraqis shelled various parts desultorily and the R.A.F. countered by improvising bomb-racks on their training aircraft and dropping whatever they could think up in the way of offensive missiles from these. Meanwhile the garrison had to hold out until relief could come from either Jordan in the west or Basra in the south. As soon as the relieving column from the west was in the offing, a mixed force of the Levies and two companies of the King's Own Regiment, which had been flown in from

Basra, made a brilliant sortie against the enemy on the plateau and then pursued them as far as Fallujah on the way to Baghdad. Alastair Graham was awarded an M.C. for his part in this little-known epic.

Despite the rather unhappy end to my tour of duty with the Levies, I had loved being in Iraq. I had in fact been there as a child just after the First World War when my father had been serving as a brigadier in charge of the Armed Arab Labour Corps. We had all been involved in the tribal uprising of 1920 and I had had my baptism of fire – of which I was inordinately proud – during a train journey from Kurdistan. In 1946, while I was in command of the 2nd Battalion of the Parachute Regiment during the post-war bout of troubles in Palestine, I drove across the desert via Rutba and Landing Ground No. 5 to Baghdad, where Alastair was serving with the British Mission to the Iraq Army, and spent a few days there and in Habbaniya where many of my old friends and soldiers had spent the whole war. It was all much the same, but it was forcibly brought home to me how lucky I was to get away when I did back in 1940.

In 1950 when I was an instructor at the Senior Officers' School near Devizes, among the foreign students on one of the courses was a certain Iraqi, Lieutenant-Colonel Kassim. My wife and I remember him well for he was a member of my tutorial syndicate and came to a party at our house, during which he took photographs. He sent us prints of these and also presents from Baghdad. He became the leader of the rebellion in Iraq in 1958 when the Amir Abdulilla and the rest of the Royal family were slain, together with most of the leading Anglophile statesmen. I don't suppose I shall ever go back there again.

I travelled the rest of the way home round the Cape under civilian auspices, arriving back in London four months after I set out. During that time our armies had achieved spectacular success against the Italians in Libya under General Dick O'Connor, himself a Cameronian, and I wondered if I had not made a great mistake in neglecting to have asked him to fit me in somewhere. After a short stay at the Regimental Depot at Hamilton in Lanarkshire, I was posted to the 10th Battalion of the Cameronians which was on beach defence duties along part of the coast of Suffolk.

The beach defences for which we were responsible never looked like being completed to the satisfaction of the higher Commanders. No sooner was one belt of wire laid than another was proposed. Minefields were continually being taken up and put down again, and now a new horror in the way of static defence was to be employed. Tubular scaffolding had to be erected along the high-water mark all round the shores of Britain. The magnitude of the task as it appeared on my particular sector appalled me. The dreary weeks of labour stretched ahead, and I knew that the men would settle down to the gloomy task and need no help or encouragement from me.

We had been waiting for the German invasion for several long months, but now most of us felt that it would never come. The Panzers and storm troops were far away on the Russian steppes and the R.A.F. had grown mightily in strength since those early days. We found it hard to believe that we would now be called upon to fight from the positions on which we had lavished so much of the promised toil and sweat, and we dreamed of other places for our blood and tears. Unfortunately, however, it looked as though the 15th Scottish Division, to which we were so proud to belong, was not at that time earmarked for any great and glorious venture in the immediate future. Earlier in the year we had been informed that we were high on the list of Divisions to be sent overseas. We were not surprised at this for we had an idea that we were pretty good and the Division had a fine record from the last war. But as the year developed bad omens came. Sir Oliver Leese, the Commander, was taken away to form the Guards Armoured Division; the Reconnaissance Regiment left us from some other formation; our petrol ration was cut down to an infinitesimal amount; transport was reduced; and, finally, we began to find drafts for other units going overseas.

The shooting on the estate, where we were housed and had our fortifications, belonged to a retired officer, who had very kindly asked me to join him whenever he decided to shoot on days convenient to us both. We had already had a good day driving partridges, but I was looking forward more to October, for it was a better pheasant country and later still the woodcock would be in. In days gone by the shooting had been good enough to draw King Edward VII, who actually used to sleep in the room which was now our officers' mess, in a long rambling wooden house called Scotts Hall. Below the house was low-lying country, which had been flooded as an anti-invasion measure. Mallard, teal and shoveller now lived here in considerable numbers. This stretch of water was a continual delight and I spent most of my spare time wading through to small islands in the middle, from which I could either shoot or watch the marshy folk going about their daily business. There were coot and other waterfowl in hundreds. There were herons, swans and snipe. There were water-voles and otters and there was one solitary goose, who must have been pricked at the end of the season and left by his brethren to fend for himself. He was now quite recovered and as strong on the wing as he had ever been. I thought about this goose a lot and often stalked him through the reeds. Each time I flushed him I was deeply thrilled by the wild power in his wings, and I envied him his future in strange places far away. I never fired at him, for something about him and his circumstances aroused all my sympathy and I felt that without him the marsh would lose some of the subtle fascination that it held for me. Perhaps in him was the embodiment of the discontent that would not leave me despite the very pleasant life I led.

One evening I returned from a solitary walk having made up my mind to ask my Commanding Officer to recommend me for the Staff College, and I went into the Company office with a vague idea of writing out an application. The clerk was there and he handed me an envelope marked Secret, which he said had just arrived. There was a copy of a War Office letter inside it soliciting volunteers for special air service battalions. Captains were required as company commanders and I decided straight away to send my name in. I had not very much idea of what special air service was, but presumed it would be something in the Commando line and just what the doctor ordered. (Shades of Mr Sethi's pronouncement!)

The next day the Adjutant rang up to say that I was to

report first to the Medical Officer for examination and then to the Colonel for an interview. I was not worried about the first, for I had been passed fit by a medical board not long before, but I had a fairly shrewd idea that the Colonel would not be overjoyed. The dull and uninspiring soldiering we were doing sometimes brought a crop of applications for posting to other units and other places, and I knew that I wasn't setting a good example by asking to leave the battalion myself. The doctor told me that special air service entailed parachuting. This had not occurred to me before and I certainly could not imagine myself as a parachutist. At that time I knew that some Commandos had been trained in this role, but the subject was still very secret, and my knowledge of parachutes and parachuting consisted solely of accounts of what the Germans had achieved by this method of moving into action. Their airborne units had been well to the fore in the invasions of Norway, the Low Countries, Greece and Crete. On the whole the press had rather scoffed at the effectiveness of the new arm and I found it difficult to take very seriously the threat of German parachutists landing behind our own defences in Britain. I think that most of us felt that the Home Guard would be more than a match for them, that their morale was invariably low owing to the highly dangerous nature of their task and that in any case a large number were killed by their parachutes failing to open. However now I found that I had more or less unwittingly volunteered to undertake the same type of training and missions, and I was rather shocked.

The doctor passed me fit and I went on to the orderly room for my interview. The Adjutant and one of the Company Commanders who happened to be present greeted me with various gibes and general rudery, which had the effect of rather stiffening my shaken resolve, and I walked in to salute the Colonel, fairly determined to stick to my guns.

The Colonel smiled rather sympathetically, I thought, and seemed to be more amused than annoyed.

'I can't imagine any sensible person choosing you to be a parachutist,' he said, 'you ought to keep your feet firmly on the ground.'

In my heart of hearts I couldn't help agreeing with him. However I was able to explain my rather vague reasons for wanting to volunteer and he was never a man to stand in one's way.

He agreed to send my name in and I told him that I would be quite glad if I was turned down. It was an extremely happy battalion. The Colonel was the only officer among us who had served in the last war. He trained and ruled us firmly and well. I knew I had been very fortunate to be posted to his battalion and now that I had voluntarily set into motion the machinery that might cause me to leave, I felt that I had been foolish and impetuous and began to regret the whole thing. As I drove back to the Company billets some distance away, through the countryside I had grown to like so much, and thought of the pleasant days' shooting I should miss and the friends I should leave, I began to feel almost wretched and I practically made up my mind to ring the Adjutant on my return and cancel my application. But just as I was getting out of the car at my headquarters a squadron of Spitfires flew over the building. It was a glorious cloud-free day and my heart filled with envy for the men up above. We often watched them in mock combat, swooping and climbing with such sumptuous ease, and now my eyes followed them hungrily far out of sight while my ears thrilled with their luxurious drone, which followed long after them when they had gone. I decided not to ring up after all.

A summons to an interview at the War Office in London came a few days later and one morning I found myself among a room full of captains and majors in a large building up there. I felt myself being looked over by the earlier arrivals as I entered, in much the same way as people all the world over must look at each other when many are hoping for jobs that can be given to only a few.

I strolled over to a group which included two other Lowland Scotsmen. The conversation dwelt on the subject of parachuting, about which great ignorance prevailed, and we found time to sum each other up and to wonder which amongst us would be the chosen. We all moved into a larger room where a fierce-looking brigadier sat on the edge of a table with a cheery colonel.

When we had settled the brigadier eyed us all gravely
and said: 'Gentlemen, from amongst you officers here
assembled we are going to select the Company Commanders, the Company Seconds-in-Command and the Adjutants of the 1st Parachute Brigade.' He paused to let the
name sink in and continued: 'We shall interview each
officer in turn, but you will not be informed of the result of
the interview here. If selected you will receive posting
instructions within seven days from now. If you are not
selected now your names will remain on our list and you
may be required later on. Those of you who receive posting
instructions will act on them as soon as they arrive. We
have a tremendous task ahead of us and very little time.
You will come in here one by one as your names are
announced.'

With that we filed out again to wait our turn in the next
room. My name was called quite soon. I went in, saluted
and was told to sit down. The brigadier asked questions.
My brigade? My Division? Any active service? Length of
service? Age? Commission regular or otherwise? Why did
I want to leave my present unit? Why did I want to parachute? My views on discipline? Was I married? I never do
enjoy interviews and I didn't enjoy this one. I felt I didn't
know enough about what I had volunteered for to be able
to answer the questions confidently. I wanted to ask a lot of
questions myself but I wasn't given an opportunity. Feeling
that I had made a very bad impression, I was eventually
dismissed, and I went round to my Club for a drink. I was
sure that I would not be selected and was glad rather than
sorry, but annoyed with myself for not having made a
better showing. The journey back to Halesworth in Suffolk, where I was met by my driver in the P.U., took about
three hours. Having got back to my Company billets, which
were so pleasant and comfortable, I felt relieved and something seemed to say: 'Well, now that's over, so settle down
and forget all mad ideas about jumping from an aircraft.'

However during the week that followed it wasn't so easy
to forget. Every time I saw an aircraft in the sky I felt a
twinge of disappointment at the thought that I would probably remain earthbound for the rest of the war. I had often
wanted to be an airman and had tried for Cranwell when I

sat for my army examination, but parental influence made Sandhurst an inevitability. Some years later I had volunteered to become an Army Co-operation pilot, but a bad fall in a point-to-point in the meantime had resulted in partial deafness in one ear and I failed to reach the standard required at the medical examination. Now that the ideal opportunity of combining flying with soldiering had appeared it looked as though I had missed it as a result of going to an interview in an undecided state of mind. In spite of all the compensations I have described, as each day passed without word from the selection board my disappointment increased. My mind kept turning back to that interview and I remembered how the brigadier had raised his eyebrows at my reply to his question on discipline. He had asked me if I thought that strict military discipline should be enforced among a formation of volunteer parachutists. Without thinking carefully what was meant by discipline I had voiced the opinion that strict discipline tended to cramp initiative. At that time the prestige of the British army was definitely low, while the prestige of the R.A.F. was extremely high. The army had Dunkirk, Norway, Greece and Crete behind it and the public had been dismayed when, after Dick O'Connòr's brilliant desert campaign against the Italians, a couple of German divisions had arrived in Africa to the great discomfiture of our most seasoned formations.

To the uninformed it seemed as though there was something radically wrong with either the leaders and soldiers or the training and equipment of the army, and a whole host of self-styled military experts began to expound their views on the subject. One particular section of the press found opportunity to deride all forms of military discipline. According to them the custom of showing respect to and saluting officers was quite out of date in a democratic country. They saw no reason why half the regulations in the army should be enforced. In their opinion no soldier should ever clean or blanco his clothing or equipment and any form of drill was of course quite ridiculous. The fact that part of the tremendous successes of the German army must have been due to rigid discipline was completely ignored, and in any case, according to these experts, we were democratic people fighting for freedom and must not tolerate any semblance of fascism in our army. Unfortunately this form of reasoning found considerable echo in the army itself. All over England one saw dirty, untidy soldiers, slouching and slovenly. One heard stories of the wanton damage done to the houses in which soldiers were billeted. In London it was the exception rather than the rule for an officer to be saluted by an other rank. The only troops in England who at that time were doing any fighting were the Commandos and, without knowing any details, one gathered that they were allowed to wear civilian clothes, to live quite independently, and that they paid no attention to orthodox drill and routine. On the whole the higher commanders seemed to tolerate this state of affairs and any who raised their voices against it were labelled 'Colonel Blimp'.

My own Commanding Officer insisted on and maintained a very high standard of discipline and turnout, with the result that most of the men took a great pride in themselves and in their appearance. I felt quite certain in my own mind that their fighting efficiency would be higher than that of some of the apparently undisciplined soldiers one noticed when on leave. Some, who found that discipline was particularly irksome, wrote letters of complaint to the press about their grievances and some editors published their letters, adding their own sarcastic comments. All this had made me wonder whether too much time and emphasis had been allotted to maintaining the old regular army standards and hence my doubtful answer to the brigadier's question at the interview in London. Now I came to think of it, and remembered his rather ferocious appearance, I was certain that in his opinion it was quite the wrong answer, and I was sure that he had turned me down.

Then, one afternoon, about ten days after the interview, posting instructions arrived, ordering me to report to Hardwick Hall Camp near Chesterfield forthwith, and I was overjoyed. The battalion was due to take part in a defence exercise early the next day, so that I had very little time to pack up my belongings, hand over the Company to my Second-in-Command and say good-bye to everyone. Matters were not helped by the unexpected arrival of the

Divisional Commander at Company Headquarters early the next day as I was in the throes of moving off, but I just managed to catch the only possible train and it wasn't until I was well on my way that I realized I was now fully committed to becoming a parachutist.

Chesterfield Station was cold, dark and gloomy when I arrived and I felt every inch a new boy when I met an officer on the platform whose duty it was to collect new arrivals and send them up to the camp in M.T. I found a bed for the night and the next morning reported to the brigade headquarters in the camp.

The brick huts were new, ugly and incomplete, with slow-moving workmen and all their paraphernalia draped around them. A high wire fence surrounded the camp. The grass verges beside the roads and in between the huts had been trodden into glutinous mud and the atmosphere of the whole place was depressing. The countryside was typical Midland, mildly hilly and spasmodically wooded, but here and there utterly despoiled by large slag heaps and mining works. The camp had been erected on sloping ground in the park of Hardwick Hall, a somewhat grotesque yet imposing building which stood on the high ground overlooking the valley. Two rather interest-awakening ponds lay below the camp. I noticed them on my way down to brigade headquarters and decided to have a closer look later on.

The Brigade Major was a guardsman with the most bloodshot eyes I have ever seen on a man, and he told me that I had been earmarked for commanding the reinforcement company of the 2nd Battalion. This was most unsatisfactory from my point of view. The battalion hadn't even begun to form as yet and it would be several weeks before there were any reinforcements to be commanded. I met the Staff Captain at the same time, a cheerful bespectacled young man who promptly drew my attention to the fact that he wore a Major's crown. It gave him more pull with the War Office, he said. Feeling confused and a little alarmed I went on to the headquarters of the 2nd Battalion to meet the Commanding Officer.

He turned out to be the Lieutenant-Colonel, E.W.C.

Flavell, whom I had seen at the interview in London. He had won a Military Cross with two bars in the First World War. He knew exactly what he wanted and in a few minutes had set my mind at ease over the reinforcement company business and had told me that I would probably become Adjutant. In the meantime I was to walk round, find my way about, meet the other officers and unpack.

I spent a disquieting sort of day. My future brother officers appeared to be so much keener than I was about the parachuting. A general air of enthusiasm prevailed in which I could not share. Most of them were territorial or temporary officers who had received quick promotion and looked askance at my mere captaincy after nine years' service. They were full of good resolutions about the luxuries they would deny themselves on the altar of physical fitness. Various wild stories were circulating about the ordeals ahead of us. Some said that a parachute descent was equivalent to jumping from the roof of an express train, and the casualties sustained were nearly fifty per cent. A number of N.C.O. instructors had been sent over from the 1st Battalion, which had been in existence for nearly a year and was billeted at Knutsford in Cheshire which was near the Parachute Training Centre at Ringway, Manchester. They were as fine a collection of physical specimens as one could find in any part of the world, racing fit and full of confidence. They told us about seemingly incredible marches they had done and of other feats of endurance that no other troops could emulate. They stressed the fact that their officers could do all that they could do and seemed to cock a questioning eye in my direction. Several times during that day I was on the point of going to see the Colonel and asking him to send me back to my unit. I felt it was all going to be far beyond me, but somehow that little pair of blue wings which the qualified parachutist wore on the right arm below the shoulder had become infinitely desirable, and I stumbled through the day to spend a restless night.

The next day I was sent for by the Colonel and told that I was appointed Adjutant of the 2nd Battalion. From then onwards I had no time for doubts. The 2nd and 3rd Parachute Battalions, the 1st Parachute Brigade Headquarters and the 1st Parachute Squadron R.E. were to be formed from scratch at our present location, Hardwick Hall near Chesterfield. Each company in turn would move to Ringway Airport to do their qualifying parachute descents, having got themselves formed, equipped, disciplined and undergone preliminary training in the meantime. So far most of the officers and the administrative staff had arrived and now we had to be prepared to accept the N.C.O.s and men, who would be arriving at any time of the day or night from various units stationed all over the kingdom. Luckily for me we were blessed with a most capable Orderly Room Sergeant who knew the proper procedure for posting and documentation of personnel like an Army Council instruction itself and he and his clerks were cheerfully prepared to work until midnight to keep our records straight or to disentangle the muddles which frequently occurred.

It was inevitable that some Commmanding Officers should seize the opportunity of unloading some unwanted material on to us, but I was amazed to see with what gusto some of them played the game. They had been instructed to send only volunteers of A.1 physical fitness and good character. Each man was to be accompanied by his record of conduct and a certificate of good health signed by his medical officer. Among those who came nearly half had no documents, a large number could be labelled lame, halt or blind, a good few were hardened criminals in the military and sometimes the civil sense, and some had been arbitrarily detailed as if for an unpleasant fatigue party. Unto us was left the task of sorting the sheep from the goats, of returning most of the goats to their detestable owners and of taking a chance with a few of them. It had been decided to form a completely Scottish Company in the 2nd Battalion and on the whole the men from the Scottish Regiments arrived in better shape than anyone else. This company was quickly formed and soon appeared to be a rather outstanding body of men. They certainly had an advantage in appearance over their English counterparts in that they all wore the balmoral bonnets or glengarries of their various regiments and it was fine to see the large silvery badges mingled with the red hackle of the Black Watch as they marched to and from their various duties. The Company

Commander was an Englishman, Philip Teichman of the Royal Fusiliers. It was his first experience with other than Cockney soldiers, but their joint enthusiasms were quite sufficient to melt the whole into a fine unit.

Fully ninety-five per cent of this company had decided to become parachutists as they thought it would be the quickest way of seeing some action. They weren't particular who they fought and if there was no one else available as an enemy, then the English would do very well. This attitude of mind resulted in some unfortunate incidents in Chesterfield, where the trainees were apt to let off steam on Saturday nights, but there was nothing vicious in their fun and on the whole the healthy rivalries which existed in their parent regiments flourished sufficiently for them to be able to battle away amongst themselves, mostly in verbal warfare, to their hearts' content. Black Watch and Cameron Highlanders dominated in numbers, with Scottish Riflemen, Fusiliers and Borderers a close second, but all were represented, including a small contingent of London Scottish who were affectionately nicknamed 'The Piccadilly All-Sorts'.

Perhaps our greatest problem in those early days was the lack of good reliable N.C.O.s. With few exceptions the other ranks were equally inexperienced and it was more by accident than design that some of them wore a sergeant's stripes. Very few were able to enforce their authority unless an officer was actually present and a large number of men suffered under the misapprehension that military discipline was out of date. This was a constant source of anxiety to our Commander, Brigadier Gale, and he had to express himself very forcibly to the officers on the subject. But if one needed any encouragement during those worrying times, one had only to go to the gymnasium or to the parachute training apparatus to watch the men at work. We could not have been more fortunate than we were with our physical and parachute training staff and under these most capable men one could see the Parachute Regiment taking shape. They knew just how to harness energy and how to combine enthusiasm with sheer hard work. 'With this material,' they said, 'we could do anything.' One felt some intimation then of what this regiment would prove to be.

In these days of October and November 1941 both battalions were having to reject such a large number of the men who arrived it looked as though we should never be up to strength. On leaving their own units men were instructed to report to either the 2nd or 3rd Battalion at Hardwick Hall, and nearly every day a small draft arrived. I often used to compare notes with Stephen Terrell, the Adjutant of the 3rd Battalion, and one day I noticed that they were increasing in strength more rapidly than we were. After investigation I discovered that he had posted a 3rd Battalion tout near the gate who instructed all the new arrivals to report to the 3rd Battalion guard-room, where his R.S.M. inspected them and, having selected the pick and the bulk of the bunch, the dubious remnant were then sent on to our guard-room. All being fair in love and war I arranged to post my own tout with a lorry well outside the gate who intercepted the new arrivals and drove them straight in to our guard-room, so that for approximately a week we were able to pick and choose. When the supply suddenly ceased, I sent an orderly down the road who confirmed my suspicion that Stephen had rumbled the ruse and had posted his own lorry nearer the station and was now sitting back waiting for the 3rd Battalion figures to start rising again. We had a good laugh together over this and thereafter we each had a representative at the gate and we robbed each other no more. Once the men had been accepted they were issued with a lanyard to denote the unit to which they belonged. The 2nd Battalion wore a yellow lanyard similar to the Commanding Officers' braid from the Middlesex Regiment. The 3rd battalion wore red and Brigade Headquarters blue. Later the 1st Battalion adopted green.

While the process of formation was going on at Hardwick, a small party of officers and N.C.O.s were doing their qualifying jumps at Ringway airport. To become qualified each man did two jumps from a balloon and five from an aircraft. After the successful completion of the series each man was presented with his 'wings' by the Air Force Officer Commanding. From the time a man started his training as a parachutist, and while he remained on the strength of a parachute unit, he received extra pay. It was arranged that the first party would do their final qualifying jump on a large open field near Hardwick, so that we could watch them. As a perfect demonstration this had to be put down as a failure owing to the inability of the pilots of the aircraft to fly some sixty miles across country and to drop a stick of parachutists at a certain place at a given time. Most of our men arrived at the right place eventually, though a few hurt themselves on landing, but what struck me so forcibly at the time was how completely dependent we were on the skill of our pilots. Somehow I had taken all that part of it for granted. I had assumed that when aircraft took off from an airport at point A they automatically arrived at a point B, and as far as I knew there was no difficulty about it at all. We had now seen that this was not so and in the weeks to come we were to realize how important a factor this was to be in everything we undertook.

The actual spectacle of the men jumping was a great thrill. As one saw the little figures leaving the hole in the bottom of the fuselage, being twisted and turned and jerked while falling, then floating down silently yet urgently and purposefully till finally hitting the ground with a thump, one said, 'There but for the grace of God go I, but let me be the next.'

That night in the mess we had ample opportunity to listen to first-hand information about parachuting as it seemed to a selection of novices. Our qualified brother officers were unanimous in their enthusiasm and even though half of them were damaged in one way or another, we all envied them tremendously. In general I gathered that there was nothing very frightening about it all, that the second jump was worse than the first, that jumping from the stationary balloon was worse than jumping from an aircraft and that one did need to be hard and fit to avoid damage to one's legs and ankles. One of the officers who went on the course had not been able to launch himself off when the time came and had remained quivering with fear on the edge of the hole in the bottom of the balloon basket until it was hauled down to the ground again. Although I think we felt a good deal of sympathy for him we all joined together in condemning him as a coward and thus we burned our boats against our own time of testing to come.

So the weeks went by with the men coming, being

trained, qualifying, going on leave and returning to take their place in the battalions. I had to spend long hours in the office dealing with reams of paper and had very little time available for getting fit. A special early morning P.T. class was held each day for the Commanders and staff officers, which had the effect of making us all very stiff and weary for the rest of the day. One really needed to take a complete fortnight off to learn the drills and master the apparatus, but none of us could possibly afford the time. We knew by now that the brigade was to form part of the 1st Airborne Division, which was to be ready for war by midsummer 1942, and a hundred and one problems seemed to crop up every day. General 'Boy' Browning, known to the regular officers as the most famous Adjutant Sandhurst had ever had, was to command the Division. We began to realize that we were destined to do far more than land behind the enemy lines and carry out raids or act as guerrillas.

At this stage of the war the Germans were knocking on the gates of Moscow, and as we listened to the B.B.C. news bulletins we had frequently heard references to the use of parachute troops by both sides during the campaign. The bulletin invariably added the information that the parachutists in question had been mopped up. We held various discussions as to the correct use of airborne troops and we carefully studied the German technique. The one German operation which stood out as a spectacular success was their capture of the Belgian fortress of Eben Emael, but unfortunately we had little data about it. We knew that they had very nearly failed at Crete and there the air opposition had been practically nil. The War Office had issued only one short pamphlet on the subject of our employment and our own men had been used once only in the south of Italy. This venture had been unsuccessful, but luck had not been on their side. Their target had been part of the Apulian Aqueduct. Having taken off from Malta, they had managed to blow up some of the supports, but insufficient explosive was available to effect complete destruction so the water supply for that part of Italy was not as seriously jeopardized as had been hoped. The raiding party was surrounded and captured en route to the coast where they

were to be taken off by a submarine. So the field was open
and it was up to each one of us to think and discuss the
experiment for all we were worth.

At the beginning of December my Commanding Officer
decided that he and I should go over to do our qualifying
jumps together. We booked rooms at the George Hotel at
Knutsford and arranged to finish in as short a time as
possible. Neither of us had managed to do more than a very
limited amount of training, but by this time one or two
other sedentary workers had completed the course successfully and we thought to chance it. Colonel Flavell was
cheerful in almost any circumstance, but then came the
morning when we found ourselves sitting side by side in the
crazily swaying basket of a balloon which was rising slowly
to a height of six hundred feet above Tatton Park, and we
smiled at each other the learner parachutist's smile, which
has no joy or humour in it. One merely uncovers one's
teeth for a second or two then hides them again quickly lest
they should start chattering. It was quiet up there, but
conversation was difficult. I found that one had to swallow
hard before making a remark and no one else was feeling
talkative. We fiddled anxiously with our harness and occasionally threw a quick agonized glance at the ground
below, but in the main we stared upwards, praying hard.

The Colonel went first and I soon followed. The first
sensation of falling drew the breath from my lungs till a
crackling sound from above and a sudden pull on my
harness told me that the parachute was open, and the rest
of it was heavenly. I had a very gentle landing and the
Colonel likewise, so we decided to go and do another one
right away. This time we were brimful of confidence and
chattered away happily all the way up, laughing at the
misery of the other two officers in the basket. As I was
coming down I heard someone shouting, 'Keep your legs
together.' A small gust of wind had given me a slight swing
and I was wriggling in my harness in a clumsy attempt to
counteract this. I landed with my feet apart and all the
weight of my body was taken by my left leg. I felt a savage
wrench in that knee and lay in pain on the ground for a few
seconds before being able to get up.

An instructor came running over to see if I needed help,

but I was able to walk without much difficulty. This time the Colonel too had had a heavy landing and was a bit shaken, so after watching a few more jumps we drove back from the training area to the George at Knutsford for lunch. By teatime my knee was very swollen and I had to be helped to bed. The next day the battalion medical officer arrived and arranged for me to be taken by ambulance to hospital in Manchester. This I thought was the ignominious end to my parachuting career and I wrote to a friend in my regiment saying that I expected to be back with them before long.

I was operated on the next day, which had the effect of drawing off all the fluid from the knee, and the surgeon told me that I should be perfectly sound in a month's time. I lay in a large ward and I found that half the other officer patients were also injured parachutists. Among them were two Poles, three Dutchmen, two Frenchmen and a Belgian. They were excellent company and the ten days I spent with them until I was able to leave passed very pleasantly, the only drawbacks being that the representatives of each nation insisted on hearing the news in their own language three times a day and that the V.A.D.s always served the foreign gentlemen with their food first. Colonel Flavell and several officers came to see me and I soon found that I was still very much a parachutist, and I became fully determined to get really fit before completing my course. One evening the Commanding Officer, Second-in-Command and Adjutant of one of the Air Landing Battalions of the Airborne Division were brought in, having crashed during their first trip in a glider.

I was driven to Manchester station in an ambulance and, having got myself a corner seat in a first-class carriage on the through train for Chesterfield, was arrested by the R.T.O. just before the train left on suspicion of having left the hospital without permission. Very bad words were exchanged between us before I caught the next train which involved two changes. After spending a night at Hardwick I went on leave for ten days.

When I returned a number of changes were about to take place at Hardwick. The 3rd Battalion were moving to Wentworth Woodhouse, some forty miles away where they would complete their formation. The 1st Battalion were coming in from Knutsford, where the officers and men had been billeted in small parties all over the town and a 4th Battalion would start forming at Hardwick in the 2nd Battalion lines until they were sufficiently self-supporting to move to Kettlestone Park, another large estate in the area. Our Second-in-Command had been appointed to form the new battalion and one of our Company Commanders had been found wanting, so it appeared that I should be promoted to command a company in the near future.

We were visited by General Eastwood from Northern Command and by General Paget, the Commander-in-Chief. There was a slight hitch in the arrangements made to welcome the latter and he and his staff walked half-way from the railway station to the camp. We never discovered who was responsible, but some changes took place among the Brigade staff very shortly afterwards. During Christmas week we slackened off and arranged some very pleasant parties. We knew practically nobody living in the neighbourhood at that time and the handful of charming V.A.D.s who ran the small hospital in the camp were in great demand. They were very anxious to be allowed to parachute and began to train in all seriousness, but permission was not forthcoming from higher authority. Perhaps someone was afraid that people would say 'Why, even girls are doing it!' At any rate we blessed them for their presence there amongst us in that somewhat gloomy place and though they may have been responsible for a large attendance on sick parades, they certainly did our morale good.

After a long weekend in Scotland over the New Year I returned to relinquish the Adjutancy and to take over Scottish 'C' Company from Philip Teichman. They were all successfully qualified and I started straight away on my own physical fitness campaign. The company were disgruntled at the time as they had been required to build a road from the camp to a site from which a balloon could be flown, and this solemn pioneering work did not meet with their approval. Philip was taking command of 'B' Company, which had also completed their parachuting course.

Some time during the third week in January, all the Company Commanders having been summoned to battalion headquarters, we were told that 'C' Company had been earmarked for special training, which would involve their moving to Tilshead on Salisbury Plain and remaining there for five or six weeks. The main question of the moment was whether Philip or I should go with them. Philip knew the company and was already qualified, but I was very keen to command the Jocks and had now begun to do so. It was finally decided that if I could qualify within a week I should go with the company. In the meantime Philip would go down to Tilshead with an advance party and if I failed to get through he would reassume command when the company arrived.

The attitude of the R.A.F. officer commanding the station at Ringway gave me a certain amount of food for thought. I found that I was to be treated with considerable privilege, that all the usual formalities and regulations which went with the course would be waived, and that I should be allowed to do my jumps in as short a time as possible. From further conversation with him I could not help deducing that the company had been earmarked for something fairly important, and it might be action against the enemy. By nine o'clock on the first morning I was waiting in the hangar on the edge of the airport with my parachute fitted and ready to go. The flight of Whitley bombers from which trainers were dropped were manoeuvring into position on the perimeter track. I had arranged to do two jumps that morning, but just as the first sticks were getting into their aircraft, a fog came drifting across the runways which was to persist all day long. It was quite a nerve-racking business, waiting hour after hour for a change in the weather that might make flying possible. At that time all that the R.A.F. could make available for training parachutists were six Whitleys, and no possible chance of doing the trip from Ringway to Tatton Park could be missed. This meant that even on days when the Meteorological Officers were as certain as they could be that no flying would take place, the trainees had to be ready at hand to take advantage of even fleeting breaks in bad weather. Ringway airport was particularly noted for its susceptibility to bad flying conditions. In the neighbourhood of Manchester absence of wind is apt to coincide with bad visibility, and as it had been found unwise to drop parachutists in a wind of over 15 to 20 m.p.h. because the incidence of casualties increased with the strength of the wind, one had to be very lucky to complete the course of seven jumps in under a fortnight. I now had five days left.

The next day was very nearly a repetition of the first. The hangars were full of synthetic parachute training apparatus and I spent the morning swinging, rolling and jumping through mock apertures. I also watched the W.A.A.F. at work folding and packing our parachutes. There was a notice in the packing room reminding them that a man's life depended on their skill or lack of it. Fatal accidents were very few, but when one did occur a very exhaustive inquiry was held, and the girls who packed the parachute, which was carefully registered, cannot have had an easy time, though I believe that the number of accidents attributable to careless or faulty packing was practically nil. It always seemed that some curious or freakish fault had occurred when a man fell to his death. I think most of us felt that this was inevitable at the beginning and that only by trial and error could perfection be attained; in any case these things only happened to other people and we ourselves were perfectly safe!

The weather cleared late in the afternoon and I landed safely at Tatton Park some ten minutes after leaving Ringway. I found that I much preferred to jump from the aircraft than from the balloon. The noise and harsh movement of the one was definitely reassuring after the silence and sickening sway of the other. After taking off my parachute I ran to the car park and persuaded someone to drive me back to the airport where I arrived just in time to catch one of the last planes. This time I barely missed landing in a large tree in the middle of the Park. The next day I did another jump late in the evening and the day after that in perfect weather I completed my course with great relief.

The Group Captain said he was sorry he wouldn't be able to present me with my wings at the end-of-the-course parade, but the smile the W.A.A.F. batwoman gave me when she helped me on with my jacket on which she had sewn my wings was fine enough reward, and I celebrated by having a party with the Colonel in Chesterfield that night.

The intense satisfaction I now felt was in great contrast to all the worries and doubts of the past few weeks, and it far excelled the mere lifting of the proverbial load from the mind. As a parachutist one was often asked what it felt like to jump and I always seemed to make a different answer. Some people find that to ride a horse at a gallop across country taking their fences as they come is a nerve-racking yet exhilarating performance. One meets some people who are in such a state of nerves before riding in a point-to-point that they hardly know what they are doing, yet nothing on earth would allow them to let another take their place.

I think the learner parachutist experienced much the same feeling, which gradually lessened with the number of jumps he did, though his confidence might be badly shaken by his being involved in or intimately connected with a bad accident. Perhaps an essential difference is that through the centuries man has been accustomed to jumping on horseback, but not until quite recently has he flown up to a height in order deliberately to cast himself down. At any rate, for the average person it was a most unusual inclination, and there was no doubt that it required guts. As a learner one had to screw up one's courage for each jump and this took a certain amount out of one which in turn required replacement or compensation.

The compensations which attended the qualified parachutist materially did not amount to anything very considerable. The value of the hard training and the risks undertaken were assessed at two shillings per man and four shillings per officer per day at a time when a packet of cigarettes cost as much as two shillings. Grateful Members of Parliament very soon had the officers' emolument reduced to the same level as the men's, conveniently overlooking the fact that the depredations of the Commissioners of Income Tax had already effected this reduction. The army pay office speedily unearthed a regulation which deprived the Commanders and staff officers of either their parachute pay or their extra duty pay to which officers holding these appointments were entitled throughout the remainder of the army. But these are pinpricks to which all who serve our country in khaki must become inured and it wasn't until we met our American cousins that we felt that perhaps we were rather underpaid.

At that time the only distinction in uniform was the pair of wings worn unobtrusively on the right shoulder instead of on the breast to avoid annoying the Air Force. We never met a real airman who didn't think that this was nonsense, but perhaps the position has now become a distinction in itself. The attitude of the general public towards us was sometimes disconcerting. The chauffeur of an aunt with whom I was staying, on hearing I had become a parachutist, exclaimed disgustedly, 'Why, that's the surest way of becoming a prisoner that's ever been invented.' Soon afterwards the widow of a general assured me on very good authority that only the very lowest types were being selected for the job and that the Government were even considering the use of Dartmoor convicts. The compensation we required was in our own chosen company and in our belief in glory and fame.

CHAPTER 3

The Bruneval Raid

Philip Teichman found it hard to disguise his disappointment when I arrived at Tilshead late in January. He told me that as far as he had been able to find out we were not in for a 'party' but that we were to train for a demonstration to the War Cabinet, and that if this was convincing, something real would follow. He had completed all the arrangements to receive the company, who were due to arrive in two days' time. I consoled him with such sincerity as I could muster.

This camp at Tilshead was the usual desolate sort of place which one associates with most of Salisbury Plain. The Glider Pilot Regiment had just begun to form and we were to share the accommodation with them. This arrangement had several obvious disadvantages both from our point of view and theirs, but nothing else was available. Needless to say at that time of the year mud presided everywhere. The morning after the company arrived General Browning came over from the headquarters of the Airborne Division about ten miles away to look them over. I was dreading this visit as I well knew what his views on turnout were. We had never been able to do very much about this at Hardwick, firstly because we had so little time and secondly because we had been unable to obtain replacements for old and battered clothing. The long train journey had left the men's uniforms in a mass of creases and the mud of Tilshead had now become firmly stuck on various parts of them, and altogether they looked pretty terrible. The General took a long time going round, speak-

ing to practically every man, but at the end he turned to me
and said: 'I think you've got a good lot of men but I have
never seen such a dirty company in all my life!'

When he had gone his staff officers descended on us and
we were given 'carte blanche'. We could have any or all the
articles of clothing and equipment we wanted and we settled down to make a clean sweep. We were given enough
transport to make us completely mobile and we were allotted as much ammunition as we could possibly want for
training. By this time the company, although still under
strength, had settled down together very well. The N.C.O.s
had found themselves, and on parade or in camp their
orders were obeyed.

Early the following morning a liaison officer came over
from Division with detailed instructions of what we were to
do. A piece of ground had been selected near Alton Priors,
near Devizes, some twenty miles away, which was similar
to the terrain on which our demonstration to the War
Cabinet was to take place. The steep hills rising from the
canal were to represent the cliffs at the edge of the sea and
we were to practise a landing by night behind the imaginary
enemy defences, the destruction of an enemy headquarters, followed by a move down a gulley between the cliffs to
the beach from which we were to be evacuated by small
naval craft. The actual demonstration would probably take
place somewhere on the Dover coast or the Isle of Wight
and the site would be selected later. We were to do the
embarkation practices with the Navy from this site. The
exact plan had already been decided on. The substance of
this was that the company was to be split up into four
different parties, to be dropped at small intervals of time,
each having a special task assigned to it and being specially
armed and equipped for its task.

I didn't like this organization at all. It completely upset
workable headquarters and instead of having three well-
balanced platoons to handle, I should have four bodies, all
different in size and fire-power, which would be difficult to
control if things went wrong. Previous military experience
had shown me that manoeuvres or operations which went
strictly according to plan were very rare indeed, and I
felt certain that a manoeuvre which had to begin after a

parachute landing by night would be nothing short of miraculous if it went exactly as we planned it.

That afternoon, having taken careful note of the plan as detailed by the Liaison Officer, I made my own, which fitted the normal company organization, and I went to Divisional Headquarters to see the General and explain my reasons for wanting an alteration. On my arrival I was greeted by the Liaison Officer, who told me that the General was away and came with me to the office of G.S.O.1. where he argued vehemently in favour of the four-party plan, and attacked my plan, which I had no little difficulty in introducing at all. I came away very puzzled, dissatisfied and quite determined to stick to my guns. The attitude adopted by the Liaison Officer was to my mind very peculiar and I felt that there was a lot more behind it than I knew.

The next morning our friend arrived at Tilshead and, having bound me to absolute secrecy, told me that the story concerning the demonstration to the War Cabinet was merely cover for the fact that we would be required to carry out a raid on the coast of enemy-occupied France towards the end of February, that R.E. had been included so that they would be able to dismantle and bring back to England the essential parts of the latest enemy radiolocation apparatus, that the plan had been specially devised in the light of the information available about the enemy defences in the area, and that if I still did not like the plan, someone else would soon be found who did.

I had no further objection to raise. It was a good plan if all went well with the drop and as we were going to have one of the most experienced bomber squadrons of the R.A.F. to take us there, we had great expectations of arriving at the right place at the right time. The elaborate precautions taken in the interests of security were of vital necessity and it did not require much imagination to predict what the enemy's reception would be if he obtained an inkling of our intentions. At that time a fully qualified company of parachutists undergoing special training was a sufficient rarity to be an object of curiosity, and although the cover story about the demonstration rang fairly true, I found that I had to be very careful in everything I said to my officers and I seemed to spend my time dodging awkward

questions. The most embarrassing ones came from the
C.S.M., part of whose duty it was to deal with the arms and
ammunition for the demonstration! The precautions were
effective enough to mislead the Quartermaster of the
Glider Pilot Regiment, who, even while reading a news-
paper account of the raid after it had occurred, failed to
connect us with it, and Q.M.s as a tribe generally know
what goes on.

We organized the Company into four parties, each
named after a famous sailor. This was to be a combined
operation par excellence with the Navy, Army and R.A.F.
all intimately concerned, and we hoped that the Senior
Service would appreciate our gesture. A small number of
sappers were attached to the Company and some men of
'B' Company had been sent down as reinforcements. We
started vigorous training at once. Nearly every night we
were to be found prowling across the plain and I am afraid
we caused the Glider Pilot Regiment a good many head-
aches, for we never knew exactly when we should appear
for meals, and they were sometimes horrified at the
amount of food we ate.

John Ross, an imperturbable Scotsman from Dundee,
was Second-in-Command of the Company and he was
responsible for our administration. This was no easy task,
for in addition to arranging meals at odd hours in different
parts of southern England at very short notice, he had to be
prepared to accept lorry-loads of stores and ammunition,
which might suddenly appear at any time of the day or
night. We were all equipped with the Sten gun which had
then just been produced and had many teething troubles. I
think, too, that we were the first troops to be equipped with
the new 38 wireless set with which the Company Commander could keep in direct communication with his platoons.
There were several other gimmicks for us to play with, and
anything we asked for was provided.

We were very fortunate in having an experienced old
soldier as Company Sergeant-Major. This was Strachan of
the Black Watch, a man who knew just exactly how a
Company should be run, and one could be sure that when
the Company was required to be at a certain place at a
certain time, be there it would. The officers made up for

their lack of experience by their intense enthusiasm, so that by the time we had completed our ground training at Alton Priors I was quite satisfied with the progress.

The next phase called for a journey up to Inveraray on Loch Fyne, but before we left we went over to Thruxton aerodrome about thirty miles away, to meet the pilots who were to fly us to our objective. They belonged to a crack bomber squadron commanded by Wing Commander Pickard, who had taken the leading part in the film, *Target for Tonight*. We were left in no doubt as to their efficiency and we felt that if anybody was going to put us down in the right place, they were the people to do it.

For security reasons we removed all parachute insignia in the train going up to Scotland so that we could embark on the *Prinz Albert* incognito. The *Prinz Albert* was the parent ship of the flotilla of landing-craft which were to take us off after the completion of our mission. This part of our training was the greatest fun although it meant long hours and frequent wettings in the icy loch. Nevertheless it was all a very pleasant change from Salisbury Plain and we thoroughly enjoyed moving about on the waters of Loch Fyne in the landing-craft. We were lucky with the weather and the change of scenery did us all a lot of good. The comparative comfort of the cabins and wardrooms on board were in great contrast to our camp at Tilshead. For once the subalterns were able to eat as much as they felt they needed, and there was no shortage of all the good things of life.

We were, however, a little disconcerted to find that the business of embarking in the dark was not quite such a simple matter as we had imagined, and we also noted with some alarm that the skippers of the landing-craft were not always able to find our positions on the shore. The possibility of being left stranded on the coast of France after we had done our job was unpleasant, and in the end we went on the raid without having had one really successful practice evacuation.

Admiral Lord Mountbatten, who was then Chief of Combined Operations, came to see us aboard the *Prinz Albert*. There was a misunderstanding about this visit because the Captain of the *Prinz Albert* thought that Lord

Louis was arriving specially to inspect his ship and the flotilla of landing-craft. It was arranged therefore that we should make ourselves scarce, so that morning we moved ashore and into the surrounding hills, where we hid until frantic hooting from the *Prinz Albert*'s siren told us that all was not well on board. We then scurried down to the landing-craft and back to the ship with all possible speed.

The Admiral spoke to all ranks, both naval and military, and this was the first inkling that many of our soldiers and any of the Navy had had as to what we were going to be required to do. Until this moment the sailors had no idea that we were parachutists and from then on they took a great interest in us, for we were the first of the breed that they had met. Throughout all subsequent events we had nothing but the most willing co-operation from both sailors and airmen and we were left in no doubt by his Lordship that co-operation had to be the thing.

Just before we left Tilshead for Scotland a young German Jew had arrived. No one but Strachan and I knew who or what he was and we posted him in with a fictitious number and named him Private Newman. He had been detailed from above to come with us as an interpreter, but I was not at all keen to accept this quaint addition to our Order of Battle. I was afraid that an unknown, untried man might become a liability if things went wrong and now I took the opportunity of telling Lord Louis that I would rather do without him. Newman was sent for and subjected to a tremendous barrage of questions in German. He seemed to hold his own and Lord Louis was satisfied. He told me to take him as I should certainly find him invaluable as an interpreter during the raid. In the end this proved to be more than true; as indeed were all the other little bits of advice I received from the same source at that time.

The next day we sailed down the Loch and round to Gourock, where we said good-bye to the *Prinz Albert* for the time being and returned to Tilshead by train. The day after we got back we did a practice drop on the open ground outside Divisional Headquarters which was at Syrancote House, Figheldean, near Amesbury. The squadron had not actually dropped any 'live' parachutists before, so that there was a good deal of disorder and confusion on the aerodrome and it wasn't until late in the day that we tumbled out on to a piece of ground which has received so many hundreds of parachutists since then. Although the ground was brick-hard there were no casualties apart from the odd bruise or sprain and the General was satisfied; but Sergeant Grieve of the Seaforth had taught his men to get out so quickly that they made the rest of us look slow and we determined to put this point right before the day.

It was now decided that during the rest of the time available we should concentrate on training with the landing-craft, and nearly every day a small convoy of five troop-carrying vehicles travelled down to the Dorset coast at a steady 40 m.p.h. In those days traffic control was not quite such a serious business as it is today. Sometimes we would overtake another convoy moving in the same direction, much to the astonishment of the men they carried, but speed was essential, as we barely had sufficient time to be in position, embark, disembark and return to our camp at a reasonable hour. Bad fortune with the weather caused several journeys to be fruitless and the last rehearsal could not have been a more dismal failure. It was planned that in darkness we should debus from our lorries on a flat piece of ground near the sea, that the aircraft should then fly over and drop our weapon containers to us and that, having been through our rehearsal drill, we should assemble on the beach and be embarked on the landing-craft. In the event the aircraft dropped the containers in one place, the Navy came in to another beach and we got mixed up in a defensive minefield some ten miles from where we were supposed to be.

This was disastrous as there were only two more days available before the first possible D-day, and the naval authorities insisted on having one successful practice before they started off. It was decided to have one further try on Southampton Water and, as luck would have it, the weather forced a postponement until Sunday the 23rd, which was in fact the planned D-day. This night the weather was perfect, but owing to a miscalculation over the tides, the landing-craft got stuck about sixty yards from the shore and though we walked out to heave and shove, hard and fast they remained, and we went home to bed.

It was calculated that there were now only four possible days left when the position of the moon and the condition of the tide would be favourable. These were Monday the 24th to Thursday the 27th of February. The light of a fairly full moon was essential to enable us to recognize the ground over which we were to operate and the landing-craft required a rising tide at the time they were to take us off. For obvious reasons the whole operation had to take place under cover of darkness. During the last few days in addition to our training we had been tidying up the plan in the light of the latest information available. This came to us in almost incredible detail: the exact location and the tasks of every enemy defensive position was plotted; the strength, the billets, the weapons, the morale and even the names of some of the Germans were known and aerial photographs together with an excellent model of the land-scape enabled us to give the men a very accurate brief of what they were to do.

The whole object of the operation was to dismantle the essential parts of the latest German Radar Station and to bring them together with photographs of the immovable parts, back to England. Flight-Sergeant Cox, an R.A.F. expert in radar, and a section of the 1st Parachute Field Squadron R.E. under Captain Denis Vernon, had been trained to carry out this task. The whole plan had to revolve round the business of getting these men to the Radar Station, protecting them while they did their work and getting them and their booty away into the boats. The enemy were in three main bodies: firstly the signallers and guards on duty at the main Radar Station itself (which was built near a lonely clifftop villa), thought to be about thirty men all told; secondly, at 'Le Presbytère', a wooded enclosure containing buildings some three hundred yards north of the villa, where reserve signallers and coast defence troops were billeted, totalling possibly over one hundred men; and lastly, the garrison of the village of Bruneval itself, through which a narrow road led from the beach to the hinterland, the beach being defended by pill-boxes and earthworks both on top of the cliffs flanking the beach and also down below, while some forty men lived

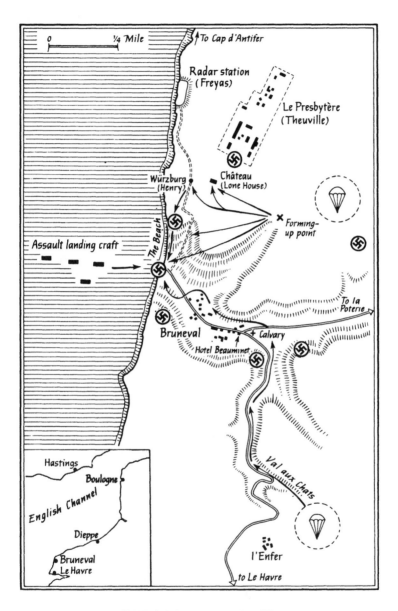

0 ¼ Mile

To Cap d'Antifer

Radar station
(Freyas)

Le Presbytère
(Theuville)

Würzburg
(Henry)

Château
(Lone House)

The Beach

Assault landing craft

Forming-
up point

To la
Poterie

Bruneval

Calvary

Hotel Beaumnet

Val aux Clairs

Hastings

Boulogne

English Channel

Dieppe

Bruneval
Le Havre

l'Enfer

to Le Havre

THE BRUNEVAL RAID

in the village and were responsible for manning these positions.

Our force, which consisted of one hundred and twenty all ranks, was to drop about half a mile inland in three main parties, starting at 12.15 a.m. First was 'Nelson' party, consisting of some forty men under John Ross and Euen Charteris. Their task was to capture the beach defences from the rear, so that we could subsequently be evacuated from the beach; then came my lot, which was further subdivided into three parties called 'Jellicoe', 'Hardy' and 'Drake'. The Sappers with Flight-Sergeant Cox were included here. Our task was to capture the lonely villa and the radar equipment while Dennis Vernon, the senior Sapper, with Cox and Co., dismantled all the parts that were needed and photographed what couldn't be removed. Finally, a reserve party called 'Rodney' under John Timothy was to be interposed between the Radar Station and the most likely enemy approach so as to prevent interference with the dismantling.

We all got a great deal of amusement out of planning the more intimate details of the raid. While sitting round the model we were able to imagine just what the enemy were doing at that moment, and as there was a fairly well-appointed *estaminet* in the village, we hoped that the Germans would choose the night in question for a carousal. We hoped to achieve complete surprise, which would mean that everybody was in position to carry out their tasks before the alarm was raised. Having decided that I would give the signal for battle to commence on a whistle just before breaking into the villa, I was wondering what I should do if the door was locked. One of the men suggested that I should ring the bell, but in the event this proved unnecessary.

All this time security was one of the main considerations. It was obvious that if the enemy had an inkling of the project we should be doomed. Only the people who were intimately concerned were allowed to know the object and the destination and the men were not told the exact whereabouts of the Radar Station until just before taking off. In spite of the fact that we were living in another unit's camp, the secret was so well kept that no one in the Glider Pilot

Regiment had any idea of the reason for our being housed
and fed by them. Some among us found it almost impossible not to boast and a few of the wilder ones caused us no
little worry. These would let off steam in the pubs of
Tilshead, and one evening their party terminated in 'borrowing' instruments from the British Legion Band and
returning to camp in style. Thereafter the guard-room door
yawned more widely and the threat of being left behind
among the reinforcements was sufficient to ensure propri-
ety until the raid was over.

On 24 February we completed packing our containers
and they were dispatched to the aerodrome. We were
completely ready. We rested during the afternoon. At
tea-time a message came to announce a postponement of
twenty-four hours owing to bad weather, and each day until
Thursday the 27th was almost identical. The 27th was
considered to be the last possible day. We were all miserable. During this last phase we had had time to brood. Each
morning we had braced ourselves for the venture and each
day after a further postponement we had time to think of
all the things that could go wrong and to reflect that with
Thursday gone we should have to wait for a complete
month to elapse before conditions would be favourable
again. On Friday morning, when I was expecting to be told
to pack up or go on leave, a staff officer arrived to say that
Divisional Headquarters had got permission to wait for
one more night. Once again we went through the routine of
inspections, tidying up, sending the containers to the
aerodrome and so on, but this time perhaps rather listlessly
and without much enthusiasm. The one man who refused
to be depressed was Sergeant-Major Strachan. He was
quite convinced that Friday was the day; and, at tea-time,
instead of a final cancellation, General Browning came
over hurriedly to tell us that we were really going at last.

Having seen the men off to the aerodrome, I sat down to
supper with the Glider Pilots. It was hard to keep silent and
yet hard to talk. The next few hours would mean so much.
One could look at each munching face and say to oneself:
'Aha! You have no idea. In two or three hours I'll be flying
off to France. I have a rather exciting appointment!' Fleet-
ingly, during pauses in the conversation, a twinge of fear

would grip one's heart and one would say: 'Lucky devils, soon going off to bed in a warm little hut, while we'll be shivering and miserable somewhere up above, going to goodness knows what.'

After dinner I went to my room to dress myself in all the usual paraphernalia. It seemed specially heavy, cumbersome and incongruous at that time of day. All accoutred, I could not resist popping my head into the mess once more to see them already dozing comfortably round the fire. I met my batman outside. We got ourselves laboriously into the staff car and were off to Thruxton aerodrome.

The Company were dispersed in huts round the airfield perimeter and we visited each little party in turn. Some were fitting their parachutes, some having tea, others standing talking, and one little party was singing. It was a lovely clear night, no wind or noise from above. Sometimes one would hear an aircraft engine cough into life and always the sound of a vehicle coursing round the perimeter on some urgent mission or other. All pretty calm in fact.

I answered a call from Group Captain Sir Nigel Norman, the brilliant man who had planned the air side of the operation.

'Good luck,' he said. 'The latest news is that there is snow on the other side and I'm afraid the flak seems to be lively.'

I couldn't help feeling annoyed that some airman had been there so recently to awaken what I had imagined to be a sleeping hive and I fretted to think we had not been given white smocks to move about in in the snow. There was no snow in England and this was the first time I had any idea there might be any in France. However, it was too late to do anything about it and I drove round once more to see the men and tell them the latest news.

When the time came, we marched out in our little parties to the waiting aircraft. Piper Ewing played our regimental marches and as the turn of each regiment came, we cheered him on and so presented ourselves to the aircrews who were to take us. They seemed to us to be a different breed. They were accustomed to their nightly sortie, and were at ease and dressed for what they often did. We paraded as a strange new bomb-load.

I had a water bottle filled with tea well laced with rum. It was the rum that I felt I needed. While we were passing this around, Charles Pickard, the Squadron Leader, came along to see us. He was already a public figure in those days, the survivor of countless bombing raids and an inspiration to all he served with. However, he made no attempt to inspire me on that particular night, for drawing me aside, he said: 'I feel like a bloody murderer!'

So many men have since described what it feels like to go by air to battle that I hesitate to mention our feelings on the way to France. This was no grand armada. We were so very much by ourselves. We knew so little in fact that it was only at the last minute that I told the men our destination. At this period of the war the Germans were to us a terrible people. Their armies knew no halting and despite reverses in front of Moscow they seemed formidable in the extreme. So many things could go wrong with this particular party, but mostly we feared their Intelligence. With all the talk of German spies, most of us felt that they must have some inkling of what we were about to do, and one could almost imagine an agent reporting from the edge of the airfield.

Emplaned in the belly of a Whitley, slow, draughty, uncomfortable, cold and seemingly most vulnerable, I had time to consider all these things, including the alarming close-up photograph of our objective which had been presented to us a few days before we were due to leave. This had obviously been taken by a Spitfire or some such aircraft at nought feet and my attention had been drawn to the fact by one of the men.

'If they're going to go flashing cameras in their faces in that sort of way, how can we possibly surprise them?' he said.

'Oh, telephoto lens, you know, telephoto lens, taken from miles away,' I replied. 'Nothing to worry about at all.'

However, we did worry as we sat in silence enforced by the alternating roar and hush of the engines. I almost longed for a last-minute cancellation or for some last reason to delay our going. My stomach contracted as the aircraft began to move and bump along the perimeter track. Then finally came the surge forward with full throttle and all doubting went. To us, waiting inside the aircraft, the past was gone, the present was there and we strained every nook and cranny of our minds into the future stretching out across the Channel, pausing, then slowly pulling back home again. My aircraft took off soon after 10.30 p.m.

It was difficult to talk. The noise and vibration were considerable. We sat side by side on the floor, which was of ribbed aluminium and not at all comfortable. We were jammed close together and our legs covered with army blankets. Some of us sat inside sleeping bags. Sometimes we sang and then above all the din the voice of Flight-Sergeant Cox of the R.A.F. filled that gloomy fuselage with ringing cheery tones. So have we sung many times since on long flights over other countries when the engines seem to play the music of an unseen band.

The aircrews kept us informed as to our whereabouts. It seemed an age before we were truly settled on the way to our objective at the correct height. Although I had attended the aircrew's briefing, I had paid scant attention to their plans. We felt this was no concern of ours. We were a cargo to be dumped at the right place at the right time, and from what we had seen of our drivers we were fairly certain that we would land just where we hoped.

The tempo in the aircraft quickened perceptibly when we took the cover off the hole. Those sitting beside it looked down into the Channel and watched the water moving gently in the moonlight. This opening made the inside of the fuselage very cold and we drew our blankets closely about us and began to count the minutes. Suddenly, we were over land. Our enemies were now only six hundred feet below us. Soon we saw lights moving slowly up towards us which increased their speed viciously as they flashed beyond the limits of our view. The noise came later. We were not hit but the aircraft moved alarmingly as our pilot swung to divert the opposition's aim.

'Action stations!' came soon after. Away went our blankets, sleeping bags, and other comforts. The noise of the engines abated to a gentle humming. I dangled my legs in the hole. Then someone shouted 'Go!'

As I jumped I was able to recognize the ground as being identical with that depicted by the model, maps and photographs. All the features one expected to see were standing out in the bright moonlight. I landed very softly in the snow. There was no wind and all was silent apart from the noise of our aircraft stealing away into the night. My first action was a natural one. It was not good drill, for now was the time when a stick of parachutists are most vulnerable and one's first concern should be to make for the weapon containers. However it had become essential and was also a gesture of defiance. We collected at the rendezvous and in about ten minutes we were ready to move off. Just as we started towards the coast the next lot of aircraft came in and we could see some of 'Nelson' landing safely.

We met no opposition nor any obstacles other than wire fences on our way. We heard a few stray bursts of machine-gun fire in the distance, but from the area of the Radar Station, which we could see plainly, there was no sign of alarm. According to plan, silently and stealthily we surrounded the villa, and when everybody was in position I walked towards the door. It was open, and I nearly forgot to blow my whistle before going in. As soon as I blew it explosions, yells and the sound of automatic fire came from the proximity of the radar set and my party rushed into the house. It was devoid of furniture and we found only one German in a top room who was firing at our people down below. Having left a couple of men inside we went to reinforce the men near the set. By this time they had dealt with the enemy on the site, and had two prisoners, one of whom was a signaller. Newman, our interpreter, questioned them about their comrades. It seemed that our original information was correct. However, they were vague about the reserves based further inland and were almost incoherent with surprise and shock.

So far so good, but fairly soon the enemy opened fire on the villa from 'Le Presbytère' and one of our men was killed coming out of the door. Dennis Vernon with his Sappers arrived soon after this and he, with Flight-Sergeant Cox, began to inspect and dismantle the parts of the radar set which they wanted. Gradually the fire from the edge of 'Le Presbytère' increased and it became extremely uncomfortable in our area. Fortunately this fire was most inaccurate and caused no further casualties, although Dennis and his men were standing up round the set, which above ground consisted mostly of an instrument like an old-fashioned gramophone loudspeaker. However, some time later we noticed vehicles moving up behind the wood. These might contain far more dangerous elements and once the enemy began to mortar us in the open it would be difficult to get the equipment away. All our small wireless sets failed to work so I had no idea how the other parties had fared and I began to feel the lack of a proper Company Headquarter organization. We had turned ourselves into an assault group for the attack on the villa and now, when I wanted some signallers, runners and my sergeant-major, they were all dispersed doing other tasks.

I told Dennis that it was time to go. His men had been loading the pieces of equipment they had dismantled on to canvas trolleys and we all moved off down towards the beach. When we reached a pillbox on the shoulder of the cliff a machine-gun opened up on us from the other shoulder and we suffered casualties. Sergeant-Major Strachan was badly wounded in the stomach. We pulled him into cover and gave him some morphia. This machine-gun opened up each time we moved, but it was possible to make contact with 'Rodney' party, who were further inland. At this stage some confusion was caused by shouting from below. 'Come on down! Everything is all right and the boats are here.' This was immediately contradicted by John Ross who was near the beach.

'Do not come down. The beach defences have not been taken yet.'

Obviously something was seriously wrong with this part of the plan and just as I was going across to see John Timothy of 'Rodney' to order him to put in an immediate attack from his positions, a man came from behind to say that the Germans had reoccupied the villa and were advancing against us from that direction. Here again we were at a disadvantage as my men were armed only with Sten guns and grenades and the unorthodox formations we had adopted meant that I personally had to lead the party back to deal with this new threat, while I had many other things to think of.

Fortunately this threat did not amount to very much, for the Germans were still very confused and were up against they knew not what. As we returned to the pillbox, we found that the Sappers were on the move again, skidding and sliding with their heavily laden trollies down the steep frozen path to the beach. The Sergeant-Major was being dragged along down at the same time. The troublesome machine-gun was silent now, so one could presume that the beach defences had been taken. All the main features showed up well in the moonlight, but one could see men and movement only when they were close at hand.

I found Euen Charteris, the Commander of 'Nelson' party, near the main beach pillbox. He told me that he and two of his sections had been dropped about two miles short of the correct place. They had had a very difficult time finding their way across country through woods and hedges to Bruneval and had fought a tricky little battle with a German patrol en route. On one occasion the rear man of a section, having realized that someone had joined in behind, found that it was a very bewildered German soldier, who just could not make out who these strange people were. Euen and his party dealt with the machine-gun on the cliffs and swept down on to the beach with great aplomb. He quickly collected the remainder of 'Nelson' and every defender who showed himself was speedily dispatched, except for a very frightened telephone orderly who was caught in the act of answering an extremely angry German Company Commander. This gentleman wanted to know what the devil they meant by making so much noise at that time of the night, and they were all going to be for it in a big way in the morning.

There was now time to take stock. So far the object had been achieved. We had very few casualties. We knew roughly where everybody was. We had given the enemy a good hammering and so far they had produced no effective counter-measures. It was about a quarter past two in the morning. All we wanted now was the Navy. I found the signallers and told them to send for the boats, but to my disgust they said they could not make contact. Then we tried to summon them with a lamp, and still got no reply. There was a slight mist out to sea and visibility was no more than half a mile. We had arranged one last emergency means of communication, which was a red Very light fired first to the north and then to the south along the beach. Even after this had been fired several times there was no sign of recognition from the sea. With a sinking heart I moved off the beach with my officers to rearrange our defences in the entrance to the village and on the shoulders of the cliff. It looked as though we were going to be left high and dry once more and the thought was hard to bear. The prisoners were questioned as to the whereabouts of the enemy reserves, but they were too frightened to be coherent, and the great cliffs each side of the little beach seemed to lean over and dominate us with ever-growing menace.

Just as we had finished tidying up the perimeter there came a joyful shout from one of the signallers. 'Sir, the boats are coming in! The boats are here! God bless the ruddy Navy, sir!'

A sense of relief unbounded now spread amongst us all as we saw several dark shapes gliding in across the water towards us and we began to assemble in our various parties to embark. The men who manned the landing-craft opened fire on to the cliffs when they were about fifty yards from the beach. The noise was terrific as the echoes ran from cliff to cliff. We shouted and screamed at them to stop as some of our men were still in position to defend the beach from a landward attack. We had planned that only two boats would come in at a time, so that we could make an orderly withdrawal in three phases, but now all six landing-craft came in together and some looked as though they might be beached, as the sea was beginning to run fairly high. Amidst the noise and confusion it was impossible to control the embarkation.

Fortunately we were able to get the wounded and the enemy radar equipment on to one landing-craft very quickly, but the rest of our evacuation plan went by the board, and it was a case of getting as many men as possible on to each boat in turn. The Germans began to emerge from some of their hiding-places when they saw we were going and lobbed grenades and mortar bombs on to the beach. As far as we could tell, eventually all our men were away. Most of us soaked to the skin, for we had had to wade and scramble through the waves to reach the boats. We were not too pleased with this finale for it had not been as we had planned it. We had not been able to check every-body in and, as we reached the gunboats which were to bring us home, we heard a pathetic message from two signallers who had lost their way and reached the beach too late.

We were taken from the open landing-craft on to the gunboats, which were now to tow the landing-craft, and we went below to warm ourselves. We learnt that the Navy had been having their own troubles, for while they were waiting motionless for us offshore, a German destroyer and two E-boats had passed by less than a mile away and by God's good grace had failed to notice them. It was no wonder that they had been unable to answer our signals and that they had been in a hurry to take us off.

The sailors made us as comfortable as they could in the limited space available and made a great fuss of us, which I began to feel we did not deserve. In worrying about the future of the unfortunate few, I almost forgot that the object had been achieved and that no operation ever goes strictly according to plan. We were considerably cheered therefore to get a message from the ship which carried the captured radar equipment to say that we had managed to get practically everything that was wanted.

As daylight came, a squadron of Spitfires flew from England to meet us for it was thought that the enemy would make every effort to destroy us on the way home, but the morning passed without incident and we vainly tried to sleep as the gunboats rolled and jerked across the Channel. I went on to the bridge as we approached Portsmouth. There were destroyers now on either side of the flotilla and as we broke away to head for *Victory* they came by at speed and saluted us. The strains of 'Rule Britannia' rang out from their loud hailers while Spitfires dived down in turn before making off inland.

At about six o'clock that evening we boarded our old friend the *Prinz Albert*. Here we found Charles Pickard with his pilots and a great welcome. The ship was crowded with staff officers, photographers, reporters and all who had taken part in the raid. The limelight was strange after weeks of secrecy and stealth. All we really wanted was dry clothes, bed and oblivion; but before that there was some serious drinking to be done.

CHAPTER 4

Aftermath

On the evening after we had returned to our base at Tils-head, I was just getting into a bath when an officer hammered on the door and shouted: 'You have to get up to London right away because the Prime Minister wants to know the details. Division are sending a staff car and the driver will know where to take you.'

How very exciting, thought I – the only trouble being that there had been no time for a detailed debriefing. We had spent the day resting and cleaning up. Though I had a fairly clear idea of what had happened, I wanted to question the key personnel thoroughly before making my report.

Individual stories always need to be checked, for imagination and exaggeration can distort the truth. However, I think that it was about ten o'clock when I arrived in Birdcage Walk to be guided below to an underground room in the centre of which our own briefing model had been put.

Soon after, various important people drifted in. One of the first was Major Clement Attlee, the Deputy Prime Minister, who asked me to tell him all about it. I was reluctant to perform before a one-man audience. He was insistent, so I began, but very soon he said: 'How do you know all this?'

'Because I was there.'

'You mean that you were actually on the raid?'

'Yes, and I have been sent up here to tell the Prime Minister all about it.'

'Good heavens,' said he, looking at me in a rather

puzzled way. 'Well, perhaps we had better wait to hear the whole story from the start.'

Soon the Chiefs of Staff and Cabinet Ministers gathered round the model, and I was glad to see Lord Louis arrive. He came up, and said nice things. The C.I.G.S. introduced me to the Secretary of State For War, Sir James Grigg, saying: 'I wonder if you have met the Minister.'

I felt like saying something to the effect that I had never dreamt of meeting such people, but would dearly love to continue doing so.

Suddenly the Prime Minister was there, siren-suited and with outsize cigar. I suppose I was conspicuous in my Cameronian Major's uniform for without further ado he came up to say: 'Bravo, Frost, bravo, and now we must hear all about it.'

However, fortunately for me, I hardly had to utter, because even in the short time that had passed since our action Lord Louis had managed to gather and absorb all the important items and aspects, and as Chief of Combined Operations he told the story, with all the background information, as no one else could have done. The accounts which had already appeared in the press had been clear and accurate, except about the purpose of it all.

Soon after Lord Louis had begun what was after all a most exciting and unusual tale, we could all hear a mumble of diversionary conversation coming from a corner of the room. Anthony Eden, the then Foreign Secretary, and Archibald Sinclair, Secretary of State for Air, were having a little private chat. The P.M. began to look disconcerted and then, having held up a hand to halt Lord Louis, he turned round slowly and said: 'Come over here, you two, and listen to this, for then you might learn something for once in your lives.'

Putting their hands behind their backs and smiling sheepishly, they skipped across to take their places near the model, and then the P.M. nodded to Lord Louis to continue.

However, soon after this, he again stopped the Admiral and asked me about the accuracy of the information I had been given. I was able to say that this had proved to be correct in every detail even down to the name of the

German sergeant, commanding the most important
redoubt. When told that the officer responsible for this,
Wing Commander Le Marquis de Casa Maury, was standing beside me, the P.M. turned his gaze upon him with such
intensity that it had an impact on us all. A beatific smile
ended the episode and Lord Louis was able to go on to the
end.

'What did we get out of all this?' now asked the P.M.

The Chief of the Air Staff, Air Chief Marshal Portal,
began to describe the possible benefits in rather technical
terms which soon brought a forcible protest.

'Now just stop all that nonsense, Portal, and put it into
language that ordinary normal mortals can understand.'

Quite unabashed, the Air Marshal explained that we
now had every hope of not only being able to improve our
own radar, but that at some future date of our own choosing we would be able to jam the whole of the enemy radar
advanced warning system.

The P.M. then went up to the model so that he could
move his fingers up the cliffs there depicted. As he did this
he said: 'This is the way they will come, if they come, up
and over the cliffs. Just where we least expect them. Now
about the raids. There must be more of them. Let there be
no doubt about that.' With which he swirled out.

Then, led by the C.I.G.S., Lord Louis and General
Browning advanced on the Chief of the Air Staff, saying:
'More aircraft, more aircraft, more aircraft.'

The C.A.S. raised his arms and fists in mock defence,
and backed slowly and smilingly out of the room. Everyone
then left, and the staff car took me to my club for my much
delayed bath.

The Bruneval raid came at a time when our country's
fortunes were at a low ebb. Singapore had recently fallen
and the German battleships had escaped up the Channel
from Brest in the very teeth of everything that could be
brought against them. Many people were disgruntled after
a long catalogue of failures, and the success of our venture,
although it was a mere flea-bite, did have the effect of
making people feel that we could succeed after all.

One very beneficial result from our own point of view

was that it put airborne forces on the map. General 'Boy'
Browning had been having difficulty in persuading people
that airborne forces could play a really useful part in the
war. Despite the successes of the German airborne troops,
the traditional conservatism of many Service chiefs stood
in the way of experiment, very largely because our more
conventional resources were already strained. Now our
General was able to get some degree of priority and the
Prime Minister, who had initiated the formation of our
Parachute troops, was encouraged to ensure that we had
the necessary support. It was also a feather in the cap for
Headquarters Combined Operations.

We got into trouble over equipment lost during the
operation. We were on a peace-time system of accounting,
and it was difficult for some people to understand that
almost inevitably things go missing in the confusion and
flurry of action against a live enemy which includes a hasty
evacuation by sea in the dark. It was not perhaps surprising
that we lost some of the wireless equipment because it had
proved to be extremely inefficient and unreliable. Our vital
communications with the Navy had not worked at all and
the inter-company sets had proved equally ineffective. The
problem of communications was to bedevil nearly all airborne operations throughout the rest of the war.

Casualties were light considering the risks involved and
the importance of the mission, amounting to two killed, six
wounded and six missing. The missing were all from the
party which had been dropped in the wrong place, so that
the men had not been able to find their way to the beach in
time. Some of them were subsequently hidden by a brave
French couple for several days, and with a little luck they
might have escaped altogether. The French family were
caught in the act by the Germans and, after being severely
mishandled, spent the rest of the war in a concentration
camp. I am glad to be able to say that they were suitably
decorated for their gallantry after the war was over.

All the wounded made rapid recoveries except for Company Sergeant-Major Strachan. He was on the danger list
for a long time, having received several bullets in his
stomach. However, after hanging between life and death
for many days, he finally made a great recovery, and to

everyone's amazement was parachuting again a few
months later and eventually rejoined the battalion as
R.S.M. Private Newman, the German interpreter, was
whisked away as soon as we got back to England. He took
part in the raid on St. Nazaire shortly afterwards and was
taken prisoner. Fortunately for him the name and number
which we had given him corresponded with the actual
name and number of a soldier who had disappeared from
the army between the wars. As a result the Germans,
having checked his credentials with the Red Cross,
accepted him as a British soldier and as such he survived
the war and now lives happily and prosperously in the
north of England.

Soon after the raid I was sent all over the kingdom to tell
various people about it. Among other establishments, I
spent a night with American Bomber Command H.Q.,
where I was initiated into the custom of drinking aperitifs
and night-caps out of tooth-mugs in bedrooms because, at
that time, drinking in the mess was taboo. I enjoyed a
splendid evening with the Polish Parachute Brigade who
made up with enthusiasm all that they lacked in material
backing. Their nation's tragedy made them all the keener
to set an example in ingenuity and for them difficulties
existed as challenges to be overcome.

   I had the honour of meeting our reigning monarch and
the Queen when they came to watch Pickard's Squadron
drop a company of the 3rd Battalion at Dishforth in Yorkshire. The Wing Commander had arranged that, as soon as
the Royal party entered the station, a message was to be
sent to the circling aircraft to start the drop. Unfortunately
at the last minute the King decided to visit the guard-room
at the gate and while he was inside the drop began. Frantic
signalling just managed to stop the last two aircraft so that
the party could at least see these two sticks performing, but
it was a near thing. However, everyone concerned much
enjoyed the Royal visit. I must admit to being captivated
and found it easy thereafter to say with heart and voice,
'God save the King'. Indeed this could be very useful at
times even though not said aloud.

I have been to Bruneval several times since. On the first occasion, General de Gaulle made the speech which initiated the formation of the Rassemblement du Peuple Français. There was a terrible traffic mix-up which forced many of the V.I.P.s to foot it across country, among them the British Ambassador and Lady Diana Duff Cooper. I never managed to meet the General, who ignored the Parachute Regiment Guard of Honour and made no reference to the part that we British had played, but I believe it was all a great success from a political point of view. On another occasion, H.Q. Combined Operations sponsored a return and some of us went over in great comfort aboard Royal Navy destroyers. Members of 44 Parachute Brigade of the Territorial Army parachuted in very adverse weather so that they came down oscillating most alarmingly, breaking telephone lines and the roof of an ambulance in the process. Nevertheless no one was really hurt and a young naval officer was heard to say: 'We shall have to revise our ideas about pongos after this.'

The last occasion was for the unveiling of a memorial to all who had taken part. This was attended by Ministers and ambassadors, including the Russian, but, most fittingly, also present was Admiral of the Fleet The Earl Mountbatten of Burma, K.G., who had masterminded our raid all those years before. Among all the memories of illustrious events that a great Captain must have had, I like to think that perhaps Bruneval did have a special place.

My lecture tour over and all the shouting done, I brought the company back to Hardwick Hall. We felt considerable reaction and found it hard to settle down. As humans will, we quickly forgot all the anxieties and unpleasantness and could only remember the thrill and excitement.

The 1st Parachute Battalion had been in existence for over a year before we were formed and many of them felt strongly that they should have been chosen for the operation. General Richard Gale was our Brigadier at the time and he deliberately chose one of the newly formed battalions so as to prove that his whole Brigade was ready for action at any time. I am sure this was a very wise decision and in time the 1st Battalion came to accept it too. They were scheduled to take part in the Dieppe raid, but luckily for them their part was cancelled, for it proved to be a costly failure. Anyway we were all thirsting for action whatever might be the cost, and soon after going back to Hardwick the whole Brigade moved down to Salisbury Plain and the 2nd Battalion went into barracks in Bulford.

Once settled in on the Plain, everybody got down to the business of serious training. We paid great attention to physical fitness and before long our men were able to travel considerable distances without fatigue. All platoons were required to be able to cover fifty miles in twenty-four hours, and all battalions to be able to march thirty miles and more for several days in succession, with some mortar men laden up to nearly one hundredweight. These semi-endurance tests resulted in a solid welding together of officers, N.C.O.s and men and it was soon obvious that a very fine instrument of war was being prepared. Unfortunately, despite the example and the directives of our G.O.C., we failed to spend quite as much time on the ranges as we should have done. We were to find that there is no short cut or substitute for skill at arms and without this skill fitness, discipline, enthusiasm and all the rest counted for little when there was a real live enemy to contend with.

Each Battalion in turn went down to Exmoor to train on its own in the wild country there. For a short time I was transferred to the 3rd Battalion as Second-in-Command. Our training on Exmoor was of great value and we marched all the way back to Bulford in tremendous form. While there it transpired that a small pack of harriers called The Quarm was about to be put down as it was being found impossible to feed them owing to the wartime shortages. They were liver and white and seemed manageable, so I decided to save them and keep them back at Bulford. I put them in with a couple and a half of what remained of the R.A. harriers' pack in their kennels at Bulford and had a lot of fun chasing hares on the Plain. Others took over after we left and at the end of the war Airborne forces handed over a going concern to the Salisbury Plain gunners.

There was an acute shortage of aircraft suitable for drop-ping parachutists; only a few squadrons of obsolete Whitleys were available, so actual parachute training was minimal. Later that year an American parachute battalion arrived in the United Kingdom with their own squadron of Dakotas. These aircraft were far superior to anything we had seen before and could carry twenty men instead of the ten which was all that the Whitley could hold. We were all very eager indeed to jump from them.

When our turn came to have a closer look, we went to Netheravon aerodrome and waited to see the squadron arrive. As they approached, the leader peeled off in a stall turn and very narrowly missed colliding with the plane immediately behind. It was a startling performance and when all the pilots had finally landed, some of them told their leader exactly what they thought of him well within our hearing. However, we all liked the aircraft immediately. It was wonderful to be able to sit in comfort on seats, to look out of the window and see what was going on, to talk and walk about and even smoke.

It took time for the necessary alterations to be made to the Dakotas before we could jump from them because our parachutes differed considerably from the American equipment. However, after various trials had been carried out, the day came when the 2nd Battalion was to drop company by company. Quite apart from the other conditions, the American pilots' technique for dropping was also new to us. They approached the dropping-zone at almost ground level until they were about one mile away when they pulled their aircraft up sharply and suddenly to seven or eight hundred feet. The parachutists, at this time, would be standing one behind the other in the aircraft and this sudden upward surge was a most exhilarating performance which always brought a tremendous cheer from the stick. Just before giving the signal to jump, the pilot throttled back and put the aircraft into a shallow dive. Then the men poured out from the door at the rear.

On this particular day, having taken off from Netheravon, the aircraft flew low, just above the roof tops of Tidworth and Cholderton, then turned round towards the aerodrome again and did their sudden upward swoops over Beacon Hill. We all jumped out over the Figheldean dropping-zone.

Mental uplift and enthusiasm were soon dispelled, however, for there were three accidents which resulted in four men being killed that day.

One man had a 'Roman candle'. This term described the non-development of the parachute after it had been pulled out of its bag. It was at that time an inexplicable event and no blame could be attached to anyone. Another man had come down with his parachute still intact, in its bag, on his back. The dog clip which fastened the static line of the parachute to the strong point in the aircraft had been forced open, despite the holding wire, and so there was no chance of the canopy's developing at all. The last accident was caused by the canopy of one man's parachute becoming entangled in the tail of the aircraft. This man, while swinging beneath the aircraft, collided with one of the men following, and they plummeted down to lie together like crumpled bundles on the ground.

Despite these disasters we all knew that the difficulties would soon be resolved, for resolved they had to be. The next stage would be getting the American pilots to learn to fly and drop us by night. So far, they were only trained in daylight operations and the number of navigators in the squadron was limited. The Dakotas were comparatively slow unarmed aircraft, most vulnerable to enemy fighters in daylight, unless escorted by our own.

Under active service conditions the ability to fly exactly to, and drop loads on, a certain place several hundred miles from home base was one that few of these pilots possessed. It took a great deal of time and experience, and there could be no doubt, therefore, that any operations we undertook in the near future would have to be in daylight.

Early in October 1942, the 1st Parachute Brigade were ordered to get ready to go overseas, and I rejoined the 2nd Battalion as Second-in Command. On the 29th of the month, the Battalion embarked at Greenock. During the period of mobilization, Goften Salmond, the Commanding Officer, had been ill and afflicted with painful sores, but he was determined to come if it was humanly possible. The doctors managed to keep him on his feet throughout, but the strain was too much and as soon as he embarked he was forced to take to his bed. The Brigadier decided that this was an unsatisfactory state of affairs and he thereupon gave orders for Goften Salmond to be put ashore and I was given command. Our voyage was uneventful for the convoy was very strongly escorted. Although we were packed like sardines on the ship it was a pleasant change from wartime England, and the food on board was very much better than that which we had been used to. We had no idea what our objective was until being told after the convoy turned into the Straits of Gibraltar. Till then most people had their money on Dakar.

CHAPTER 5

Maison Carreé

On 12 November 1942 the 2nd Battalion of the Parachute Regiment landed at Algiers as part of the First British Army which was to thrust eastwards across North Africa to occupy Tunis and Bizerta. The rest of the 1st Parachute Brigade had already arrived by sea and air. I was ordered to march them to a suburb of Algiers called Maison Carrée and there to arrange to billet them with the help of the local French authorities.

The next few days were spent unpacking at the billets or the airfield, doing odd jobs and trying to keep fit for an imminent operation in awkward circumstances. Although the local French seemed to be friendly, many were dubious about coming back into the war with us as allies. Moreover most of them were anti-de Gaulle and his Free French movement and so there was the possibility of a difficult emergency suddenly arising. This made it hard to keep training as rigorously as I would have liked. A further problem was the presence of American troops billeted in neighbouring houses, for at that time in the war their ways were not our ways.

The Eighth Army had won their great victory at Alamein and were now advancing through Libya, and on the Russian front the Germans had suffered many reverses. Indeed it had begun to look as though the tide had really turned.

It was now also essential for me to get to know my officers better. I had been away from the 2nd Battalion for several months, but having been with them as Adjutant and Company Commander before doing my stint with the

3rd Battalion, I knew most of them quite well.

Philip Teichman, the Second-in-Command, had originally been senior to me and my rival for command of 'C' Company prior to the Bruneval Raid. He therefore had reason to feel vexed that I should yet again supersede him and it was asking much that I should have his loyalty. We were very different types. He was a lawyer by trade and although a keen territorial officer, was very much a civilian at heart. Nevertheless I felt that I could trust him implicitly. Jock Short, the Adjutant, was a most forthright character who would never find it easy to change methods and habits. I had quite different ideas to those of my predecessor and I fear that Jock found it hard to accept the changes I sought.

'A' Company was commanded by Dick Ashford. He had been a rival contender for the adjutancy when the battalion first formed and had stepped into my shoes when I took over 'C' Company before the Bruneval Raid. He was socialistically inclined and disliked regular officers on principle. Not a cosy subordinate. Frank Cleaver of 'B' Company was another promoted ranker, but with all the traditional loyalties, and was a great man to have about. The 'C' Company leader was John Ross who had been my Second-in-Command for Bruneval. He was still of tender years for his rank and responsibility, but a great heart beat beneath a somewhat dour exterior.

There were no weak links among the subalterns. Perhaps Ken Morrison and Pat Playford were outstanding for I felt that they could tackle anything. Dennis Rendell was cheerful and dedicated, Henry Cecil one of the more amusing contributors to our life in the mess, while Euen Charteris, the Intelligence Officer, was the acme of ebullience though seeming to need twice as much food as anyone else to keep going.

We found that the French were prepared to be very helpful and friendly and by the evening the whole battalion had been very comfortably settled in. Most were fitted into the various schools which were sited in different parts of the town. On the whole they were well built and roomy buildings with water laid on and all usual conveniences. Battalion Headquarters and the officers' mess were put in the

largest girls' school we could find, as it was hoped that this
would be the cleanest place available, and it was indeed a
very attractive building with all the necessary niches for the
various parts of headquarters. The schoolchildren were
delighted with our invasion. The shopkeepers and wine-
sellers rubbed their hands and most of the townspeople
found much to amuse themselves by watching us moving
in. All our heavy baggage and stores were being brought
from the docks by huge and ancient *camions* with solid
tyres and charcoal burners. We had not one single vehicle
of our own, but I was very fortunate in having acquired one
motor-cycle and this machine was in use continually from
dawn till dusk.

That evening, as I was sitting in my newly established
office thinking that things had really gone very well indeed,
I was suddenly confronted by a very angry American colonel. He had arrived in Maison Carrée soon after the initial
landings, having had quite a battle with the local French
forces. The situation had been confused for some time and
even now he wasn't on firm ground with the local French
Commander. As a result, he was inclined to resent our
sudden, and to him unannounced, arrival. The Americans
assumed that the French would be better disposed to them
than to us and were perhaps piqued to find that this was not
always the case. Whereas we were assuming that there was
no immediate threat to our security, the Americans were
taking no chances.

Leading elements of the British First Army were struggling with Axis Forces in Tunisia some five or six hundred
miles farther east. It had been the intention that the 1st
Parachute Brigade would drop near Tunis or Bizerta,
either or both, with a view to preventing the enemy from
coming in to Tunisia. However, the Germans reacted to the
Allied landing so quickly that the opportunity for a *coup-
de-main* was too fleeting to be risked. The 3rd Battalion,
part of which had flown from England to Africa via Gibraltar, had occupied the small port of Bône unopposed. The
1st Battalion had dropped on the borders of Tunisia and,
having rallied the French troops in that area, had advanced
to meet the enemy near Medjez el Bab, a town of which the
name means 'the key of the gate' and a real key-point it

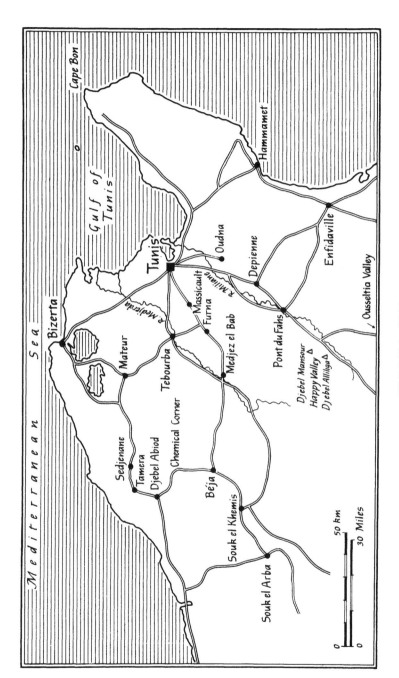

TUNISIA: 1942

proved to be. We of the 2nd Battalion had to possess our souls in patience waiting for a suitable job to come.

It wasn't very easy to find a worthwhile job for us to do, and as every single man who could be made available was urgently required up forward, we feared that we might never get our parachute operation, but would be sent for in a purely infantry role. The very extended communications and the number of headquarters between the front and ourselves made it extremely difficult to plan an operation, quite apart from actually mounting one. Our Brigadier, Flavell, would go to Allied Force Headquarters every day to see if there was any worthwhile target, but by the time information had percolated down through 78th Division, 5th Corps, First Army to A.F.H.Q. it was apt to be a little out of date for our purpose. In those days nobody knew what airborne forces could be expected to do and we certainly didn't know ourselves; though of one thing we felt quite certain: that there was practically nothing we couldn't do.

One evening the Brigadier came in to see us. At last there was an idea. I was to fly up to Tunisia and have a look at the small port of Sousse with a view to dropping the battalion nearby and capturing the place. It was thought that there were very few, if any, Axis troops in that area and we should have to hold it only until an infantry brigade arrived from Malta. We should then advance with them northwards towards Tunis. This plan seemed to have distinct possibilities, and we received first-hand information from various Frenchmen who had been at Sousse recently. The French troops who had been there before the landings had come over to our side *en bloc*, so there would be no complications about doubtful allies. The next day the Holy City of Kairouan was mentioned as a possible additional commitment for us. It might be possible to drop part of the battalion at Sousse and part at Kairouan and we should be able to keep contact by using the railway running between the two places. Anyway, it was reckoned that there were infinite possibilities and, as far as we were concerned, we were willing to have a go at anything.

Early one morning I reported to the flying control at Maison Blanche airfield. The Duty Officer told me that there was a Bisley waiting for me and I found the pilot beside his aircraft on the edge of the airfield nearby.

'Look,' he said, 'this is not on. There are Messerschmitts and Focke-Wulfs where we are going and if they see us we won't come back.'

'Well, I've got a recce to do and having done it I must come back again, because, without my information the next airborne operation can't take place.'

'You ought to be going in a Beaufighter. You would be there and back in the time it will take us to do one leg of the trip and if we did see enemy fighters we would have some sort of a chance. I think I will just get on the phone to see if there hasn't been a mistake.'

He was back a few minutes later.

'No,' he said. 'No mistake. You must be expendable. So off we go for better or worse.'

It was a most uncomfortable flight. There was thick cloud the whole way and at anything over nine thousand feet the aircraft started to collect ice. The tops of the mountains on our route were up to eight thousand feet, so there didn't seem to be very much in the way of margin. I made my eyes tired peering out into the whiteness, expecting at any moment to see the sides of a great craggy Atlas mountain looming bang into our nose and I wondered just how much one would know about such a sudden ending. I had a most uncomfortable little seat to the side of and slightly behind the pilot and had no chance of dozing off. Over Tunisia the cloud faded away.

'Makes it all the easier for Heinrich,' grinned our pilot.

Sousse was unmistakable on the edge of the sea, with green orchards on its outskirts, and roads running in from several directions. There was a big open space to the south of it which looked like a mud flat, and this, I thought, would do very well for our dropping-zone. We came down to ground level to have a close look at it and I was sure that it would do. It might have been a little on the hard side, and if any sort of a wind was blowing, we should be dragged a good long way before being checked by formidable cactus hedges which surrounded the mud flat.

Having come down, the pilot decided to stay down and fly low until we were out of danger from enemy fighters.

We had another job to do on the way home. An American parachute battalion had been dropped at a place called Tébessa, which was an important road junction on the extreme right flank of the Allied forces in Tunisia. The position was very isolated, at least a hundred miles from any other, and so, as these Americans had come out to Africa under the command of 1st Parachute Brigade, my Brigadier thought it would be a nice gesture if I called in to see how they were getting on. We flew up a railway line towards Tébessa and as we approached we climbed to about a thousand feet. Then, having recognized the town-let and the landing-ground, we circled it and began to come down. We could see what we took to be a Dakota on the edge of the landing-ground and a fair number of American soldiers moving about.

Suddenly we realized we were being shot at. Bullet-holes appeared in the wings and the pilot shouted: 'We've been hit. My controls are soggy.'

'I believe those are German troops down there and that's a Junkers, not a Dakota,' said the gunner.

I sat still, miserably, saying nothing. I could not believe that the Germans had suddenly managed to capture the place. Then we were down to a rough landing; one of the wheels was obviously punctured and we pulled up with a jerk, one wing sagging.

At once troops appeared with weapons at the ready and we were ordered out. However, they *were* Americans. They reckoned we were Germans coming in to drop a bomb and so they had opened up. There were no markings under the wings of the Bisley and as the Americans had already been caught by an enemy aircraft which looked very like ours they were taking no chances. My visit was practically useless because their Colonel and most of the battalion were probing forward and the only officers I met did not know what 1st Parachute Brigade was anyway. It was bitterly cold there, being several hundred feet above sea level, and I was most anxious to get away. There was no hope of the Bisley's being able to take off until various things were done to it, and a spare tyre and other parts would have to be flown from its base. The Dakota pilot wasn't at all anxious to go anywhere without a fighter escort. However, at last he listened to my entreaties and agreed to take me back to Maison Blanche. I claimed that on the morrow I had to lead the airborne operation which would pave the way to an early finish of the campaign, and the thought that if he didn't take me he might delay his own return to the U.S.A. was what won the day.

This leg of my journey was as pleasant as the other was horrid. We flew just above the clouds in the sunlight and I was able to lie on a big heap of sacking with my head near a window, watching the changing shapes and colours of the cloud and making music in my mind from the rising and falling noise of the engines. It was getting dark as we approached Algiers, and at first the airfield was a little reluctant to receive us, but at last we were down and I went to report to Brigade Headquarters straight away. Before I even had a chance of relating my adventures I was told that my recce was no longer of any value as the plan had been changed; we were now to drop at Enfidaville, which was about thirty miles north of Sousse, and there would be another nice Bisley to fly me there tomorrow.

I felt that I was quite justified in being cross with Brigade. However, there was nothing one could really say as there might have been some very good reason for confirming the map in this way. In any case, having only just got command, I didn't want to appear reluctant about anything to do with operations. I was very tired and went to bed full of forebodings, but the next day we went to Enfidaville and back without incident, returning over, and about ten feet above, the sea. At Brigade Headquarters I was told that the Enfidaville show was no longer on.

The next few days were very trying. We had got wound up to go and now we began to feel flat and rather out of sorts with each other. Among our number were a few who were apt to be really wild when given any encouragement and by now they had discovered where they could buy the liquor which had the most effect for the least money. When primed, some of them were quite formidable and the average rather inexperienced N.C.O. of those days was not really capable of dealing with them. Our original Americans had been replaced by American parachutists, and now each evening quarrels arose which were sometimes settled with savagery. At Blida airfield some French parachutists had been training for many years, and hearing about the evening battles in Maison Carrée, they began to arrive in batches and joined in impartially wherever a fight could be found. We were no longer the only British troops in Maison Carrée, for a large headquarters had been set up not far away, and the Military Police attached to it began to put their spoke in. Unfortunately the 'Red Caps' had a somewhat adverse effect on the behaviour of our delinquents and I became rather harassed by it all. Some of the local French were glad to make capital out of the incidents which occurred and, indeed, there were young men among them who were always ready to attack a soldier when they could find one on his own. One evening, Mickey Wardle, the brigade Intelligence Officer, was set upon in a lonely street by two hostile youths. He was getting very much the worst of it when, fortunately for him, a large Grenadier Guardsman appeared on the scene. The guardsman introduced himself characteristically with his tremendous stamp of foot and a shout: 'Permission to join in, sir.'

On the morning of the 28th I was briefed to take the battalion to an enemy airstrip at Pont du Fahs in Tunisia and to destroy any enemy aircraft we found; to move to Depienne some twelve miles further on and deal with another airstrip there; to repeat the performance at Oudna, another twelve miles on; and finally to link up with the First Army which we would find at St. Cyprien.

It seemed quite a lot one way and another. We should have no transport unless we could capture some and we had a long way to go carrying all the ammunition, food, batteries and other stores we needed for at least five days. However, we were not the least worried; there was talk of a combined thrust by the 6th Armoured Division, and we imagined ourselves being 'Primus in Carthago', gloriously. There was no information about the local inhabitants in the area in which we were to operate and we imagined that they would be friendly. To help them be nice we were given a large sum in francs, and even if this only went on buying eggs, it seemed that life for us among the 'tribes' was expected to be without serious problems. Very little was known about the likely opposition either. We knew that the aircraft on the landing-grounds to which we were going were causing a deal of trouble to First Army, and we also knew that the enemy required every man they could lay their hands on to hold our thrust. We could only guess at the strength and speed of his counter-measures and hope that he would not be able to spare any armour. Our anti-tank performance left a great deal to be desired as we depended on the Boys anti-tank rifle, which could damage only the tracks of enemy tanks, and the Gammon bomb, an untried weapon which one had to be close enough to the target to throw. Anyway, I felt that if we looked like getting into trouble we could always take to the hills and live to fight another day.

We were to be flown by American crews in Dakotas which had already dropped three other battalions in Tunisia. However, our mission looked like being a bit more hazardous than the others and everyone was insisting that our armada should include adequate 'pursuit'.

A troop of the 1st Parachute Field Squadron RE and a Section of the Parachute Field Ambulance were included in our order of battle. The Dakotas normally lived at Blida, an airfield some forty miles away, so the details about the arrival and parking of aircraft were not easy to come by and eventually a very sketchy plan was brought along by Brigade late in the evening. According to this, the aircraft were going to be parked up on both sides of the main runway for our emplanement. Having made all the necessary arrangements, loaded our containers, issued the ammunition, given out the various codes, distributed money, written the orders, inspected the troops, and said our prayers, we went to bed fairly exhausted.

At dawn of the 29th we were all up and working. For once there was a fair amount of transport to take us and our belongings to the airfield and provided the aircraft arrived according to plan we had no problems left to face, but this was not to be. Not only did aircraft park on only one side of the runway, but each one had two lots of chalk numbers on it so that it was impossible to decide which lot of men were meant to go in which aircraft. It had rained during the night. Soon lorries and aircraft began to get stuck in the soft mud at the edge of the runway, and, cursing mightily,

officers and men grappled with their containers as they
splodged through the muck looking for their aircraft.
There was nothing one could do to lessen the confusion as
we had no means of communicating with anyone apart
from shouting, and everybody was doing that already. The
Brigadier and I went to hear the pilots being briefed and,
as we were making our way back to the runway, hoping
desperately that the loading was somehow being done, new
information came to the effect that neither Pont du Fahs or
Depienne was being used by enemy aircraft. This meant a
last-minute change of plan and it was decided that we
should now drop at Depienne, march to Oudna where we
would deal with the enemy aircraft and then link up with
First Army at St. Cyprien. The pilots had to be rebriefed in
a hurry and there was no time for a detailed study of the
map to find a suitable dropping-zone. It was agreed that we
would fly low and slow over Depienne, and that when I saw
a suitable-looking open space, I should jump and the other
aircraft would take their cue from us. There was no chance
of warning the whole battalion of this change in the plan,
but as there should be plenty of time to give out fresh
orders at Depienne this didn't matter. 'Take-off' was
scheduled for midday and as the time drew near, a few
sticks were still not ready. At the pre-arranged time my
aircraft lumbered down the main runway and we missed,
by a hair's-breadth, hitting a medical stick which had had to
reload from one aircraft to another as their first mount had
got irretrievably bogged.

Airborne, we circled, cursing as we watched the slow
unwinding of the muddle down below. There was a dead-
line time and if we were not all on our way by then, we
should have to land and go through the whole ghastly
business again next day. Although the inadequate planning
and subsequent confusion were not our fault, many of us
chose that day to be particularly stupid. When we had been
flying for nearly an hour I saw the last aircraft coming up to
join us and then we all headed for the east.

CHAPTER 6

Oudna

It was clear and cloudless as we flew between the peaks of the mountains, but it was a rough passage with sudden gusts of wind buffeting us and every now and then these blew in through the open door. Our neighbours in the flight rose and fell unceasingly and there was no peace or rest for us inside. Up above us were American Lightnings and far away on the flanks came British Hurricanes, but no enemy approached. After the mountains we saw the plains and we lost height until we skimmed the dry brown earth. With only a few minutes to go I went forward to see the pilot.

"It's easy today and I know exactly where I am,' he said. 'Are you going to be able to make out O.K.?'

'If it is like this at Depienne we shall have nothing to worry about,' I replied.

Below us the country appeared to be smooth and level with no obstacles except an odd dried-up watercourse and a few clumps of cactus. I was standing at the door as we swept over Pont du Fahs, which had been our original target, and as a result of our study of the place it seemed quite familiar. Then came Depienne and as soon as we had passed over it I jumped. Having landed, I made for a small mound at the edge of the dropping-zone and sounded a note or two on my hunting-horn (the one which I had been given when I left Habbaniyah) to let people know where I was. The battalion was dropped far and wide and a deep gully separated some sticks from their weapon containers, causing considerable delay in the process of assembly. Dominating the whole scene was a great rocky peak rising abruptly some five thousand feet above the surrounding plain; this, the Djebel Zagouan, was so prominent a landmark that it helped us to keep direction during the whole operation. Gradually the battalion sorted itself out and headquarters gathered at my mound, but far too many soldiers were taking a long time to collect themselves. I thought that perhaps it was the sudden lessening of the tension they had felt in the aircraft and relief at being, as they thought, safe on the ground. This time the confusion seemed to be more than usually pronounced, and then I remembered that most of the battalion had expected to arrive at Pont du Fahs and they were now experiencing difficulty in finding their rendezvous. I sent orders to the companies by wireless that they were to take up positions on the edge of the dropping-zone, and summoned the company commanders.

It was now after four o'clock in the afternoon and suddenly three armoured cars appeared on the road leading east from Depienne. To our great relief they were friendly and belonged to the 56th Recce Regiment. I had not been told to expect any of our own forces in the area so soon and therefore this meeting was very encouraging, even more so because the troop commander was most optimistic and trundled on down the road in the direction we would take later on.

I took stock before the company commanders arrived. About six men were injured and one killed as a result of heavy landings. As the French people of Depienne proved to be more than helpful, it seemed best to leave the injured in the village from which they could be evacuated when the opportunity arose. Some form of transport we must have, even if it meant requisitioning every vehicle we could find no matter how vital it was to its owners. Already we had collected one or two mule carts from the natives, who had appeared from all directions, bent on scrounging as many parachutes as they could. Brigade had ordered me to salvage our parachutes, although this entailed leaving much-needed men behind when we moved, and now we literally had to fight off the would-be looters, for they were most persistent. Some held their ground until shots were falling right among them, and it was maddening to have to waste valuable ammunition in this way. With a shock I realized that the battalion was already rather weary, for there had been no let-up for several hours and the time of waiting for a task in Maison Carrée had not served to harden them. I decided that we should make no move until well into the night so that we could start our march comparatively fresh. Another advantage to be got by waiting was that we might deceive the enemy into thinking that our task was to hold onto Depienne. Several months later I learnt that a German patrol had actually watched us landing.

The troop of armoured cars came back through our positions about an hour later and told us that there was an enemy road-block near a place called Cheylus. They said that they hoped to catch up with us at Oudna the next day and that they would do what they could for our dropping casualties. I reckoned it was about twelve miles to Oudna and that if we started at midnight, we should be able to attack at first light, having done the whole approach under cover of darkness. We could avoid the main road by using a track which was shown on the map as being a reasonable route and, with any luck, we should meet no enemy on the way. When the company commanders arrived I discovered that one stick of 'C' Company had not turned up, so I decided to leave the rest of that platoon at Depienne with the unenviable task of salvaging the parachutes. Having given out orders for the move and fixed the timing, we rolled ourselves up in any parachutes that were handy and tried to sleep.

We formed up and moved off before midnight. We were very glad to go, for as the sun went down it had become cold, and we only had light camouflage smocks over our shirts. By this time the companies had managed to collect quite a number of mules and carts and a certain amount of the heavier equipment had been loaded on them. Even so, some of the men were carrying as much as a hundredweight on their backs. We had to be self-supporting for four or five days and we knew that our stocks of ammunition could not be replenished. There was no system of supply-dropping in Africa in those days.

Lieutenant Ken Morrison was leading the column. He was an outstanding officer in whom we all had implicit trust, and now, as always, he went unerringly despite our maps, which were very far from truthful, as so often proves to be the case in little-known countries. Later the moon came out, and its light was welcome, for gradually the track became steeper and rougher in places and some were having great difficulty in getting their mule carts and trollies over the course. The bad going caused the column to stretch out snake-wise, and sometimes gaps would appear, caused by the jamming of cartwheels in ruts. All shoulders within reach would be put to shove until the spindly wobbly wheels could be made to revolve again. An alarming factor for me was the inadequacy of our wireless. The signallers seemed to lose touch with each other far too frequently and all through the night one was forced to listen to yet more 'short tuning calls'.

Some time before dawn I called a halt. We were well into the hills and it would not take us long to get to Oudna once it was light. As soldiers will, they quickly slept, deep in heather by the side of the track. I felt too cold.

Soon after dawn two German aircraft flew above us, but apparently failed to see us. The sun put heat into our shivering bodies and as we moved steadily on, the local Arabs, by now fully awake, shouted from village to village across the hills. We also noticed little fires being started on some of the hilltops, but much though I disliked their activity there was little I could do about it. We collected a few more carts and paid for them with the francs with which we had been quite liberally supplied. Gradually our maps began to make sense and in the distance over the plains the outskirts of Tunis suggested themselves. During most of the night streams of tracer, feeling up towards our bombers, had shown where the capital lay. In the backs of all our minds was the proud hope that somehow or other we should get there.

By eleven o'clock we were deployed on low hills which commanded a view of the airfield we had come such a long way to deal with. What might be described as a landing-ground was there all right, and on the edge of it was one crashed German aircraft. There did not seem to be anything else, but we could not see round all the corners so the only thing to do was to go and have a look. We had not

Mr Sethi, the Indian clerk of No. 2 Assyrian Company of the Iraq Levies, who made an uncanny prediction about my future

The hunt staff of the Royal Exodus in Iraq. *From left to right:* Pat Uniacke, myself, Nashmi (my head groom, who had a mind of his own), Alastair Graham and Gordon Arthur

Men from the Kurdish Company of the Levies training. Kurds and Syrians lived in different villages in mountainous Iraq

Assyrians in their walking-out clothes. These splendid men were great ones for a party

The chalet at Bruneval with the radar device showing above the ground. Only a small number of troops occupied the chalet, which was unfurnished. The D.Z. can be seen in the distance

The German defence layout designed to protect the beach and village at Bruneval. The R.A.F. and the French underground provided information correct in almost every detail

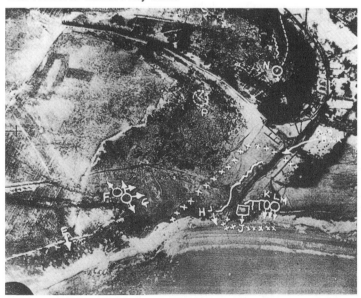

German prisoners captured during the Bruneval raid. One was a radar techni-
cian who was able to give valuable information

With Lieutenant-Colonel Johnny Goschen on board the *Prinz Albert* after the
raid. He was AA and QMG of the Division

At the R.A.F. Station, Dishforth, Yorkshire with Their Majesties King George VI and Queen Elizabeth soon after the raid in 1942. Wing Commander Pickard, who commanded the bomber squadron which flew us to Bruneval, is seen talking to the Queen

With Admiral of the Fleet the Earl Mountbatten of Burma who, as Chief of Combined Operations, master-minded the raid. Several years after the war we were invited to the unveiling of a monument at Bruneval to commemorate the action

Left: Waterwork building at Prise de l'Eau, Oudna, in Tunisia. The 2nd Battalion laid an ambush here during the operations in December 1942

Right: The track leading into the battalion positions adopted after the abortive attack on a landing ground at Oudna. The Germans advanced up this route

Left: Sidi Bou Hadjeba. After being threatened from both front and rear the battalion moved on to this prominence and held off the enemy till nightfall

Right: Looking west from the top of the Sidi Bou Hadjeba. Medjez el Bab, where the nearest British troops were thought to be, was about 40 miles away

A platoon post in the Béja sector, Tunisia. Often there was no cover and the men lived alongside their weapon pits which frequently filled with water

Left: Cork Wood. This hill feature was held by the 2nd Battalion for twelve days in February 1943 under almost continuous attack

Right: The Pimples at Djebel Abiod. These rocky features changed hands several times whilst 1st Parachute Brigade were preparing to attack past them early in the final offensive in Tunisia

'Monty' addressing troops of the 1st Airborne Division near Sousse before the invasion of Sicily. The soldiers loved his impromptu speeches and cheerful badinage often took place

British transport at Primosole Bridge, Sicily

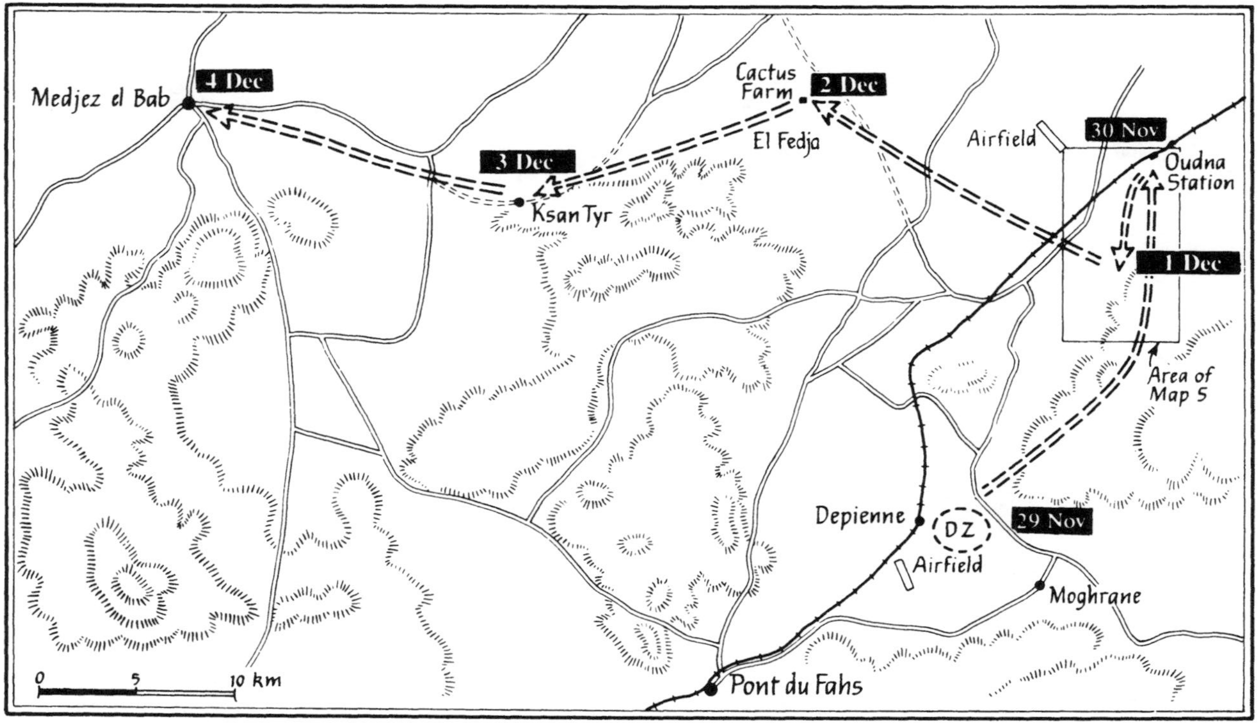

Oudna Station

30 Nov

Airfield

1 Dec

Area of
Map 5

29 Nov

Moghrane

DZ

Airfield

Depienne

Pont du Fahs

2 Dec

Cactus
Farm

El Fedja

Ksan Tyr

3 Dec

4 Dec

Medjez el Bab

10 km

5

0

OUDNA OPERATIONS: DECEMBER 1942

managed to glean very much in the way of information
from the Arabs, some of whom spoke French, but they
implied that there were no enemy in our area and that the
Luftwaffe had gone. They had heard a lot of fighting
farther north and as far as they knew everything had moved
up there.

Our briefing had been very hurried, and, owing to the
distance Algiers was from the front, information was apt to
get out-of-date so quickly that I was not at all sure what the
rest of the army was doing. There had been mention of a
thrust by the 6th Armoured Division and our meeting with
our own armoured cars of the day before made me feel that
there was little need for caution, so I decided that, after we
had eaten, we could press on to the airfield with the whole
battalion. While we ate bully and biscuits I passed on the
orders and detailed Frank Cleaver's 'B' Company to keep
a good watch from the high ground on the left flank from
which the main road was visible. I hoped we should see our
armoured cars patrolling forward as they had said they
would the day before.

In the event, they saw some armoured cars about a mile
away, and waved the yellow silk triangles which we all wore
round our necks as recognition signals to other troops of
First Army. However there was no response.

Dick Ashford's 'A' Company moved down the valley in
open formation, while John Ross's 'C' Company, followed
by Battalion H.Q., made their way along the high ground
on the left with Piper Ewing giving tune. We must have
been a brave sight moving 'à la Field Day', so far behind
what the enemy considered to be their front line. The
miscellaneous transport was woven into the pattern, and it
seemed that nothing would ever stop our steady progress,
when all of a sudden the noise of mortars and machine-
guns came from the direction of the airfield and, with it, the
bursting of bombs and the spattering of bullets among the
advancing soldiers.

Two or three were hit and those with them went to
ground. 'C' Company on the left forged on, and soon it
seemed that there was movement from the enemy also.
'A' Company started again under cover of their own
weapons and soon they were over the edge of the airfield

and in among buildings near a railway station. It was obvious that the Luftwaffe was not using the airstrip and I tried to send messages to 'A' and 'C' Company Commanders to stay where they were while I had a chance to decide on the next thing to do. However, stopping them was not so easy, and though I got through to the signallers at where the Company H.Q. should have been the only reply obtainable was: 'There's nobody here but me.'

Everyone else seemed to be having a look-see and so, having sent a runner to 'C' Company to tell them to stop, I went off to 'A' Company in the valley below and on the edge of the airfield.

They had a few casualties and had nearly captured some of the enemy. They could not tell me much about them as we were all so new to battle and each man's story was different. However Dick Ashford had the company under control, except for one platoon which, with its enthusiastic subaltern, Dennis Rendell, was thought to be well on the way towards Tunis.

Leaving them I moved to where I thought the leading elements of 'C' Company would be. As I approached, I heard the very ugly noise of heavy engines being revved up, and against this background came the cracks of high velocity guns and the impatient ripping sound of strange machine-guns. Tanks had been lurking near an old Roman viaduct and as soon as our men left the rocks and boulders on the slope of the hill this unwelcome column trundled into action. Ken Morrison was still in the van and now he, with a valiant few, wriggled towards them, intending to grenade them at close quarters. Ken was killed in so doing, and only one survived.

We had come to deal with the German aircraft which now came to deal with us. First on the scene were Messerschmitts which wove and dived and sought for us before they fired. After each attack we watched them climb and, as we watched, another attack would come from some unexpected direction. We could not afford to reply as our ammunition had to be kept for surer targets. However we must have been almost indistinguishable from the scrub in which we lay, for though there were at least two hundred of us gathered in a small area, none was hit and, indeed, when the Stuka attack followed, their bombs fell far away.

As the evening wore on, the tanks and aircraft left us more and more alone and before dusk we started withdrawing to the high ground at Prise de l'Eau, where we had paused during our advance in the morning. This was suitable for a position with all-round defence; a good deep well was available and we could look down into the valley along which we hoped to see our own armoured troops advancing on the following morning. Unfortunately not all of 'C' Company got the orders for withdrawal, and Dennis Rendell's platoon of 'A' Company which had forged on across the airfield was out of touch with its Company H.Q. Thus, when we took stock at Prise de l'Eau, our effective strength had already been seriously depleted. The platoon of 'C' Company, which we had to leave behind at Depienne to salvage the parachutes, never joined us and was in fact eliminated by the enemy while they were trying to carry out their futile task.

The optimistic mood in which I had set forth on the operation was now fully dispelled and apart from worry over the rapid decrease in our strength, I had two other serious problems. The ammunition of those men who had been in action had been used up at an alarming rate and now that the sharp cold of the night had settled upon us, our wounded need extra attention.

During the training periods in England, no special study had been made of the paramount need to conserve ammunition on airborne operations. It was tacitly assumed that such operations would not last long and that parachute troops would be reinforced or relieved by ground troops before replenishment of ammunition became necessary. We inclined towards a raid complex and felt that our technique should be 'quickly in and quickly out'. Like normal infantry, who carry reserves of ammunition in transport close behind them, when we met the enemy we aimed to win the 'fire fight' before manoeuvring, and used up ammunition we could ill afford. Each man carried one hundred and fifty rounds and there was no reserve. Now already we were beginning to run short.

I had envisaged being able to leave small parties of wounded at such places as Pont du Fahs, Depienne and

Oudna when the operation had first been proposed, but the last-minute change of plan had altered things. Fortunately we were blessed with a most capable and resourceful officer, Jock McGavin, who was in charge of a section of the parachute field ambulance which had dropped with us. He managed to get the wounded into an Arab hut just outside our defended perimeter.

I was sure that the enemy would follow us up early the next day, so I ordered a small ambush to conceal itself near the track at the foot of the hillocks where we were, close to the well at which the waterbottles were refilled. At intervals all through the night our signallers tried to get in touch with First Army H.Q. It was very disconcerting to be completely out of contact, particularly having met our own armoured cars the day before. Nevertheless, we still felt that friends would arrive on the morrow, and that then we should be able to go forward again. We were scantily clad. The bitter cold of the night, which was in such contrast to the temperature by day, made any sleep almost impossible. The soldiers lay huddled together like new-born puppies. Philip Teichman and I lay back-to-back to give each other what warmth we could, and we covered ourselves with maps. Streams of flak rose continuously from Tunis as our bombers attacked. Further north artillery fire rumbled.

No dawn was ever more welcome and after 'bully and biscuits' we co-ordinated our positions and began to dig deeper. Cover was sparse on these brown hills and I feared that the enemy would have very little doubt as to where we were once he came forward. As there were no aircraft on the ground for us to destroy, I had decided that our next move should be towards where we thought that units of First Army would be. We had been told to make for St. Cyprien which was well to the north and not many miles from Tunis. However, bearing in mind the armoured thrust which we were expecting, and encouraged by the contact we had had with our own armoured cars on the day we landed, I felt that we should stay where we were for the time being, and continue to try to get in touch with First Army by wireless.

At about ten o'clock a small column of vehicles, some of which were armoured, approached us from the direction of the airstrip at Oudna where we had been the day before. There was a well-defined track leading up the valley, and soon a small spearhead detached itself and came up to the well, where the ambush position was, at considerable speed. Unfortunately, this surprised a party filling water-bottles and in the confusion our ambush achieved little, though afterwards it claimed that an officer leaning out of the top of an armoured car had been killed. At any rate, this forward party went back to where the rest of their column had halted and then began to shell and machine-gun us from about two thousand yards away. We hit back with our mortars as best we could, and after one bomb had landed slap in the middle of a group of vehicles and men, they withdrew to what they considered a safe distance, and though they continued to strafe us intermittently, they ceased to be a menace for the time being. Now 'C' Company, which was holding ground behind us, facing in the direction from which we hoped our own ground troops would arrive, reported that two tanks and an armoured car were approaching, and that they were displaying yellow triangles, our First Army recognition sign. A little later we were told that three of our men from an outpost had contacted the tanks and that they had climbed aboard them and were now coming nearer waving their triangles.

At Battalion H.Q. we all heaved a mighty sigh of relief, and a feeling of great joy swept over us. All our troubles seemed over and we should soon be on our way with more ammunition, our wounded taken care of, and with the tremendous moral support of some of our own armour. John Ross, the commander of 'C' Company, came over to confirm and to discuss the developments, as I thought. However his face was grave.

'I thought I had better come personally,' he said. 'The tanks behind us are in fact German. They must have picked up the yellow triangles from the Depienne party. They have taken my three chaps prisoner and have got them covered all the time. They have sent one in to say that they have us completely surrounded and that there is no point in our continuing to fight. They are waiting now to hear what we have to say.'

Sickness, rage, and utter weariness were my feelings

then and, just to plumb the depth of disillusion, while John had been speaking, the signallers received the only message we got during the whole operation, and this was to tell us that the armoured thrust on Tunis had been postponed.

I decided that we must move without delay to fresh positions from which we would be able to make a clean break as soon as it was dark. The map showed that the highest features in the immediate vicinity lay about one mile to the north of Prise de l'Eau and that these features fell away to the plain across which we would have to march. Having sent a warning order to the companies, we set about destroying equipment which was no longer of any use. The amount of mortar ammunition we had been able to land with and carry was woefully inadequate and had been practically all used up, so we dealt with the tubes as best we could and also the wireless sets. During the thirty-eight hours we had been in action, our sets had had to be on almost continuous watch, and now the batteries were finished. To show the Germans that we were in no surrendering mood, I sent a small party with Gammon bombs to get into a place from which they might have a chance of knocking out one of the tanks which was lurking outside 'C' Company's perimeter. Lastly, and most wretchedly, we had to tell McGavin, who, with his section of field ambulances held our wounded, that we should have to leave them behind.

As we moved, the enemy in the valley increased their volume of fire, and some of this found its mark, sending splinters from the rocks to cause horrible wounds. I passed one man whose face had been almost sliced from his head and he held it on with both hands as he was guided along, blind and stumbling. Our requisitioned mule transport was no longer of any use, for now part of our climb was to be on hands and knees, but already much of it had taken fright and, together with the haversacks of some of 'C' Company, our precious set of bagpipes had been galloped off with.

The sun shone down with full force and after climbing for quite a short time we began to feel raging thirst. We had noticed our need for large quantities of liquid during the active periods of the day before and now this had increased considerably. The battalion had not been able to do any serious training for several weeks. Embarkation leave and the packing-up period had been followed by a fortnight on a very overcrowded transport and the life we had been forced to lead in Maison Carrée was one that would have been more natural to a docker or a furniture remover. Perhaps we should have realized what a problem water was going to be, but we had gleaned all we could from anyone coming back to Algiers from the front and the possibility of soldiers being hamstrung through the need for water had not been mentioned. Moreover, we had not appreciated the effects of the sudden transition to which the airborne soldier may be subjected. From comfortable billets with beds, clean clothes, hot water, extra rations and a very fair share of drink, after a restless night followed by a dawn and morning heaving and wrestling with heavy equipment, he faces an uncomfortable and hazardous flight, during which he is alone and vulnerable in the air with an unknown enemy below, and then finds himself struggling over hostile territory with no creature comforts to hand. There were only the barest necessities for the airborne soldier then and everything that was needed had to be carried, or wheeled along on little canvas trollies.

Anyway we now found that moving over the hills, heavily laden in the heat of the day, was more than we could do if we were to be able to fight, and so I decided to halt when we got to the northern slopes of a hill which, according to the map, was called Sidi Bou Hadjeba. By the grace of God there was another well in the middle of where the new battalion area would be.

We deployed on two summits of the hill with 'B' Company on the right and what was left of 'C' Company on the left. In reserve and looking out to the left was 'A' Company. While the companies were sorting themselves out, I lay down on a hillock to the rear and had a look at the plain below us. There was quite a lot of activity including the movement of armoured cars and pieces of artillery. This time I had no illusions as to who they were and was pondering the most likely direction of the enemy's attack when Keith Mountford, who was then one of 'A'· Company's officers, came up beside me and asked what I was looking at. I remember saying in a nonchalant way which I was far

SIDI BOU HADJEBA

from feeling: 'Just studying form, Keith, studying form.'

At about three o'clock the attack began. Infantry were carried up from the valley below in half-tracks and light tanks were brought up to the positions from the direction of Prise de l'Eau. Under cover of fire from these tanks more infantry advanced and now both sides raced for the top of the hill. I went up with one bren-gun team, but before we reached the crest, a burst from a German light machine-gun caught us. Both the leading men were hit and also Padre MacDonald who was immediately behind us. I waited to see the bren get into action and from my vantage point saw several duels between our own teams and the Germans, who were armed with a similar weapon, but which had a much higher rate of fire. Admittedly the Germans were fresh compared with us, but there could be no doubt that their weapon handling was superior, for time and again they got into action first, and while our men were still groping for good fire positions, the opposing gun numbers would bring long and accurate bursts to bear. Nevertheless we managed to prevent them from being able to call the top of the hill their own and, despite the help their tanks could give them, we clung firmly to the reverse slope and were able to enfilade any who became too adventurous.

Meanwhile every kind of missile, except the more heavy ones, fell amongst us and they came from all points of the compass. There had been no time to dig or prepare defences, so that we were woefully vulnerable and our casualties mounted rapidly. Frank Cleaver, 'B' Company Commander, was suddenly struck down while he was talking to some of his H.Q., though none of the rest of the group were touched. One old and battered mule remained of those that we had requisitioned and he was used by Ronnie Gordon, the Battalion M.O., for moving the more badly wounded men to a collecting point. Ronnie seemed to be covered in blood from the men he had tended, but there was not a great deal he could do. He had practically nothing to staunch wounds or relieve pain and while the battle lasted it was not possible to send anyone back to McGavin.

Despite the odds against them, the proximity of the light

tanks infuriated and challenged some of our more intrepid characters, and they made the most determined efforts to put them out of action. After it was all over, various claims were made which we had no means of proving or otherwise; nevertheless some of the tanks were made unserviceable, and one in particular lay passive and inert between the two forward companies throughout the battle.

Just as the enemy pressure was at its height and I for one was beginning to wonder how much longer we could hold, the Luftwaffe reappeared. This time the Messerschmitts seemed to take particular care to discover our exact whereabouts. We had no ammunition to spare for them and, lying doggo, let them circle, but when they dived and fired it was not at us. For a time the opposition on the ground was almost silenced for the Luftwaffe had made a grave mistake, and pressed their attack hard into the valley where our assailants' H.Q. and forming-up places must have been. This vital breathing space came when we most needed it and now, as the hours of darkness approached, all knew that we must use its cover to the full if the battalion was to survive to fight another day.

CHAPTER 7

Retreat from Oudna

We now knew that the plans for the thrust on Tunis must have misfired to some extent and that therefore St. Cyprien was probably not the best place to make for. Massicault was a few miles farther west, so I decided to head for that. Every now and then we had heard gunfire coming from that general direction, and I presumed that we would be most likely to make contact with troops of First Army there. Now the question was, how to go? We could go together in one big battalion party, or we could split up into smaller groups. It was not going to be a simple matter to get through, and small parties might find it easier to pass undetected, while a big party was very difficult to control, especially as we no longer had wireless working between companies. Eventually I decided on a compromise and based the orders for the withdrawal on moving by company groups.

It had been impossible to collect many of the wounded during the heat of the battle and, now that we had to go without them, we could not leave them where they lay. With great reluctance I decided to leave one of the platoons behind to search the battlefield after we had gone, and this very unwelcome task was given to Pat Playford of 'B' Company and his men. It meant that they were almost certain to be made prisoner, but the coming cold of the night, and the uncertainty of the behaviour of the local Tunisians, required that our men be collected and protected despite the cost. 'C' Company had practically ceased to exist, and among those killed was Henry Cecil, one of our best-loved and most cheerful subalterns.

I gave the signal on my hunting-horn to start the withdrawal just after it had got dark and the companies
slithered past the battalion check-point one by one. Long
after the time they were due there was still no sign of 'C'
Company, so we had to go on without them, for we could
afford no delays and must cover as much ground as possible
in the hours of darkness. The enemy allowed us to slip away
without further let or hindrance.

Later we were told that the Germans had a saying, 'The
night is the friend of no man.' As the campaign wore on we
were to note a seeming reluctance on their part to continue
battle after last light, and many times we were very thankful for it.

The way down to the plain was very much steeper than it
had seemed in daylight and was an unpleasant foretaste of
what the rest of the march was going to be. I hoped that
when we reached the plains the way would be easier, but
unfortunately much of it had been ploughed, and ploughed
in such a way that huge slabs of solid earth were balanced
on top of one another; these tripped us up and turned our
ankles, and sometimes brought us cursing to the ground.
We marched on a compass bearing and so could afford no
detours, and we forged our way across wadis and through
cactus hedges in stumbling heaving columns.

We had to pass very near some of the areas where we had
seen enemy movement during the day, and as before,
whenever we were near native villages the dogs came out to
bark. In fact our route seemed to be clearly reported to
anyone who cared to listen, and I felt that the enemy would
surely make some attempt to follow us up, but of this there
was no sign. Occasionally we heard firing to the right or left
and this we attributed to one of the other company groups,
but apart from the ack-ack fire over Tunis there were no
further signs of battle.

We kept to our normal marching custom, having ten
minutes rest in each hour, and when this time came, the
men sank to the ground where they had stopped. As the
night wore on it became more and more difficult to get
them on the move again and sometimes violent methods
had to be used. There was no moon in the early part of the

night and in the darkness some who left the immediate area
of the column for personal reasons were not seen again.
Rasping thirst was again our greatest affliction and we
longed for the crossing of the River Medjerda where we
should be able to drink. When we reached it, the first of
those who drank cried that the water was salty and unfit to
drink, but we had to have something and though it was very
unpleasant and brackish, it did quench our thirsts, and its
very brackishness discouraged us from taking more than
was strictly necessary. Indeed I now believe that the salt
made it more refreshing.

In the early hours the moon appeared and made things
very much easier, but it became obvious that we should not
be able to reach Massicault before dawn. It was essential
not to get caught out in the open in daylight, and so, shortly
before dawn, we halted in a dry wadi while a small recce
party went on ahead. They soon returned, saying that they
had found a large Arab farm a short way ahead which they
thought would be a good place to lie up in during the day.
We moved on at once, and this farm turned out to be just
what was wanted.

It was called El Fedja and it lay on the southern slopes of
a gentle rise, surrounded by thick cactus hedges which as
obstacles were as effective as barbed wire. There was
plenty of cover, abundant water and fairly solid buildings.
The crest of the hill was quite close and above it, and this
made an excellent observation post from which all the
immediate country could be watched. Once the defences
had been arranged we were able to look to ourselves.

The Arab owner made himself as helpful as possible. We
bought eggs and other fresh food and for the first time were
able to make some kind of a cooked meal. We were also
able to wash, paying particular attention to our rather
battered feet. It was very warm and sunny and it was grand
to let the air get to our bodies and saturated underwear.
Some sampled prickly pears and regretted it, for this so-
called fruit needs skilled preparation and the prickles cause
discomfort for a long time when firmly stuck in tongues and
lips.

While we were all enjoying this respite, an Arab boy
came in to say that there was a similar body of troops in

another farm a few minutes away. Euen Charteris with one of his men went off on borrowed ponies and found Dick Ashford with 'A' Company. Dick was told to bring his company to join us, and together we made a fairly formidable little force again. When they had gone to their allotted sectors I could feel that every approach to El Fedja was well covered, and were it not for the acute shortage of ammunition, we would have been quite secure. Dick Ashford's march through the night had been much the same as ours and he had covered much the same distance. Already that morning he had seen considerable enemy activity, and a motor-cycle and sidecar had come right up to the farm in which his men were resting. As far as he knew he had not been seen, but it was obviously only a matter of time before we were located again.

The Arab farmer told us that the nearest First Army troops were at Furna. This was farther West than Massicault and his information rang true. If only we could make contact and get more ammunition, supplies and equipment we would feel a proper fighting force again. After a short rest the indefatigable Charteris set forth once more, determined to come back with some support; with him went all our prayers.

Suddenly, there was a complete change in the attitude of our Arabs and in a twinkling their friendly smiles were gone. Feverishly they began to throw their possessions together and, quickly gathering their womenfolk, they were off with scarcely a backward glance, obviously wishing no further contact with us and now reproaching us for the upset we had caused. The reason was soon made clear, for on a ridge a few hundred yards away a party of Germans had appeared, and among them were men with binoculars which were trained on us. From now on, every few minutes we were to see more and more enemy movement, and this at all points of the compass so that it seemed as if a web were being spun all round us, ever more tightly.

The enemy were a long time in starting unpleasantness and seemed to be taking a lot of care. We had to conserve every single round of annunition and had none to spare for the rather fleeting targets that their little groups presented. We remained silent and showed ourselves not at all.

Perhaps this misled them; it certainly seemed to mystify them and it may be that the Arabs had given them an exaggerated idea of our strength. With every few minutes they delayed our own chances increased, and always we hoped that, either through Euen Charteris or by some other means, some First Army unit would learn of our predicament and do something about it.

At about three o'clock mortar bombs began to land in our positions, but they were not nearly so effective as they had been on the rocky hills of the day before. The ground was soft enough for reasonable slit trenches to have been dug, while the buildings and cactus hedges caught most of the splinters. Soon, heavy machine-gun fire was added to the mortaring and before long some of the buildings were blazing, but we suffered few new casualties. One unfortunate sapper was killed by a bomb which landed close beside him, yet the only visible sign of damage was that his eyes were forced clean out of his head.

At battalion H.Q., Ronald Gordon, our doctor, suddenly announced! 'Good heavens. It's my birthday. What the hell of a day to have as a birthday. What a day to choose.'

'If you survive this one you *should* have many happy returns,' said we, rather unkindly, and after a quick whip round we were able to give him three sticky pieces of chocolate as a birthday present.

At about five o'clock, a small enemy party which included some officers approached so close to 'A' Company that there was no chance of missing them, and the whole lot were wiped out. However this furore drew attention to the fact that the enemy were much too close for comfort and I knew that I must now decide how we were going to get out, then make a plan and stick to it.

We had been watching and plotting all enemy movement during the afternoon and there seemed to be one place where there was considerably less than elsewhere. Very fortunately, this was in the direction in which we wanted to go, being on the route into the hills leading to Furna. The Germans, although originally encircling us, were now rather more concentrated on the eastern side with their rear towards Tunis.

This time I felt it would be better to keep together as one large body, for then we would have our maximum possible strength concentrated at the same time and place to effect the breakout. We made a very simple plan for the withdrawal, which involved parties passing through Battalion H.Q. when the hunting-horn was blown, forming one long column, with the head organized especially to assault. Reorganization would take place in the hills on the way to Furna.

It now seemed clear that if we could avoid being bounced before dark, we should be able to get away, but there was one very dangerous place in our perimeter. Heavy fire had already forced our picket off the high ground above the farm, and though our defences were as strong as we could make them in that area, a burning building was producing smoke and embers which were not only distracting to the defenders, but were also making quite an effective smoke-screen for an enemy attack. Here we had what was left of the mortar platoon and some other stalwarts under the R.S.M. The best sub-unit we still had was the troop of Royal Engineers, who had come on the operation to blow up installations and dumps on the airfields which we had been told to destroy. Possibly they had been less involved in the previous fighting, but now they were in much better shape than anyone else and it was very nice to have them there.

As the evening drew to a close our hopes continued rising, for still the Germans hesitated. Once again 'A' Company repelled the enemy in their sector most successfully, and all were carefully obeying the orders about not opening fire until kills were certain. Just as darkness fell, the long-awaited assault came in from the hill above us; this was met by a withering fire which repelled it most effectively, and in the breathing-space thus given, it was time for us to go.

The first parties came out at a gallop and were directed towards a large haystack which had been selected as a landmark. Now we took the freshly wounded, and by this time the walking wounded of the day before were getting stiff, so the leading parties drew well ahead of the rearmost. Moreover the leading parties met no opposition and their very impetus carried them onwards. This was to make our meeting up very difficult, for each moment it was getting darker. When we were well clear of El Fedja, I again sounded my horn, this time the signal for all to rendezvous. After several minutes we could only muster one hundred and ten of the two hundred we had had in El Fedja, and as many besought me to stop my horn-blowing lest the enemy should hear and follow, we formed up with what we had got, and set off on what we hoped might be the last lap.

On the way I had doubts about going to Furna. Euen Charteris had not returned and it seemed probable that he had run into trouble. There was very little we could now contribute to First Army, and the best thing we could do might be to get somewhere to rest for a day or two and re-equip. Medjez el Bab was the only place we knew to be firmly in Allied hands, and as we had become little more than fugitives, I decided to make for Medjez.

I halted the column and called the officers together so that we could discuss the problem and make fresh plans, but even as I was speaking, we all fell asleep and were woken by the cold about half an hour later. The going was then much easier, and we made very steady progress. At about three o'clock in the morning we became aware of another marching column on the track ahead of us, and by the greatest of good fortune they turned out to be the men we had missed after the breakout from El Fedja.

Dennis Vernon with his sappers was leading this party, and he said he felt that another fairly extended halt was becoming essential. He had not had quite such a good track to move along as we had, and the march had told more on his party. We found another large farm with many out-buildings and plenty of water, and nearly everybody was able to get about half an hour's sleep. This farm was being managed by a very charming French lady, who had two extremely charming daughters, and their invitation to the officers to take breakfast with them was most welcome, particularly as champagne was served.

Those wonderful women did our hearts the power of good. They told us that they reckoned they lived in no-man's-land and that they never knew which side was going to appear next. Now, even before we had finished our meal, one of our hostess's employees galloped in with the news of a German armoured column making its way towards us. This time I knew we must not stay. There were not as much as one hundred rounds between the whole lot of us, and we could not afford to be invested again. We were under twenty miles from Medjez and it was reasonable to suppose that someone would be keeping an eye open for us.

There was a certain amount of cover in the shape of olive groves for most of the morning, and on our left were foothills, into which we could move if enemy armour should approach. We no longer liked to see lone Arabs watching us from the hilltops. We had been told that the Germans rewarded them for information and now, if they seemed to be taking an unusual interest in us, tired though we were, we found ways of discouraging them. At noon we halted in an olive grove near Ksar Tyr and while resting saw three armoured cars prowling by the road junction there. The battalion had grown wary in the last few days, and it was no longer necessary for the officers to say anything when the enemy drew near. All ranks froze where they stood or lay, and absolute silence prevailed. The prowlers made off down the road to Tunis before we restarted our march. Now there was less than ten miles to go, but we could see there was no cover and we should be quite defenceless if any enemy armour appeared.

After we had covered about two miles we saw some armoured half-tracks moving across open undulating country to our right. They were not more than a mile away, and when they saw us, they approached with their heavy machine-guns covering us all the way – but they were unmistakably American.

I imagined that they would have been warned to keep a lookout for us, but they seemed to know nothing about us, though they agreed to take the walking wounded and a small recce party with them back to Medjez and to report our whereabouts by wireless. I went with this party as I hoped to be able to organize some kind of help for the rest of the battalion, which should not be very far behind us. By various means I got myself to the H.Q. of the 78th Division, which was fighting the battle up forward, and here everyone was preoccupied with a battle which was raging near Tebourba. This was on a route to Tunis other than the one that I had understood was to be the main axis for the thrust, and possibly served to explain why so little interest had been taken in our abortive mission. I was told that if we had achieved nothing else we had at least drawn off a considerable number of enemy mobile and armoured troops from the main battle, and it was agreed that a sortie would be made on the following day towards where I thought the rest of the battalion might be.

Medjez was being held by an odd assortment of troops, the main body being French Colonials. It had been considerably damaged, but was still quite attractive, at any rate to us, the newest arrivals, and when I got back from division I found the battalion billeted, fed and mostly asleep. There were A.A. guns and even tanks dotted about, and at last we could feel able to relax. However, not for long, for I was woken at four o'clock to be told that a full-scale attack was expected, that German parachutists were going to drop, and that all available Luftwaffe were going to bomb Medjez any moment now.

Once more the hunting-horn proved invaluable and with its penetrating help we soon had the battalion roused and on the move again. I went to the French colonel and with him settled on the positions we should adopt to defeat the parachute attack. It never came, and through this false alarm we missed being able to take part in the sortie which had been arranged the night before. Later that morning we were taken to a place called Sloughia to rest.

CHAPTER 8

Oudna Aftermath

Sloughia was a little Arab village a few miles outside Medjez on the banks of the river and here we were able to get clean and refreshed despite its muddy banks and bottom, and generally recover from our unpleasant experience. The inhabitants had been moved away and we enjoyed a day of almost perfect rest. Survivors arrived in dribs and drabs. Most of H.Q., the Support and 'A' Companies, were with me, as was also the sapper troop. That afternoon John Ross arrived with only a handful of men, which was all that was left of 'C' Company. There was hardly a man from 'B' Company. Philip Teichman, the Second-in-Command, and Jock Short the Adjutant had been with them; both had been killed when they were isolated and attacked by an armoured column. Euen Charteris had been intercepted and killed while he was trying to make contact from the farm at El Fedja. He had been a magnificently enthusiastic Intelligence Officer, whom I had always thought would bear a charmed life, specially after his amazing performance at Bruneval. However, I was soon quite delighted to hear that Douglas Crawley of 'B', who had been temporarily blinded on the Bou Hadjeba, had been led all the way back to Medjez by Ronald Stark, another officer of great determination. Both were to serve with great gallantry and distinction with the Brigade throughout the war.

The most unpleasant thing about this abortive operation was having to leave our wounded behind after every action. We had been quite unprepared for this. I had envisaged that units of First Army would be coming up close behind, as indeed had been implied in my briefing from Brigadier Flavell. However, instead of this, we had been virtually abandoned among an apparently hostile Arab population to compete against mobile armoured troops who were fully supported and informed by their own air forces. On two occasions I had felt bound to leave part of my fighting strength to protect our wounded, but in the event our German opponents turned out to be of the parachute fraternity and they took considerable trouble to look after our men whenever they could.

We heard later that McGavin, our surgeon, and Mac-Donald, the padre, who had stayed with the wounded and had been taken prisoner, were considered persons of great interest by both the Germans and the Italians. It was intended that they should be exhibited in Rome and Berlin and they were flown to Rome from Tunis in a transport aircraft, which was full of blankets and also carried a certain amount of petrol. The padre had been wounded in both arms and so was helpless and uncomfortable, yet this intrepid pair determined to continue to make their contribution to the war effort. When the aircraft landed in Rome, the sentries got out to inquire where they were to take their prisoners, and McGavin then poured petrol over the blankets and set light to them. When the mixture was well and truly ablaze they both jumped out and the whole aircraft soon disappeared in flames. Great rage ensued which our pair did not assuage as they found it necessary to roar with laughter, and frantic Italians took them off to shoot them out of hand. They were saved in the nick of time by a German Air Force officer and, after some very unpleasant days, they were carted off to Germany, but not before McGavin had broken both his legs when jumping off a train and the padre had enjoyed a short spell of freedom by escaping through a lavatory window.

My main reaction to having had the battalion cut to pieces on such a useless venture was astonishment. I could well understand the difficulties of finding a really worthwhile mission for our battalion when the situation forward in Tunisia was fluid and could change considerably while the information and the requirement were being processed through the long chain of command from Béja and Constantine to Algiers, but once the use of the battalion had been accepted by the Forward Headquarters, one would have thought that they would have made every reasonable effort to support us, to verify information, to get and keep contact and, when their own optimistic appreciations had proved to be so false, they would have redoubled their efforts to do some of these things. In the event it seems that they did none of them.

However, the real mistake was ever to have had the task accepted on such flimsy information. If it had been considered reasonable for me to have flown reconnaissance missions over enemy territory, surely the R.A.F. could have been asked to fly an offensive mission to confirm or otherwise the need for a whole battalion to be dropped for the purpose envisaged. Furthermore, there were several Frenchmen farming in the general area and surely other Frenchmen could have been asked to contact them for information. At that time the telephones were working and normal movement by civilians was almost unimpeded. The fact of the matter was that the British Army had no idea of how or when the new airborne capability should be used and our own Brigade Headquarter set-up was woefully inadequate to ensure that really dreadful errors should not occur.

We were left at Sloughia for barely twenty-four hours and were then required to move back to Medjez to protect a landing-strip on the hostile bank of the river. A flight of Spitfires was to be based on this as it was thought that such bold handling of our best aircraft would achieve local air superiority. However, the casualties incurred on their first sortie put paid to this particular nonsense and we went back across the river with all concerned the next day. We had been joined by the remnants of the 1st Battalion of the Hampshire Regiment who had been badly mauled in the battle for Tebourba. This was the débâcle taking place at the same time as our operations in the Oudna area.

We dug defensive positions in the general area of the railway station at Medjez and made ourselves as comfortable as possible. We were at a considerable disadvantage compared with the Hampshires, for they had greatcoats, blankets, transport and even typewriters. All that part of our equipment was still five hundred miles away near Algiers, but given regular rations and water, we considered ourselves fortunate. We enhanced our warmth and elegance by borrowing clothing from a French Army store nearby. Baggy trousers meant for Zouaves and blue jackets for Spahis came in useful, but we could always be identified by our red berets for no one among us was prepared to swap his for even the most fetching of 'kepis'.

One morning a staff officer arrived to take note of our immediate needs and, having had my list for weapons, wireless sets and equipment, he said: 'But what about vehicles?'

'Vehicles!' I exclaimed. 'You don't mean to tell me that you are actually going to give us some transport?'

We had grown so accustomed to our total deprivation that I had come to regard it as normal. In fact it was amazing how much one could achieve without what is now considered quite essential. All through the war airborne forces had to operate with the very minimum possible scale of motor transport, yet their overall mobility was seldom jeopardized and in some circumstances was even enhanced. There were two needs that were always irreconcilable with this: ammunition forward and wounded back.

Stomach upsets now became our worst enemy. Our doctor, Ronnie Gordon, couldn't really explain why. We may have all picked up germs on our way back from Oudna. We had to drink wherever we could find water and we had soon run out of purifying material. So when a whole battalion of Coldstream Guards arrived to relieve us I shuddered to think what their opinion might be of ourselves as we were at that time. However, Stewart-Brown, their Commanding Officer, was kind and understanding for he had knowledge of what had happened to us. Our leaving was enlivened by the arrival of elements of the 10th Panzer Division who made a reconnaissance into the outskirts of the town just as our troop-carrying vehicles arrived to take us away to Souk el Khemis where we were to rest and refit.

It was a relief to all of us to be 'out of it' for a little while, for we badly needed a chance to sort ourselves out. In the rest area near Souk el Khemis we met the 1st Battalion. They had had a very different kind of battle, having fought in close co-operation with the ground troops, except for the initial drop. They had been very successful in all that they had been asked to do and had already collected many prisoners and enemy equipment. Their very success rather accentuated the disappointment of our own disaster and their eagerness to return to battle was in contrast to our dismal knowledge that it might be several weeks before we would be fit to fight as a parachute battalion again, or indeed as any kind of battalion.

We quickly absorbed any reinforcements that were going and welcomed our administrative 'tail', but we needed three hundred fully trained parachutists and we understood that they did not, at that time, even exist. There was talk of building us up with normal infantry reinforcements, but there would be many difficulties and complications if this were done at this stage, particularly as they would outnumber the trained parachutists in the battalion.

The writing of detailed reports on the operation and the careful composition of the citations for gallantry awards took far longer than I had thought possible. We had not been able to keep a war diary and now that we had a lot of remembering to do, it seemed that many things were remembered differently by different people. At this time, too, we wrote to the next-of-kin of those who had been killed.

On 20 December we moved up to the 'line'. It was the quietest possible sector, where the only enemy activity came from the air. Nevertheless it was very good for us to be in use again, despite our small numbers, and we were greatly heartened by the arrival of fifty reinforcements. A surprise visit from General 'Boy' Browning, the commander of the 1st Airborne Division, left us in a very much happier frame of mind, for he fully understood what had happened to us and he promised that somehow we should be brought up to strength again as soon as possible.

Just before Christmas, all the First Army's strength was gathered for another big attempt to capture Tunis. Even now this total amounted to not very much more than one division, but 1st Guards Brigade had had time to settle in and they were to make the initial break-in. 1st Parachute Brigade was to go through after an American unit had consolidated the ground gained. This was a feature later to be known the world over as Long Stop Hill.

In the event, the first part of the battle went as well as could be. Coldstreamers bounced the Germans holding Long Stop under cover of darkness and signalled back for the Americans to come and take over; but this was easier said than done. Long Stop was a savage little feature, quite an effort to climb in daytime and no fun at all in the dark and the rain. Nevertheless the Americans got up after the feature had been captured and when relieved by the Americans, the Guardsmen came down.

In the early morning the Germans began to counter-attack and at the same time some of their forward machine-gun posts, which had been bypassed during the night, came to life. Thus the Americans were hard pressed before they had had a chance to consolidate. The German commander obviously realized the importance of Long Stop, for it completely controlled one of the most direct roads between Medjez and Tunis and without it there could be no First Army thrust on Tunis at Christmas.

The main strength of the German defensive tactic was his counter-attack. The bulk of his riflemen were kept out of the immediate front line and were available to counter-attack or reinforce wherever danger threatened. They knew the ground over which they might be required to move, they had plenty of ammunition handy, their mortars and artillery had already registered their own front positions, so that when unleashed, they were very formidable indeed. The Americans came down off the hill.

1st Guards Brigade were told that they would have to retake Long Stop and so for the second night in succession the Coldstream marched out to assault. This time the Germans were fully expectant and had increased their strength in the forward positions. After suffering some two hundred casualties, the Coldstream came back to Medjez.

So ended the Christmas thrust. It began to rain in earnest and all the armies began digging seriously. Nearly all movement was confined to the roads and mud was everywhere.

Now began one of those periods which are always so particularly galling to armchair critics. All the armies paused to consolidate for the mid-winter months, to find out as much as possible about their opponents and to prepare for offensives as soon as the weather and their own effective strengths made them possible. It was both amusing and annoying to get letters from home, which implied that we were just settling down to enjoy ourselves, and that we were so lucky to be where we were. Friends in the Eighth Army were inclined to have a dig at those whom they knew in the First and some prophesied that as soon as Rommel attacked we would retreat headlong, hotly pursued all round the coast of the continent, both by Rommel and by the Eighth Army, which would be hard on the German's heels.

Movement in vehicles along the roads in daytime was apt to be fairly hazardous because the Luftwaffe was extremely expert at strafing roads and at that time they seemed to have the upper hand over the R.A.F. It had been thought that it was always dusty in North Africa and so the mark of Spitfires allotted for the campaign were fitted with dust eliminators. This modification reduced the performance of our aircraft by some thirty miles per hour and as they were opposed by the latest mark Focke-Wulf and Messerschmitt, which of course were unencumbered by dust eliminators, they were operating at a distinct disadvantage. Sometimes two enemy aircraft would dive right through a flight of our Spitfires, shoot up a column of lorries on the road and then climb imperviously back before attacking our aircraft on their way home.

The battalions on both sides were indeed far-flung. In some cases the enemy's main positions were thirty miles from ours and some of our battalions were as much as twenty miles from other friendly forces. Our brigades were usually given the task of holding centres of communication and vital ground which dominated the approaches to them. Thus only by very vigorous patrolling could contact be obtained, for, without this contact, our commanders had no means of discovering what the enemy was up to. A certain amount of news percolated through from Tunis, Bizerta and Sousse, and the R.A.F. usually reported any large-scale enemy movement, but information about the enemy front-line troops could only be obtained by our infantry patrols.

Thirty miles there and thirty miles back is a fairly tall order for any patrol. In that semi-mountainous country with the going made treacherous by the very heavy rain, with unreliable maps and hostile eyes watching, they could be ordeals. The Germans were much less adventurous than we were and usually the aim of their patrolling was to lay mines on unguarded roads. Such mining was often very effective and it was nerve-racking indeed to have to drive along lonely winding narrow roads, early in the morning, when every bit of loose gravel could cover a mine. On the other hand, our patrols were required to come back with prisoners, or at least some form of identification of the enemy formation opposing them, and this meant that our men, having covered thirty miles carrying enough food and ammunition for three or four days, had to do battle with an enemy who lay fresh, concealed and often fully prepared. Thus the odds were heavily weighted against our men and it is not surprising that there were occasional disasters.

This vital task might well have been done more easily by more mobile troops, either armoured or horsed cavalry. However, we had no vehicles, either tracked or wheeled, with the performance required and, although the armoured cars of 56 Reconnaissance Regiment and the Derbyshire Yeomanry did fearless and energetic work along the roads and tracks, none but heavily equipped infantry could get to the hilltops. The French still disposed a number of horsed cavalry regiments, but these were concentrated under French command most of the time. Once when I was motorcycling late in the day between Béja and Djebel Abiod, I passed a group of about fifty horsemen as I came round a corner. I thought it would be most unwise to stop, but as soon as I arrived at my head-quarters, I caused inquiries to be made. There was no knowledge anywhere of any bodies of Allied cavalry in the brigade sector or divisional area. It seemed that I had had a lucky escape, for either they were a party of the enemy or they were brigands, and at about this time it was by no means unknown for lone drivers or riders to disappear.

We tried sending out small reconnaissance patrols of two or three men, who were briefed to lie up near the enemy, to watch them and so gather detailed information from which large company-sized raids could be planned. However, these small patrols were particularly vulnerable to unfriendly Arabs, they had no means of sending messages back and by the time they had returned and their hard-won information could be acted on, it was often found to be out of date. Later we learnt to be quite ruthless about clearing our operational area of all civilians, friendly or otherwise, and the enemy had to rely on his own eyes alone. The Germans used to make good use of Arab ways and Arab clothes, but the British soldier is reluctant to wear disguises and likes to show his colours plainly. However, we should have achieved more and suffered fewer casualties if we had been more unscrupulous in this respect. A handful of 'friendly' Arabs attached to each unit would have reaped rich rewards, both as regards information and more concrete results.

Despite the weather and other disadvantages, life was by no means too unpleasant. Advantage was soon taken of every available type of cover. Farm-houses and all farm buildings were filled to bulging-point, men burrowed into haystacks, culverts became dormitories and crude shelters sprang up everywhere. Eggs and chickens were on sale along the roads and fresh vegetables could be found to bolster the excellent tinned rations provided. All messes stocked cheap rough wine and the monastery at Thibar distilled stronger fare. As usual most of the N.A.A.F.I. whisky and gin went down the throats of those who were well behind the line. The main grumbles were over the uncertainty of the mail and the shortage of reading material. Quite a number of letters going in both directions went astray, but most of this was accounted for by the sinking of ships. No one ever had enough to read. All newspapers and periodicals from home were read from cover to cover and passed from hand to hand until they fell to bits.

Every now and then the weather relented and when the clouds rolled away the sun showed us a lovely rolling, rich and varied countryside. In the far distance were blue hills, some smooth, some craggy, glistening with falling streams. In the heart of the British sector was the great Djebel Zaghouan, dominating everywhere, rising with savage abruptness to six thousand feet from the surrounding plain. Otherwise the hills sloped gradually down to the valleys and in various sheltered folds were farmsteads, the buildings white with red roofs and surrounded with poplars, fruit trees, vineyards and gardens. Well below the farms were the watercourses, marked by juniper bushes and flowering shrubs. Many of the farms were most attractive places with well-planned gardens, adorned with strutting peacocks and flocks of gaily coloured pigeons. Little windmills generated their electric light and some had modern drainage. Up in the northern sector the hills were covered in cork oak and it was all much wilder, the farms were poorer and there were fewer of them.

There has always been some controversy as to how the battle cry of the 1st Parachute Brigade came to be adopted. This was a shout of 'Waho Mahommed'. As far as I am aware it was merely copied from the local Arabs during this phase of the campaign. These people, who lived near and sometimes within the brigade sector, were continually calling out from one hilltop to another. Like all hill people they knew how to make their voices carry and, as every Arab's name in that part of the world seemed to begin with Mahommed, all their shouted conversations began with:
       'Waho Mahommed.'
       'Waho.'
       'Waho Mahommed bil Munchar,' and so on to the text of the message.
       It was too much to expect that the soldiers would refrain from joining in. Some became expert at imitating the more guttural sounds and, before long, as soon as our neighbours started up, the air became jammed with real and bogus Arabic. Long after the Arabs had moved and wherever the brigade went, a concerted cry of 'Waho Mahommed' brought extra spurts of energy, in action or play. Some authorities not in the know feared that the whole formation had secretly embraced Islam, but it was in fact just something to shout when shouting seemed to be a good thing to

do. Anyway, it became a custom in the rather indefinite way that customs do and one had to hope that nobody's feelings were hurt.

We were the only troops out there who wore camouflaged smocks. These smocks had a fork piece which was meant to be fastened in the front by two press studs. These studs had a way of getting damaged or torn off and then the fork pieces hung down behind in a most unmilitary manner like a tail. This much amused the Arabs, and despite all our other distinctive characteristics, they always referred to us as 'the men with tails'.

Early in January the rest of the brigade were withdrawn to go back to base to prepare for a parachute operation. We were still so under strength that our brigadier, very reluctantly, agreed to leave us behind and planned to use an American battalion in our place. This was of course a bitter blow. None of us could ever forget that we were parachutists first and foremost and we longed to go to battle again by air. However, we were told that two hundred reinforcements were coming in the near future and so the sooner we fully absorbed them the better.

The battalion was allowed to concentrate in the town of Béja the day before the welcome reinforcements arrived. Many of them had been anti-aircraft gunners and had little experience of infantry work. However their heads were high, they seemed to be as anxious to join us as we were to receive them and as the new rifle companies began to swell, the battalion took its proper shape again. As soon as they had been equipped and documented we moved up into the line.

Apart from patrol activity and the occasional air raid, there was nothing much to disturb the tranquillity of those January days. John Marshall, who had been the Brigade Major, came up from base to be our Second-in-Command. He had the gift of managing to be cheerful in literally all circumstances and was a very able, experienced regular soldier. Father Egan, the Roman Catholic padre to the Brigade, had made his home with us and gave our headquarters an atmosphere of great respectability. However the real authority on all domestic matters was our Adjutant,

Willoughby Radcliffe. He was several years older than any
of us and was a very successful solicitor in private life. He
was a great authority on many subjects, particularly on
graceful living, and soon our small mess became a very
comfortable centre in our particular part of the world. We
found that quite apart from our own personal inclinations,
it certainly paid to try to run a reasonable mess under
nearly all circumstances. Those with precious gifts to give,
such as gunners, sappers and Service Corps men, are more
apt to call on a unit that can make them feel at home than
one that requires them to sit in a wet ditch while mutual
wants are discussed. A unit that becomes a popular port of
call picks up and learns a great deal that can be extremely
useful to it and all ranks benefit thereby. Moreover, it
could be a refreshing change for officers from the forward
companies to come back for a meal or some other form of
comfort and it all went to help that intangible called
morale.

Our 'B' Echelon, where the quartermaster reigned,
which might be between two and ten miles behind, held an
embryo sergeants' mess and men's rest centre and here we
tried to get each man out of the line for two days at a time as
often as possible. These measures had a most marked
effect later on, when the battles raged.

One day it became known that some Tigers, the most
formidable tanks in the world, had arrived to assist the
opposition. More German reinforcements were flown in.
Part of the Afrika Korps were reported to be arriving in the
southern part of Tunisia, and, by the end of January, there
could be little doubt that the semi-peaceful period was
nearly over.

CHAPTER 9

Happy Valley

Our troubles began on 2 February, when we handed over the pleasant and familiar positions we held just above the village of Munchar in order to relieve a Guards battalion which had been moved from the Medjez area to face a threat elsewhere. Their move had been a very hurried one and they had had to leave quite a lot of equipment and men behind. Needless to say, this rear party was occupying all the best part of the area, but before any serious argument could arise our orders were changed, and we scrambled back into the troop-carrying vehicles, which were still waiting, only partially unloaded.

Our new assignment was to be under American direction. For some time a rather crack German unit called the Hermann Goering Jaeger Regiment had been able to dominate the Goubellat Plain in front of the very extended positions held by an American combat team, and the plot was that we should be put secretly into an area lightly held by them, so as to be able to surprise the German marauders when they approached during the night. However, apart from one company, the battalion never had a chance to set foot in the American sector, for before we had time to debus, fresh orders steered us farther south to the extreme right flank of the First Army.

In the early hours of the morning of the 4th, I found the brigade headquarters under which we were now to serve. There was a crossroads in the Ousseltia valley, over the hills to the south, and it was considered most important that the enemy should not be able to use it. The Commander,

Brigadier 'Swifty' Howlett was roused to brief me. The talk went something like this:

'If you are attacked, you must be prepared to accept heavy casualties. It is vital that you impose as much delay as possible.'

'Yes, I see.'

'There are reports of ten infantry battalions with about a hundred tanks up the road in front of where you will be, but I don't suppose they would use all that lot.'

'Those seem to be rather heavy odds. Can you let me have some anti-tank guns?'

'No, I am afraid all mine are fully deployed and dug-in, but I will send you six tanks.'

'Thank you very much, sir. I am sure they will make all the difference.'

'Not much I'm afraid. You see, they are no use against German tanks.'

'Oh.'

'And I'm afraid you are going to have quite a time getting your battalion there at all, because we have mined the tracks, so you will have to find a way over the hill for as much as you can, as quick as you can. Meanwhile, we are clearing the mines and will get the rest of your stuff up to you as soon as possible.'

The Brigadier certainly did not enjoy having to pass on such unpleasant news, but he was careful not to encourage any self-pity and this made it easier for me to face my own officers with a confidence I was far from feeling. I kept the details about the possible scale of opposition to myself.

We managed to get one company over the hill in the darkness, largely because the brigade were able to produce a guide. Soon after dawn, some bren carriers arrived to take the battalion order group forward, as most of the mines had been cleared from part of the track. We approached the crossroads very gingerly and got out of the carriers just short of it. The whole area was fairly liberally sprinkled with trip-wires connected to mines, which fortunately we noticed before any harm was done. There was complete silence and the place stank of death. We saw and stalked a stationary German armoured car, but found it empty and out of action. There were a number of hurriedly shovelled-in graves, and, most sinister of all, the fresh track-marks of one of the huge new Tiger tanks which had recently arrived in Tunisia.

Having given out orders I moved everyone back to the carriers and started off to the assembly area, where the battalion would be waiting for us. I was in the leading carrier, with two others following, and this time we went at speed. Suddenly I noticed that the surface of the road in front of us had recently been disturbed. We were too late to stop, but as soon as we were over it, I turned to shout a warning to the next vehicle. At that moment, the third carrier bucked savagely on to its side as a sheet of flame appeared beneath it, immediately followed by a tremendous explosion. As it turned over, several figures were catapulted out; we got out and ran towards them. 'Dinty' Moore, commanding Headquarters Company, and Dick Ashford, commanding 'A' Company, were both dead when we reached them and the men with them were very badly injured. Now we carefully examined the road before going on. We found three belts of mines. My carrier had been over them all twice.

Dick Ashford had been with the battalion since its original formation and his keenness was a byword. 'Dinty' Moore was one of those characters one does not easily forget, ever ready with the appropriate comment for the occasion and a great man for summing-up. Both knew the parachute form and both would be sadly missed. They were our first officer casualties since December, and their going made that beastly place seem much more beastly still.

However, the attack never came. The ten battalions and the hundred tanks went elsewhere. We were shelled and suffered a few more casualties, among them our one ardent Communist. On 7 February we were relieved by some men from Kent and we moved away from that dreadful crossroads to spend the night in the hills behind. Since moving from Munchar on the morning of the 2nd we had been separated from all our kit, including the bare necessities. This was because the various changes in orders had caught most of us on the hop. We were beginning to look very scruffy indeed. The nights were cold with ground frost in the hills and our thin clothes, without blankets, groundsheets or greatcoats gave us scant protection. The men as usual slept in huddles, but feeling jealous of my dignity as a commanding officer, I could find no one to huddle with and so I kept on the move until I had to sleep. On waking I found I was actually frozen to the ground. On this particular morning of the 8 February, I heard a nearby orderly sergeant with a muezzin-like tone rouse his company thus:

Arise and shine, my little ones,
The moon has gone, the stars do wane,
Arise, for lo, the morning comes
Another day has dawned again.

That day we returned to be under command of the 1st Parachute Brigade once more.

Nothing had come of the projected airborne operations aimed at cutting off the Africa Korps from von Arnim's army in the north of Tunisia. There were various difficulties of all sorts and kinds and finally the brigade was hurried back again to the First Army front. Soon after their return, the 1st Battalion took part in a very expensive battle in an endeavour to capture a feature called Djebel Alliliga. A number of other units were involved, and despite very gallant fighting on the part of all concerned, the venture ended in failure. Now the brigade was in position south of Bou Arada.

We took over from a French battalion, who left us their anti-tank guns and crews, and French artillery remained in support. There were also two horsed squadrons of the Spahis behind us in reserve, who had the task of moving forward on our left flank if that were to be threatened. Guarding our right flank, which was otherwise very much in the air, were two dismounted squadrons of Chasseurs d'Afrique. Thus we were nicely mixed up with our Allies and, despite their old-fashioned methods, we soon developed a great respect for them. Their customs and way of life were often very different from ours and some of their officers laboured under a sense of disillusionment and distrust, but we worked hard to break this down and we soon had many friends. So poorly were they equipped that the battery commander had to direct the fire of his guns by standing on top of the nearest hill and shouting fire orders through a megaphone.

We took an immediate liking to our new area. It was most reassuring to be back with our own brigade after wandering about at the behest of so many masters and now we were in a fertile, undulating valley which enclosed several thriving farms. The farms stood on high ground surrounded by watercourses. Trees and bushes provided cover where it was wanted, and domestic animals abounded. The civilian families still lived in their farms, so that in contrast to our last place this was completely alive, and before long we were calling it 'Happy Valley'.

The main snag was that we were very dangerously spread out. We had taken over the positions from a big French battalion and the total distance between our right and left extremities was nearly three miles. Bearing in mind that by normal reckoning, a battalion front in those days should not have been much more than a thousand yards, it will be seen that our elongated front was much greater than was really desirable. Nevertheless, we had been made responsible for the sector. There were three dominating hillocks which we could not afford to let the enemy take, and so we had to have one of our companies on each. Almost equidistant from, and behind, the hillocks was another smaller one, and on this I placed our medium machine-guns and our Command post, which controlled the fire of the artillery and mortars. Good motorable roads connected everything up and though we were overlooked by the enemy main positions, they were far enough away to be fairly innocuous. We had been told that our particular enemy were Italian and Austrian and not inclined to make trouble. We were shelled occasionally, but never accurately, and thus, by and large, I was a mildly unworried C.O.

Not for long. Suddenly, there came a morning, when, whilst on my rounds, I was summoned to meet General Charles Allfrey, the Corps Commander. I was severely criticized for having the battalion spread out in penny packets, for not having dug in properly and for not having warned the men that an attack was likely to be launched on us in the near future. I was very nearly sacked on the spot.

I saw no point in arguing there and then. I could think of

no better way of deploying the battalion in view of the task
we had been given. During the time we had been there we
had had very few tools to dig with, as no transport had been
available to bring up defence stores. Moreover, I had been
told by Brigade that the possibility of an enemy offensive in
the sector was remote. The next day my gloom was much
alleviated by a visit from Major-General Keightley, the
divisional commander who, himself being a cavalryman,
understood our difficulties when it came to static defence
and digging. After this episode, the brigadier, in his wis-
dom, decided that John Ross and myself, who had been in
the forward area almost continuously since the end of
November, could do with a change, so with ten days' leave
in hand, we hopped lifts by road and by air all the four
hundred miles back to Algiers.

Apart from enjoying ourselves there and at Boufarik,
where the brigade's rear base was ensconced, we tried to
find someone at Allied Forces Headquarters in Algiers
who might be interested in airborne operations. With one
accord we longed for the opportunity to go to war again by
air and we hoped most ardently that when the time came
for First Army to reassume the offensive, we might be
dropped well ahead in our proper role.

Quite apart from being used in a major offensive, there
seemed to be so many targets for company groups of parachutists in the rear areas of the enemy-held territory. The
trouble here was that each senior airborne commander,
very naturally, always wanted to maintain his own force
intact until a mission was found big enough for him to
command in person. Thus company group operations were
always condemned as 'penny packet' warfare, and apart
from the Bruneval raid and operations done by special
forces, our regular parachute formations were always used
in bodies as large as the aircraft available allowed. It
amused John and me to find quite a large number of French
troops guarding every road and railway bridge right back to
within a few miles of Algiers, for all these, who were very
badly needed up forward, were tied down by the threat of
the possible arrival of small parties of Italian parachutists.

Having had no success with any planner at A.F.H.Q. in
Algiers we called in at H.Q. First Army at Constantine on

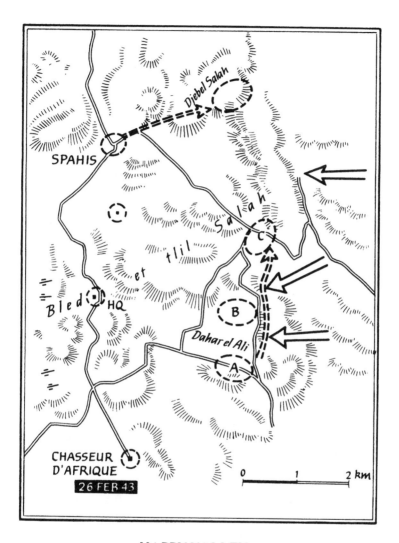

HAPPY VALLEY

our way back. Here we were told quite bluntly that 1st
Parachute Brigade was considered to be far too useful as an
infantry formation to be frittered away doing anything else.
However, they were very complimentary and lent us a car
with a very cocky driver to take us back to the battalion.
The nearer the front we got, the scarcer became the traffic
and the more sombre his mood. As we turned the final
corner on the hill which overlooked the battalion position,
he slowed to a crawl, fearful of the lack of signs of activity,
so different from the friendly bustle of division and corps
administrative areas. Nor were there any signs of any activity until we were a hundred yards short of Battalion Headquarters, when down came a very neat little stonk close
beside the track. The driver declined an invitation to stay to
tea.

John Marshall had been commanding in my absence; he
now told me that things had been much more active lately.
Patrols had been meeting more opposition and the enemy
were much more alert. The enemy had attacked with varying success in many other sectors, but farther south they
had broken through the Americans. The Guards Brigade
had been rushed to a place called Thala to stem the first
phase of what was in fact Rommel's last offensive.

The battalion had made great strides with the defences
since we had been away and by now wire fences had been
erected and minefields laid. Ten days in the same place had
allowed the men to settle down properly and all the details
of communications and administration had been tied up. I
soon found that the best way to go round the battalion
positions was to use a horse borrowed from the Spahis, for,
as we had discovered when we came back from Algiers, the
enemy were much more observant and any movement by
vehicles was apt to be swiftly punished. The weather had
much improved and it was really very pleasant to hack
round the area to see the form. Large coveys of *chikor* – hill
partridges – flourished and flushed, making me curse the
fact that for the first and last time in my life I had not
brought a shotgun overseas with me.

Our normal battalion headquarters was at the bottom of
the valley, actually well in front of the command post, but it
was completely screened from everywhere and seemed

safe enough. It was centred on an old farm which had Roman remains in the garden and was a relatively lovely, peaceful little place with a sluggish river running by. It was sometimes difficult to realize that it lay in the middle of a battalion area which might be attacked any day or night. By now all civilians had left and so the best beds in the house were ours. Cuisine had reached new heights and we were by no means ashamed to have some of the senior French officers to a meal. By this time, N.A.A.F.I. were well established and so we were able to get most of the things that help to make life pleasant.

Early in the morning of 26 February, we heard the sounds of intensive fighting away to our left flank. Before long we were informed that the 3rd Battalion was being hard pressed, as the enemy had managed to get right up into their positions during the night. By nine o'clock our own forward positions were under shellfire and large numbers of infantry could be seen advancing down the slopes of the hills to our front. They looked very very small and ineffective in the distance, so we took up our places at the command post with no feeling of alarm. We all knew we were as fully prepared as possible, plenty of ammunition had been stocked, the defensive fire-plan had been carefully worked out and neatly fitted in, the positions had been properly dug, revetted and concealed. Moreover the men were fit, fresh and should know exactly what to do. Wireless communications with the companies were working perfectly and I was able to have a running commentary from each company commander in turn.

The enemy first bumped against 'C' Company on the left, but had no success against their forward positions and, foiled, groped their way round the flank. There was a deep gully in this area and it was not easy to see them, but our supporting artillery knew where they were and pinned them nicely. To seal them off, as had been planned, I got the Spahis to move forward, leaving their horses behind, and from a fairly commanding feature, the Djebel Salah, they were able to make certain that our left flank was secure for the rest of the battle.

Next, 'B' Company in the centre of the battalion sector was attacked. The assault was launched from some high ground which we normally occupied, but had given up as it was too far forward to be supported by any other weapons. Again the enemy, having failed to make any impression frontally, felt their way round the flanks of the company and into the gaps between the companies. These gaps were so large that the companies could not support each other, but the gaps were more than adequately covered by the machine-guns and mortars sited in depth to the rear. From the command post we could watch most of the enemy movement and manoeuvre, and could ensure that the fire from all our supporting weapons fell in the right place and at the right time. Thus, although the battalion was defending such an extended front, before the battle was half over I felt confident that we were going to have little difficulty. Apart from achieving no success against our positions, the enemy were doing us no harm, for it was not until well into the evening that the first casualty was reported. Throughout the day everything worked perfectly and everybody seemed to be in tune. The enemy's little scrabbling rushes in the valley between 'C' and 'B' Companies were noticed, and punished, almost as soon as they began. There could be no doubt that by the end of the day they would be very weary, hungry, thirsty, and quite a lot of them killed and wounded. Their own artillery and mortar fire was almost ineffective, whereas ours got better and better, and before darkness came, our French anti-tank gunners, tired of waiting for something to do, threw off their elaborate camouflage and let our opponents feel their solid shot.

The situation at nightfall was that we with our French supporters were intact and sound in every way, but the enemy were scattered about in front of, and between, our forward company positions. We still were not absolutely certain who the enemy was. We knew that the positions on the hills facing us had been held by Alpini and that there were Austrian troops in the area as well. During the attack the enemy had shown little determination or skill and it seemed probable that the very unwilling Italians had been responsible for most of the performance. However, we knew that sometimes German units were mixed with Italian and our inward sections reckoned they had seen both types of uniform during the day.

The two squadrons of Chasseurs d'Afrique, which held reserve positions on our right flank, had been most excellent and vigorous when patrolling and had frequently brought back prisoners from their various forays into enemy territory. I therefore felt confident that their commander would be only too glad to take part in any skirmish that was going and so, having detailed two of our own platoons to get ready, I went to see the Frenchman to organize a strong right hook.

Much to my chagrin and disappointment he firmly refused to commit any of his soldiers, pleading that he had to have permission from his own French superior before taking part in such an operation, and so we had to make do with our own resources. There was not sufficient time to organize more than the two platoons already standing by, but in any case it would not have been easy to plan, lay on, and subsequently control a much larger force. I put Captain Ronnie Stark in command, with orders to go out through 'A' Company, to sweep across our front fairly close in to the forward companies, and then to come in through 'C' Company.

Ronnie Stark was one of our oldest members and a most imperturbable, forthright officer. We heard him from time to time during the night as he forged his way through no-man's-land, with grenades and stens in chorus, and when he appeared at Battalion H.Q. soon after dawn with more than eighty Italian prisoners, he made it all seem a quite natural everyday occurrence. 'B' Company picked up a couple of Austrians near their positions and in the morning we gathered a great number of weapons and various types of equipment.

We now learned that German tanks had penetrated right through to our 'B' Echelon on the previous day and that the three quartermasters of the brigade had put up a sterling defence until they were relieved by some of our own tanks. The 3rd Battalion had had a very sticky battle and had required vigorous help from our Parachute Engineer Squadron and elements of the 1st Battalion. Farther left, the Irish Brigade had been in serious trouble, and it was through them that the German tanks had gone. Still later, we learnt that the enemy had launched a general offensive

all along the front and in some places the Germans were
very successful indeed. Rommel, with the Afrika Korps,
was now firmly linked up with von Arnim in Tunisia, and
this was part of the last big Axis offensive in the battle for
Africa.

All the other much more important events which happened elsewhere along the front caused our own very
successful defensive battle in Happy Valley to be quite lost
sight of. At Brigade Headquarters they said: 'What! Were
you fighting too?'

Later I managed to discover that our assailants, both the
Austrians and the Alpini, had lost well over one hundred
and fifty killed and wounded. Unbelievably, our own
casualties consisted of one killed and two wounded. Thus,
altogether, we had scored a total of two hundred and thirty
for three despite having to hold a three-mile front.

The factor mainly responsible for this impressive little
victory was the handling of the battalion's mortars and
machine-guns. An officer known as 'Bombs' Panter had
looked after our mortars since the battalion was formed
and he had made himself an expert in support weapons.
This battle was a wonderful demonstration of the efficiency
of these weapons and from now on everyone in the battalion realized what could be achieved by making full use of
their characteristics of long range, accuracy, sustained fire
and weight of fire.

The morning after the battle, I went forward with John
Marshall to look at part of the ground where the enemy had
been. There were plenty of traces of their occupation for
they had not been exactly tidy. We were keeping a good
lookout for there was no one between us and the enemy,
but we were both considerably shaken when suddenly a
high velocity shell cracked just above our heads, especially
as it came from our own lines. We jumped into the small
truck we had with us and drove back to where we reckoned
we had been fired at from. Not far from the track, in 'A'
Company's position, we found a Frenchman cleaning a 3.7
anti-tank gun. We asked him what the blazes he thought he
had been doing and after a long pause, he turned to us with
a charming smile and said, 'Accident?'

The following day we got orders to move. We handed

over to American troops and, bidding a sad farewell to our French comrades, now tested, proved and well beloved, we drove out of Happy Valley and went on our way.

CHAPTER 10

Battle of Tamera: Phase One

John Marshall went ahead to try to discover what our next task was to be. The usual crop of rumours predicted that we would now move back to our base to prepare for another parachute operation. We did our best to discount these rumours, for it was common knowledge that the German offensive was by no means spent on other parts of the front. After struggling to sort out the usual transport muddle, I hurried on after John, calling at Corps Headquarters on the way. There I learned that we were bound for the northern sector, where the enemy still held the initiative.

I found John with 139 Infantry Brigade near Djebel Abiod. This was now being commanded by Brigadier 'Swifty' Howlett, who had briefed me for the defence of the Ousseltia valley a few weeks before. Once again it was his unpleasant duty to give me a most unenviable, and indeed 'soldiercidal', task. During the last few days the enemy had dealt severely with 139 Brigade and had pushed them back along the northern road for several miles. The Brigade had been forced to relinquish the village of Sedjenane, which was also a road junction of very minor importance; however, now those in authority wanted it back. It was estimated that there were four German battalions, with some tanks, in and around Sedjenane. The 2nd Parachute Battalion was required to advance and retake it without delay.

The whole of this northern sector differed from the rest of the country in that the hills were covered with cork oak woods. In most places, these woods stretched right down to the roads and villages, and so there was plenty of cover everywhere. I considered that we ought to be able to infiltrate into Sedjenane without much difficulty, and that we could do a good deal of damage to the enemy when we got there. But if there were any plans to reinforce us I was not made aware of them, and naturally I felt that to remain in Sedjenane for any length of time would be disastrous. Therefore it was in no very cheerful state of mind that we did our planning as we waited for the battalion to arrive.

We waited for a considerable time and the people up there began to look at their watches frequently and pointedly. There were several there with vested interests, who were only too anxious to see a Parachute Battalion interposed between the enemy and their own sadly battered troops. After a while, I thought I had better go back to try to find the battalion. After motoring for about two hours, I found a small party of our soldiers at a place called Chemical Corner.

It transpired that Headquarters 46 Infantry Division, under whose orders we came after leaving Happy Valley, wanted us to clear some Germans off high ground overlooking the town of Béja. They had stopped the battalion en route and apparently countermanded the Corps orders. Although I wondered who would ultimately be blamed for the change in plan, I certainly welcomed it, for I felt that anything was preferable to the Sedjenane venture.

Johnny Lane, the senior Major, had already made some plans by the time I resumed command, and I gave out orders during the night. By 5.30 on the following morning two companies had climbed to the top of the Djebel Zebi, and, encountering no opposition, they swept on to occupy the next feature, Kef Ouiba. These manoeuvres proved that fears for the immediate safety of the town of Béja were groundless, and it seemed doubtful if the enemy had ever been there in more than patrol strength.

A composite force consisting of a company of infantry, a troop of tanks, and a troop of a reconnaissance unit, moved forward on our left flank during the morning. Their task was to protect our left flank and to hold a crossroads in the valley below.

Soon after 46 Division knew that we had been successful

so far, they ordered us to go on to capture a feature known as Spion Kop and to hand it over to the Argyll and Sutherland Highlanders, who were in the general area. We were to be allotted the bulk of the divisional artillery, and to this end a gunner officer with his paraphernalia was sent to us post-haste.

The main difference in the new task was that whereas we had climbed to our present positions under cover of darkness, to reach Spion Kop we would have to slither down steep forward slopes in full view of anybody who happened to be on it, cross the road in the pass below, and then face a stern, forbidding climb of about fifteen hundred feet in daylight.

We needed to know a great deal more about the enemy's exact positions and so opened the proceedings by searching out all the most likely places with our machine-guns and mortars. At the same time, part of 'C' Company went on down the hill to draw the enemy's fire. The Germans reacted by opening up heavily on the force at the cross-roads on our left. So doing, they showed us some of their own positions quite clearly, for we had an excellent view of Spion Kop. We called loudly upon the divisional artillery to play their part, for here were targets plain to see and their destruction would make our task much easier later on. Notwithstanding the most determined efforts of our Gunner O.P., not one round of gunfire did we achieve.

We were forced to be very conservative with our own stocks of machine-gun and mortar ammunition, because it all had to be carried up by hand. We had no tracked carriers, jeeps or even mules. After several minutes of the German bombardment we saw movement on the road to our left and to our amazement this developed into a general retirement by the composite force below. I went down to see the form, for without that cross-roads there could be no success for us with Spion Kop.

With heads bent low and eyes averted, the infantry trudged along on either side of the road. The light scout cars and tanks made a brave show of covering them on their way. I found the Infantry Company Commander with the troop of tanks.

'We have been told not to accept casualties. That mortaring will catch us up there and we have had no time to dig.'

'But what about your task?' I asked him. 'What about the support you are supposed to give on our left? You know we cannot function properly without the use of the cross-roads you are meant to hold.'

Meanwhile his column continued to move on rearwards. There was no point in haranguing anyone. No one seemed either to know or care much about the purpose of the day. Eventually it was agreed that the tanks would remain until darkness fell, and, having at least achieved this, I climbed back up the hill. By this time the enemy had turned their attention to 'C' Company, who were worming their way up the lower slopes of Spion Kop. We were still unable to get any artillery fire, and my attached gunner told me that he thought all available guns were doing a counter-battery shoot elsewhere.

It was enough. I called 'C' Company back in the gathering darkness and arranged for the battalion to close on the road behind. Transport would await them at our starting-point at Chemical Corner. I drove off to Béja to try to discover what the Divisional H.Q. thought of all this.

I couldn't find much enlightenment. I could find no one who would tell me why we were deprived of all support. The General was fully absorbed with other things and Spion Kop was no longer worrying him. I had not before realized the extent of the Germans' success nearly everywhere. 1st Parachute Brigade at Bou Arada had been about the only place that had not been breached and elsewhere the line was being patched as best it could. I met a double D.S.O.'d brigadier, Chichester-Constable, who had been relieved because his brigade had been overrun by a greatly superior number of Germans. He had known that the attack was coming and had asked to be allowed to take up more easily defendable positions a few miles to the rear. Instead, one of his battalions was taken away to deal with a breakthrough elsewhere. When the attack arrived, the whole sector was overwhelmed. All heavy equipment, including the guns, had been lost, and though many of the men made good their escape, a dangerous gap had been left to plug. On such occasions scapegoats must be found for sacrifice or the impression might be given that those immediately above were not sufficiently ardent. For this particular burnt offering a brilliant future had been predicted, but he was unlucky, and good fortune is a gift that soldiers cannot do without.

I caught up with the battalion while it was still on the move and the next day we rejoined our own brigade which, by this time, was already in action along the north road.

We were to take over from a battalion of the Lincolns. They had been heavily engaged for many days and had been very considerably reduced by casualties. They were defending high ground to the south of the road, deployed on a feature called Sidi Mohammed el Kassin. This large hill was covered with cork oak woods and the sides were very steep. It was a key position, for its loss would mean the cutting off of the rest of the brigade, which was deployed on both sides of the road further forward. The day before, a strong German patrol had penetrated the Lincolns' positions and had taken several prisoners, which meant that the enemy had a fairly clear knowledge of the defensive layout. That night, in the failing light, our soldiers moved up, and gradually the Lincolns came down. Every single item – tools, reserve ammunition, barbed wire, food and water – all had to be manhandled up, and the battalion toiled and scrambled throughout the night and felt far from poised to meet the enemy as night gave place to day.

At dawn on 8 March our battle began. My headquarters was beside the road, in the valley below and behind the battalion. A tremendous crescendo of noise came down from above. The echoing hollow crumps of mortar bombs were intermingled with the sharper thumps of artillery shells, and both ripped into the trees and tore them savagely. Distinctive above all was the noise of the German machine-guns. These had a much higher rate of fire than our own, and in comparison our bren-guns seemed to strike an almost apologetic note.

This was the first time I had had my headquarters in a position from which I could see practically nothing. Even higher up we should have been able to see little more, because the trees were everywhere. I felt terribly shut in and constricted. We selected fire positions and put the

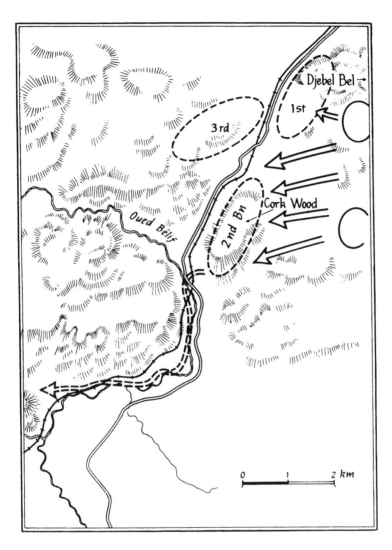

TAMERA: PHASE I

wireless sets in a culvert under a railway line which ran alongside the road.

News from the companies at the top came back sparingly. The company commanders had had no time to feel their way about before the attack came in, and now they were still groping. Brigade were thirsting for information, for the 1st Battalion was being attacked as well, and it looked as though the enemy intended to cut the road between them and us. The first calls from the companies were for more ammunition. It always seemed incredible how quickly ammunition was used up, and already some of the forward platoons, which were in very close contact with the Germans, were beginning to find themselves dangerously low. We had been given a few mules by this time and some were sent forward loaded with small arms, but by now shelling and mortaring of the battalion area had become general, and it was difficult to ensure that the mules and their native drivers made really determined efforts to get far.

Time stood still. After what seemed a veritable age, our watches told us the unpleasant fact that it was still only eight o'clock, and there were many hours of the long day ahead to cope with. By about nine o'clock the first of the wounded began to trickle back, but there was very little they could tell us. The Germans were able to crawl to within twenty yards of our positions and it was impossible to say how many there were. However it did appear that they were not over-zealous, and having got it among our positions, they were apt to stay where they were without attempting to exploit.

At about ten o'clock, Johnny Lane, commanding 'A' Company at the sharpest end of the battalion position, came through by wireless. 'We appear to be completely surrounded now, but do not worry, I can assure you we shall be perfectly all right.'

There was little we could do to help, but it was most reassuring to feel that people like Johnny had such confidence. We had not been able to arrange adequate supporting fire as no one quite knew exactly where everyone else was. The guns and mortars were practically blind through paucity of communications and could do little more than scatter their missiles into areas where they thought the enemy might be.

As the day wore on, the enemy came close to achieving his objective. Although he failed to turn us off the hill he was able to infiltrate and establish small parties in between the 1st Battalion and ourselves, and indeed, between our own forward companies and Battalion Headquarters. As demands for ammunition grew more insistent, Willoughby Radcliffe, desperately frustrated at having to remain below, took it upon himself to organize and lead a small mule train loaded with ammunition for 'A' Company. On the way they ran into one of these enemy parties. In the ensuing battle for the right of way, Willoughby was killed. News of the death of an outstanding man travels fast and his going was a harsh blow. At about the same time Geoff Rothery, who commanded H.Q. Company, was killed while conducting a tremendous machine-gun duel from the hill above. He was another original parachutist and was to be very sadly missed.

The most encouraging item of the day was the attitude of some of the prisoners taken during the fighting. One complete platoon, having been severely handled, put up their hands and their leader said: 'We were told that the English soldiers on this hill would offer little resistance. Now we find your parachutists here. There is no end to damn propaganda.'

When afternoon eventually came, the general bombardment lessened, though outbursts of German machine-gun fire continued to remind us where they were. Officers from Brigade Headquarters drove up to see us and officers from the 1st and 3rd Battalions up in front could also pay calls. The Brigadier reckoned that the enemy infiltration between the 1st Battalion and ourselves must be eliminated before the end of the day and, accordingly, 'A' Company of the 3rd Battalion was ordered to thrust across the road to link up with part of our 'C' Company, which would move down towards them. Considerable success attended this very well-led manoeuvre, for over sixty Germans were rounded up, including a number of men from a regiment called Barenthin, who were considered to be specially formidable fighting men. Sergeant Fleming, one of the oldest members of that company, led the 'C' Company part of the force. The 3rd were very unfortunate to lose Taffy Evans, a Welsh rugger Blue, who was in the forefront of their 'A' Company.

Gradually we could think of food. Those of us who smoked had got through packets and our mouths were furnaces. Less than a hundred yards down the road a meal was cooked and weary men from the companies came back to carry it up the hill. However the enemy had not had their last say, for just before it grew dark, a flight of Stukas dived on 'A' Company and dropped their bombs among them, making huge craters and smashing acres of trees, with a numbing and bewildering effect. This final parting shot brought our day's casualties up to nine killed and thirty-five wounded.

As a sharp riposte to this last unpleasantness, John Timothy descended on a small party of German machine-gunners who were digging in near his platoon. Having killed six of them in one quick rush, he returned with two brand new MG. 34s.

The morning of the 9th began quietly. Shelling and mortaring were sporadic and we managed to do a lot of sorting-out. I climbed the hill with a small escort to co-ordinate the fire-plan rather more closely. The right flank of the battalion position was fairly open and one could look across rolling, hilly country for several miles. The hills were slate-grey with wet rocky outcrops glinting in the sun. Two thousand yards away to our right was a long narrow hill and the far slopes of this were occupied by a company of 139 Brigade. Suddenly we noticed furtive movement, and then recognized small groups of men moving slowly along the ridge. There could be no doubt that the Germans were probing. Two of our machine-gun sections, which were in position further to the right, soon had their guns in action. Although it was not possible to see the streams of bullets landing, the reactions of the enemy showed us quite clearly that our crews were on the target. All forward movement stopped abruptly, for we dominated their route, and as long as we could see them, they were checked.

It was an excellent lesson in the effectiveness of long-range machine-gun fire and demonstrated, so clearly, the economy of effort achieved. The four guns were manned by a total of twelve men who, sitting comfortably, hidden and protected, some two thousand yards from their foes, could kill and wound many times their own numbers. Moreover, the infantry company, which was sitting at the far end of the ridge, could be given almost complete protection in daytime.

The Germans were not inclined to accept this state of affairs and before long the bullets from their machine-guns were falling all round us. We could only just hear their guns firing in the distance, and then only after their bullets had arrived. At one moment we were laughing as the branches of a tree were cut above us, then we all felt the sharp pain as a bullet passed clean through the nose of the youngest soldier amongst us, Private Grafton. Our machine-guns were to remain up there for another ten days. They won every duel they fought with the German guns and because they so ably commanded a vast area, we could make other use of the men, who would otherwise have been required to guard and patrol it all.

When I returned to Battalion Headquarters later, I found 'Bunty' Stewart-Brown, Commanding Officer of the Coldstream Guards, waiting. His battalion had been sent up from the Medjez el Bab sector, and it was most reassuring to have this famous regiment close at hand. The 'Warriors of London' had achieved a great reputation during the campaign and this had come as almost a surprise to some of us. We all knew their virtues, for they had been well rammed in by Guards Drill Instructors during the training eras. 'The discovery that their performance in the face of the enemy was of the same high standard as their performance on the barrack square gave some of our cynics much food for thought.

During this day, the 1st Battalion carried out a reconnaissance in force towards the village of Sedjenane. Although it proved to be firmly held, the enemy were thin on the ground en route, which should have proved that the main enemy strength was still south of the road and round about the Djebel Bel. During the evening, the Coldstream departed, the guns of 70th Field Regiment moved up to the valley immediately behind the battalion, all the infantry of

139 Brigade withdrew, and 1st Parachute Brigade stood alone and ready.

The attack came with the rain. Perhaps it was fortunate, for although it was extremely uncomfortable for the defenders to have to sit in trenches which gradually filled with water, the attackers, heavily laden with extra ammunition, weapons and tools, slid back two paces for each one they took. The bombardment was far heavier than before and now the noise of our own guns was much closer and almost continuous.

In addition to being able to talk to my own company commanders whenever I wanted, I could also hear the other two battalions talking with Brigade. As we listened and talked, we marked the places on our maps where the enemy were. Gradually a complete picture built up and it was possible to see, quite clearly, what the enemy intentions were. In fact we soon achieved a remarkable degree of skill at talking on the air so that communicating thus with each other became almost second nature. Corps H.Q. detailed a monitoring programme in case we were giving away vital information. However, being strangers to our ways, the monitors could make nothing of our talk and considered that the enemy might just as well be hearing double-dutch.

Once again the enemy was making a determined attempt to reach the road between the 1st Battalion and ourselves, but at the same time, a major effort was aimed at 'T' Company of the 1st.

Wounded men came back in dribs and drabs and sometimes little batches of prisoners. They wore camouflaged smocks rather like our own. They were wet, cold, tired and seemed very hungry. It was nice to know that our opponents had their troubles too. They showed no truculence, or any kind of unpleasantness, and seemed anxious to be taken away and out of the war as soon as possible.

Although we were having a hard time of it, the 1st Battalion bore the brunt and as the day wore on it seemed that something would have to give. In addition to the shot and shell, at times German infantry attacked in waves, and as fast as they were felled, fresh men appeared from new directions. Eventually numbers told. They swarmed over

'T' Company and, having digested that, they forged on for the Battalion Headquarters. Then Alastair Pearson, their well-proven commander, having gathered a posse of those whose job is normally to weave and spin, charged in amongst them, and by the evening, the 1st Battalion, though holding a smaller area, was just as firm as ever before.

There was a gap between the three battalions and it was not possible to cover all of it with fire. Part was thickly wooded and the enemy decided to dig in there and lie low. In reality, it was a confession of failure, because there was little they could do from that position. It was cleverly sited in one way, in that our guns were unable to reach it. When they tried to the following signals were sent back through the company net:

'The last two rounds from the battery landed in the rear of the company area. Crest clearance NOT being achieved.'

'Check crest clearance. Shells landing in company area.'

'Stop those bloody guns.'

'Will you stop those ********* **** **** **** guns.'

The rain continued all day long, mud and slush spreading everywhere. More Germans came in, defeated and bewildered, and by the end the brigade had collected over two hundred. We always felt that the taking of prisoners was the real measure of success. It is easy to claim large numbers of killed, but when it comes to the point, it is very hard to count them. Live prisoners are a tangible harvest and many of these were ready to talk, so that valuable information came our way. The odd Pole was to be found among them. Such had usually been press-ganged, not too unwillingly, to fight the Russians, but after being wounded, had been drafted indiscriminately to Africa. Some of the Germans who spoke English voiced indignation that we should be fighting against them instead of against the Russians.

Most of us gradually discovered that we no longer hated German soldiers. Fairly frequent close contact had shown us that most of them were very human beings, with many of the same needs, fears, habits, strengths and weaknesses as our own. We had met no cases of 'Hunnish frightfulness', and on the whole they were a chivalrous foe. Admittedly we came across the occasional quite unrepentant Nazi, but it often seemed that these were just as unpopular among the other Germans as they were with us. Anyway in this campaign, we were all a long way from our homes and the causes of the war, and our mutual exile was at least a telling point in common.

There was, however, one thing we could never get used to, and that was their smell. It was a clean smell. It was a strange mixture of a food of some kind, of untanned leather, and of chemical soap. It clung to their clothes, their equipment, their vehicles, and even some weapons. Sometimes one could smell them quite a long way off and we found the smell in their dug-outs so strong that it was unbearable to use them. On one occasion I asked our Provost Sergeant to get me a pair of braces as my own had broken. I found it impossible to wear the pair he purloined from a prisoner because nothing would remove the smell. Yet it was a clean, efficient smell. Perhaps in other circumstances one would not have minded. Perhaps one would not even have been aware of their different smell. It may have been that we were so keyed up to kill each other that nature had given us special power to detect our own potential destroyers in this way.

There would always be a little group next to the wounded, waiting by the Aid Post for transport to take them to the rear. One wounded officer had some interesting things to say about the eastern front. His remarks went something like this:

'You English have no conception of what fighting against the Russians is like. The bombardment which precedes an attack is tremendous and, if you are not properly dug in with overhead cover, which you never appear to be, you suffer a great number of casualties. Fortunately for you, we do not seem to have any artillery in this campaign. Then, when the infantry come, they come in hordes. You simply cannot kill them quickly enough. We have had to put two of these L.M.G.s with each section and even when the scene of carnage in front of our positions is indescribable, still they come, and eventually you have to move to avoid being trampled on.'

The 11th of March was a peaceful day. However there was no end to the work on developing our defences. We had beaten off two attacks, but there were still many weak and vulnerable places for we were considerably stretched to cover the whole of the feature. Moreover, in this close country, the siting of L.M.G.s to cover all possible enemy approaches was an extremely difficult task. Often the adequate covering of one way in would leave a dangerous gap elsewhere, and there would be an outraged protest from those who found themselves exposed. It was rather like fiddling with a curtain which does not quite cover a window, but we improved our positions with each hour that passed, and although our numbers shrank each day, my confidence in our ability to hold grew stronger. On this day, we were strengthened by the arrival of a troop of our Parachute Engineer Squadron. These staunch old friends took up positions on our left flank, just where we had been most vulnerable before, and we nicknamed their position the Citadel. By this time the soldiers had christened our feature Cork Wood and many felt that they had established an everlasting right to it.

As the Commanding Officer, it was one of my duties to go round the forward positions once a day. It took at least two hours to get round and I often found that I was in a hurry. I therefore walked about everywhere and never deigned to crawl up to any of the positions or use a covered approach. I came to think I was rather brave and that my apparently careless movement could be good for morale. However one morning after I had been particularly flamboyant with map and binoculars on one of the most exposed places, as I was passing out of earshot, I heard the following: 'Right. Now everybody get well down. Jerry now knows that somebody is definitely here. Maybe other places too, but definitely here. We are going to cop it. All right for the Colonel, he's gone.'

A few seconds later, when mortar bombs were bursting all round them, I wondered about many things and half hoped that that particular N.C.O., right though he certainly was, would cop it.

That afternoon, Stephen Terrell brought his 'A' Company of the 3rd Battalion to try to winkle out the Germans

who had established themselves between the 1st Battalion
and ourselves. He was supported by a troop of tanks, but
handicapped by lack of precise information as to the
enemy's whereabouts, and after a confused little battle, the
3rd had to pull out. Somewhat unkindly, Stephen maintained that we had kept his men under a withering fire
throughout, especially when they were trying to disengage.
We decided to try to mortar the enemy out the next day.
All available hands were put to carrying bombs up and we
soon had a dump of several hundred. However, that night
Ian Alexander, one of 'C' Company's platoon commanders, made another attempt. Although he was driven back
and suffered a few casualties, the next morning the erstwhile enemy pocket had disappeared; better still, they had
left several weapons and a useful quantity of ammunition
behind. We were gradually collecting a complete armoury
of German and Italian weapons and by now each section
had an M.G. 34 to pair with its bren-gun.

   Just before dark that evening, the Luftwaffe dropped
supplies for their troops who were living south of the
Djebel Bel. We shelled the containers where they lay; and
we sent out patrols with orders to intercept the German
collecting parties, but they evaded our men and had succeeded in gathering most of it in by the morning.

   The 12th was a nice fine day and we were able to hang up
clothing and blankets to dry. All that we wore and slept in
had got thoroughly damp and most of it was covered with
sticky red mud. But the fine weather also brought the
Luftwaffe, who began to make frequent appearances. Messerschmitts and Focke-Wulfs could make rings round the
old mark of Spitfire which the R.A.F. had provided and the
German aircraft used to dive right through the Spitfire
screen, when there was one. Some light anti-aircraft gunners were sent up to help us and they were positioned
on either side of the road. Whenever German aircraft
appeared they pumped their shells very ineffectually into
the sky behind them, and now that we had plenty of
ammunition, all who were suitably armed joined in too.
The attacks came very suddenly. One moment there might
be peace and quiet in our valley, with everyone relaxed,
smoking, talking, letting the sun get at their bodies. Then

suddenly, and literally like bolts from the blue, the sharp black silhouettes would snark over the treetops, pumping cannon-shell, being pumped at by the Bofors guns, being cursed by us as we reached for our weapons and unleashed round and burst after them, then would come the thud and crash of bursting bombs, and finally it would all die away with the diminishing hum of the German engines getting farther and farther away. We came to rather enjoy these episodes, for none of us was ever hit, and we would have given our all to have managed to bring a German aircraft down.

During lulls in the battle we wrote to the relations of those who were killed. It was very difficult to find the right words and as death became more familiar, it was hard to avoid being matter-of-fact.

The road and the valley behind us were always busy. The advanced dressing station of our Field Ambulance was sited only a few score yards away. Here lived Lieutenant-Colonel 'Mac' McEwen, R.A.M.C., a fighting doctor if ever there was one. He had been a gunner and an airman in the First World War, and had qualified in medicine afterwards. He had sought and found adventure in time of peace, and now he fretted under his non-combatant status, and in fact never really accepted it. He felt that the best contribution he could make to general aggressiveness was to have his medical arrangements as far forward as possible, and here, under constant bombardment, his surgeons and doctors plied their trade. Despite shell splinters through the tent walls and fresh wounds received by those inside, some wonderful work was done. Many limbs and even lives were saved by this early treatment and later, when we were to visit the hospitals far back at base, we saw concrete evidence of this. No formation was ever served better by its doctors than 1st Parachute Brigade, and the foundations of all the medical arrangements had been well and truly laid.

Life in one of the forward sections of the battalion was very much more dangerous and uncomfortable than life in the area of Battalion Headquarters. During the daytime in quiet periods, it was always possible to relax, and provided food arrived regularly, and N.A.A.F.I. supplies were kept flowing, there was plenty of professional duty to keep everyone fully occupied and free from any danger of boredom. Prolonged bad weather brought many problems, for damp boots and clothing brought on every kind of skin disease, given half a chance. We had evolved a drill that made the maximum use of the bowl of hot water with which we managed to shave each day. After the face and neck, we treated the armpits. This meant that one was more or less stripped to the waist. Then on with the shirt and off with the socks for action on the feet with particular attention to in between the toes. Finally off with the pants so that one could squat over the bowl to deal with nether regions. This was a most undignified performance, but I having set the example, there was no excuse for anyone else, and in this way we kept remarkably clean, fresh and free from skin troubles.

The nights were long and no lights could be allowed to make them shorter. Here again, even during quiet periods, there were many duties to be found, and as the numbers shrank through casualties, it was difficult to find enough men to undertake all the calls made upon them. After prolonged rain, when the trenches were full of water, it was very difficult to find anywhere to sleep, and all had to be ready to jump into their trenches the moment shells or mortar bombs were thought to be on the way. Fortunately, during this campaign, our enemy was normally inactive at night, but the dawn was his favourite time to attack and it was essential to be completely prepared for him then.

The area of Battalion Headquarters always got its fair share of shelling and though the soldiers in front used to grin with glee when they heard the strafing behind, they were often quite glad to get back to their own well-prepared trenches rather than stay in the rear when they had been sent there for something or other.

Dogged endurance was what counted in the end. Our parachute soldiers had volunteered, been trained and conditioned for the assault. Now when it came to just stolidly sticking it out, they took it in their stride, determined that no human enemy would make them shift.

One felt more sorry for the stretcher-bearers than for anyone else. Every day must have been a purgatory of toil, acute discomfort and danger as, having climbed up the slopes, they would have to slither down the steep muddy tracks, anxiously trying not to stumble and thereby increase the pain of the wounded men they bore.

Signal linesmen were also among those whom no one envied. As a result of bombardment, the telephone lines would usually be cut. As soon as this happened they would have to emerge from whatever sheltered them to follow the line to wherever the break could be found, repaired and then tested. Although our wireless was seldom interfered with, it was essential to have an alternative means of communication.

That afternoon, General Charles Allfrey, the Corps Commander, came up to see us. The Corps Commander bore an immense responsibility at this stage, for it was vital to the whole course of the war that First Army did not give ground in the face of the Axis offensive. Substantial reinforcements were on the way, both from England and the 8th Army, and provided the enemy were not allowed to gain much elbow-room, final victory in Africa would come soon.

I did not stay to greet the Corps Commander as I had unpleasant memories of our last meeting in 'Happy Valley' so I left John Marshall to do the honours. In fact he had come to congratulate the battalion and to see for himself how they were standing up to their ordeal. The soldiers he spoke to chose to make light of the situation. Remarks such as: 'It's a piece of cake, sir,' and 'Send up some more,' gave him the impression that they could stand a good deal more and it now transpired that that was just what they were going to have to do. He immediately appreciated the importance of the Djebel Bel and decided that an effort must be made to take it. The following day, a battalion of the Sherwood Foresters were sent up to attack. When very near the summit, the German counter-attack drove them back and it became obvious that only a really major effort could establish and maintain our troops on the top. After their battle, the Foresters relieved the 1st Battalion, who went back to rest near Tabarka.

Early on the 14th another heavy bombardment shook the ground and our positions on Cork Wood. We all thought this heralded another attack, but none came, for while thus trying to neutralize us the enemy attempted a very wide flanking move round the other side of the long ridge which our machine-guns commanded. They were too far out for us to interfere with, apart from getting the gunners to lob a few shells at them. Later on a light aircraft landed out there. This was a Fieseler Storch, which was capable of incredible landing and taking-off feats. One could presume that it brought a senior officer to see what the form was, for the going must have been almost impossible. Heavy rain fell intermittently and all-pervading slushy mud made all movement away from the roads very difficult indeed. Even mule transport must have been uneconomical, as the mules had to carry their own food in addition to their loads. Nothing more came of this wide left hook, but the shelling continued all day. Towards the evening it grew heavier and the steady trickle of wounded showed that it was being carefully planned and observed.

Suddenly a wave of German soldiers charged in, L.M.G.s and rifles being fired from the hip, grenades hurled in all directions, streams of tracer from the M.G. 34s, and all to the accompaniment of Teutonic shouts and cheers. It may have been that their wide flanking movement was a feint to delude us, for there was no doubt that after a long day of continuous shelling, and our absorption with their flounderings in the distant mud, we were not quite as flexed and ready to beat our opponents off as we might otherwise have been.

Anyway, these assailants seemed to be a fresh and noisy lot who did not quite know the ground, for although they penetrated the small salients between the companies, they made little attempt to do any mopping-up or to exploit in any way. After a great deal of shouting, they fired a large number of Very lights into the air, meanwhile edging slowly up the hill between 'A' and 'C' Companies. 'C' Company captured a small group and rang up to tell me that they were 10th Panzer Division Grenadiers. This was bad news, for this division was normally opposite the Medjez sector, and it was most alarming to think that the Germans were still bringing fresh troops to force the issue against us in the north.

There could be no question of letting this lot dig in during the night. If we did, they would be all over us at first light, and yet there was no reserve at all to spare, nor was there anyone we could safely move. The bombardment had mostly lifted to our own Battalion H.Q. area, and signallers, telephone lines, stretcher-bearers and vehicles were all being hit. The rest of the brigade sector was quiescent and everything depended on us. Our own guns could do little to help us because of the crest of the hill, but our mortars fired literally hundreds of bombs and the crews worked in a daze.

Then, in the distance, we heard the busy drone of several aircraft and we glimpsed perhaps a squadron of slow lumbering Stukas, and above them Focke-Wulfs. From the Germans on the ground a fresh stream of coloured lights went up and, not to be outdone, our own N.C.O.s replied with every signal cartridge they possessed. The Stukas circled once and then dived, one behind the other. The bombs from the first landed absolutely slap in the middle of the Panzer Grenadier party and so did practically all the rest. Many Germans were literally blown to bits and the limbs of some of them were stuck high in the trees near where they had lain. The rest fled. Only a few minutes after the Stukas had gone our patrols reported our positions clear of any live enemy. It was a fantastic stroke of fortune. The mangled remains confirmed the presence of 10th Panzer Grenadiers. Surely it was we who could claim: 'God with us.'

That night the 3rd Battalion was relieved by the 2/5th Leicesters, who had been re-equipping and resting.

The next two days passed fairly quietly and it seemed probable that the enemy were regrouping. He had now made three determined attempts to capture Cork Wood, he had also tried frontal attacks down the road, and he had tried to get round the left flank. As far as we could make out, he had used the equivalent of a division and had suffered heavily in the process. We had identified the Barenthin Regiment, which we thought consisted of three battalions. Many of the men were connected with the German Air Force and some were parachutists. Closely

connected with the Barenthin was the Witzig Regiment.
They were highly trained parachute engineers commanded
by a Colonel Witzig; he was famous for the airborne capture of the Belgian fortress of Eban Emael, which occurred
during the German break-through into the Low Countries.
Then there was the Tunisian Regiment of three battalions,
which we considered to be a very average lot. Lastly had
come the 10th Panzer Grenadiers, for whom we had a very
healthy respect.

Well away on their right flank, between the road and the
sea, a rather more gentle battle had been taking place.
Here a regiment of Bersaglieri had been opposed by a
newly formed French formation called 'Corps Franc
d'Afrique'. The men, though stout-hearted, were very raw,
but were firmly held together by a most gifted leader in the
shape of their commander, le Commandant Durand. The
remnants of one of the British Commandos were also
available. Air reconnaissance reported that considerable
movement was taking place ahead of us and it might have
been reasonable to suppose that the enemy was about to
switch to the right.

Any respite was welcome to us and though we continued
to improve our defences, we also tried to make ourselves as
comfortable as possible. All through the battle we had
maintained our small officers' mess down beside the road.
Each night we had made brave attempts at having dinner
served, and each officer in turn had come down to have a
bath and a reasonable meal. The bath was of canvas and
was set up on the grass beside the road. Sometimes bath-
time coincided with the evening hate and this happened
when Johnny Lane was in it. He quietly donned his steel
hat and went on scrubbing himself, while shrapnel rattled
off the trees. As often as possible, the men came down to
wash in the stream below, and a few were sent back to our
'B' Echelon for two days at a time. The constant shelling
and mortaring was beginning to tell and some of the
weaker brethren were showing signs of what used to be
known as shell shock. We had very few cases within the
brigade and those we did have were genuine mental breakdowns.

From now on, the shelling of our rear areas became far

too uncomfortably accurate, and the enemy seemed to be able to strafe us just when it hurt most. We used to change our routine, in case he was merely making intelligent guesses, but he still neatly caught us immediately a body of men assembled for a meal or any other purpose. I was certain that there must be an enemy observation post on the hill behind us, and we made several searches to try to find it. Every now and then we came across small parties of Germans wandering behind our lines and one or two staff officers fought quite stirring little engagements on their way to visit forward battalions. We never found a party with a wireless set and each day the shells fell closer. One evening I was hit in the thigh by a small fragment. I was shown scant sympathy by Ronnie Gordon, our battalion doctor, who gouged the piece out with a grubby thumbnail and told me he thought I should survive.

The weight of shelling and mortaring we endured can have been as nothing compared to that which our fathers had to withstand in the First World War, for now both sides were trying to keep operations as mobile as possible, so that massive artillery programmes lasting for days on end could play no part. Nevertheless the accuracy of modern weapons and means of control meant that once the enemy knew, or had a good idea of, where you were, he could make life very unpleasant indeed and there was never a minute during the daylight hours when one could say: 'Well, you are safe for a bit now, chum.'

On 17 March the enemy attacked again. This time the whole weight of the assault was aimed at the infantry in front up the road, and the French away to the left. We were left alone. It was difficult to discover what was happening, because the infantry battalions did not use their wireless sets as freely as we did, and we missed the intimate contact we had grown used to with the 1st and the 3rd. Instead of groups of prisoners being marched down the road, little parties of stragglers appeared. Small groups were being made leaderless through persistent casualties to officers and N.C.O.s, and, in the resulting confusion, positions were being abandoned. There could be no doubt that unless these battalions were withdrawn in the next few hours they would soon cease to be.

I came to the conclusion that unless a withdrawal was ordered, we should be forced to fight our way out during the next few hours, and I bedded down early so as to be fresh for manoeuvre. I was summoned to Brigade during the night and my driver drove while I was still asleep in the back of the truck. Unfortunately he fell asleep when we arrived, so we both slept outside the Headquarters during most of the night. Dawn woke us, and I rushed in to find that we were required to withdraw almost at once. There was no time for the staff to tell me what other moves were being made and I tore back to the battalion to get it under way.

We adopted the simplest possible plan with no frills; in brief, the battalion was required to rendezvous at the railway viaduct over the road and river, at the back of Cork Wood. Less than an hour was available from the time the forward troops got their orders, but, in the event, all went according to schedule. Some even found time to do a certain amount of booby-trapping, and later we were to discover that some of these traps had worked.

As we were packing up the final bits and pieces of Battalion Headquarters, Dennis Vernon, our affiliated sapper, ran down the road to ask if he should blow a prepared demolition, which would have the effect of completely blocking the road. I was all in favour for this would prevent the enemy following us up in vehicles, but there were no specific orders, and so I thought I had better get permission from Brigade. After a little discussion and delay, I was told to blow. I shouted to Dennis and he galloped back up the road to touch off the explosive. I heard a rumbling roar as the side of a cliff and a slice of the road tumbled into the valley below, and I thought no more about it.

When I arrived at the rendezvous I found most of the battalion there. Many looked several years older after their ten days of the battle during which more than a hundred and fifty killed and wounded had been plucked away from their sides, but nearly all were in tremendous form and some very sorry to go. Our precious transport was still waiting by the viaduct, as the road was being heavily shelled, and those in charge were waiting hopefully for the shelling to finish. I sent them off, one at a time, at full speed, and though the shelling continued throughout their passage, they all got to the far end with but a few holes in their canvas covers to show for it. As for the battalion, we could withdraw either down the river-bed or across the hills. There were some bare patches on the hills and I feared that if the enemy were quick to occupy Cork Wood, we would present an easy target on the hill opposite, so I opted for the river-bed, and in one long snaky column the battalion made its way.

The river was deeper, faster, and fuller than I had expected and our slithering, sliding, jerky march was a ghastly ordeal for many. Every now and then a salvo of shells poured in among us, but we could at least be thankful for the cover afforded by the banks. We were also delighted to note that more than half the missiles failed to explode at all, and we attributed this to the softness of the ground, though even in these harrowing circumstances, the wags would shout: 'Many thanks, Czecho-Slovakia.'

It was here that Dicky Spender, one of 'C' Company's platoon commanders and a poet of some renown, composed his last short poem:

> Thud,
> In the mud,
> Thank Gud,
> Another dud!

Unfortunately, not all the shells missed their mark, and it was a nightmare trying to bring any wounded with us. One man had a leg horribly smashed with the foot turned completely round. We managed to get him carried up a ditch towards the enemy, to the road, where he was picked up by a passing vehicle.

As the column forged slowly on, those at the back cried for more speed. The enemy were hard on our heels, and every now and then bullets from their advanced guards tickled up the rear. Dennis Vernon's demolition on the road had turned out to be a rather vital factor. I heard later that a few seconds after the road had been blocked, a half-track full of Panzer Grenadiers had hurtled round the corner into the debris and had come to grief. This was most

probably a fairly high-powered reconnaissance party which
would have been capable of arranging to do us a great deal
of harm. As it was, their follow-up was rather slow and they
were content to fire at us from a distance.

It was very hard going indeed. Sometimes even the
larger ones among us sank in up to our necks and the
smaller ones had to swim or float. The sun shone fiercely
and despite the cold of the water, we poured with sweat.
Half-way along the column a man began to go off his head.
Having thrown away his rifle and equipment, he screamed
and sang alternately, and finally tried to swim under
water. Nevertheless progress was made, and the further we
went, the less attention the enemy paid us.

Finally we rounded a sharp bend in the river and were
able to clamber out and up to the railway line, which led to
our new positions. Here we were met by John Marshall,
who had brought the transport round by the road. I was
telling him about our horrible journey and saying how
thankful I felt to be out of the shelling at last when there
was a tremendous crump fifty yards away, as a heavy one
burst and left a huge crater. We resumed the march with all
possible speed. We were making for three rocky hillocks
which jutted up steeply from the valley, and commanded a
river junction and railway bridge at a place called Nefza.
These three hillocks were soon being called the Pimples,
and very important they proved to be.

We trudged on, trying to match our steps to the railway
sleepers. The sole on John Marshall's boot was coming off,
so that every now and then it caught under a sleeper and
nearly fetched him down. Just as we were beginning to feel
relief at getting away from the enemy's constant ministra-
tions after such a long association, there was a slow, singing
whine over our heads, and a solid thump as a shell burst
slap on top of the first of the Pimples. No more came, so
perhaps their gunners had run short of ammunition at last,
but it was salutary to think that some malignant eye had
watched us all the way, that our destination had been
appreciated, and that, after all, there would be no respite.

It took three or four hours to settle the battalion in on the
Pimples. They consisted of solid rock and it was extremely
difficult to get any depth into the positions. The biggest and

most forward was on the enemy side of the river, and the top was fully overlooked from the hills to the immediate east. I was obvious that the Pimples were going to be no fun to hold, but they were not going to be much fun for the enemy to attack either. In the event, we were not called upon to endure longer, for the following evening we handed over to the Leicesters.

CHAPTER 11

Battle of Tamera: Phase Two

A rather splendid disused tin mine was our home for the next few days. There was a niche for every man among the excellent buildings and luxuries were heaped upon us. Greatest of these was a mobile bath unit, which provided streams of gorgeous hot water. Fresh, clean clothing and new boots felt strange and ticklish after the mud-ingrained, soggy things we now threw away, but there was time to fit and stretch them, a gift of time off from the war. There were no interruptions to meal-times, no disturbances in the night and, above all, no need for any hurry, at any rate for a day or two. Our administrators took great pains over our food and no little trouble over our drink. Great demi-johns of wine were on sale for all and the N.A.A.F.I. had been made to stand and deliver far more than they ever meant to let us have.

Possibly, more needed and welcome than anything else, was an abundance of newspapers and magazines. Our Brigade had taken much trouble to get these for us and avidly they were read. They helped more than anything else to take a man out of his immediate past and into a world he could hope to rejoin. I sometimes forgot that though I might see all that happened in the battalion area, and even most that happened in the brigade sector, many of the men enjoyed a very limited view. They had many stories to tell and many questions to ask and as they sat in the sunshine, cleaning a part of a weapon or piece of equipment, the bits and pieces were put together to make an understandable whole.

I felt we could now hope to go straight back to our base to prepare for an airborne operation. Despite all the difficulties, I was sure we could play a significant, even if minor, part in the coming offensive; but that even if this was not to be, we could certainly not afford any more casualties to our trained parachutists. We had been told that no less a person than the Prime Minister had been agitating for our withdrawal from the purely infantry role, and we imagined that there would be only a short interval between the end of the African campaign and the opening of a full-scale attack on some part of Europe. However, apart from these considerations, I felt that the employment of comparatively small groups, up to the strength of a company, could greatly influence and disrupt enemy movement at a vital time, and thus be of tremendous help to the orthodox offensive. This was of course the pattern, in ever-increasing measure, in all other campaigns and already quite a large number of small operations had been mounted by various organizations in support of the 8th Army. There were many difficulties to be overcome if we were to be used, but the main ingredients were all available; parachutes, equipment, aircraft, airfields and, last but not least, ourselves. John Ross and I had seen evidence of the disruption caused on our own lines of communication by the mere threat of the use of Italian parachutists. I am certain that we could have caused immense disruption if used where good cover was available nearby, and this northern sector was one possibility, as was the hilly country to the south.

However, orthodoxy is ever a firm tenet of the British Army's faith. 'Trojan Horse' tactics are always apt to be overruled in favour of the direct approach, and so no one had much excuse for being surprised when we were warned that we should be doing a full-scale infantry night attack in the next few days.

Our main trouble was going to be that we were very weak in numbers to mount an attack. The rifle companies averaged about fifty men and there were only two officers left in each. With such numbers a battalion can hold ground fairly comfortably because ammunition for the L.M.G.s can be stocked heavily during quiet periods, but in the attack, attenuated numbers mean limited ammunition available on the objective, just when it is vital to have plenty.

We had a vacancy for a captain in the battalion and there were two almost equally matched contenders for it. Dicky Spender and Victor Dover were about the same age, had the same service, and had been with the battalion the same length of time. I found it very difficult to decide, but they solved the problem by agreeing to forgo promotion until one of them became a casualty. The first to be hit would immediately get his batman to sew on another pip, and go back to hospital as a captain senior to the one who remained to enjoy the resulting vacancy. We all used to laugh at their rather sinister, cynical wrangling, with the exception of one of our best officers. For him there was no cheer or joking. He seemed to have a premonition.

While all the normal preparations for action were put in hand, I went back up to the Pimples to make a detailed plan for the attack. The Pimples had changed hands several times since we left and had finally been recaptured by a quite brilliant night attack led by the redoubtable Alastair Pearson himself. Alastair had a wonderful flair, both for planning and leadership. His battalion had a great technique through experience, and their battle procedure was as good as could be, but it was the almost uncanny instinct of their leader that so often brought them success when others failed.

At this period, the 3rd Battalion were holding the Pimples. They were unable to give me any detailed information about the enemy positions on the hill in front of them, so it was not possible to make a really effective fire-plan. They reckoned that the Tunisian Regiment was immediately in front of them, but thought that the Witzig Regiment was not far away.

I also found it very difficult to pick out and fix on a clear-cut objective. It was a brigade attack with the 1st Battalion moving on our left and further out still was to be a Tabor of Moroccan Goumières – always known to us as the Goumes. In support we were to have the whole of 46 Division's artillery. Thus there was very little choice in the number of courses open to us, and in the first phase, we had to establish ourselves on the top of the hill which the enemy now occupied. The maps were inclined to be vague and all the upper part of the hill was covered with trees. However I eventually chose a prominence which was at the apex of a spur running up the top from the river below, and I reckoned that this spur should help us to keep direction during the night. Having captured this large, wooded, unreconnoitred feature in the dark, and having dealt with all the enemy, whose strength and dispositions were unknown, we then, in conjunction with the 1st Battalion, were to swing righthanded to recapture our old positions at Cork Wood and beyond.

It was by no means a simple operation for there were many unknown factors, but we knew that success or failure depended on our ability to withstand the German counter-attack when and where it came. Time and time again during this campaign, attacks which had been initially successful had been turned into expensive defeats by the vigorous, purposeful and concentrated German counter-attacks. As the Witzig Regiment were in the offing, presumably in reserve for just this purpose, it was vital that we should be in position, dug-in, and fully prepared to meet them at first light after our night attack was delivered.

While I was with the 3rd Battalion, just behind the foremost Pimple, known as 'Bowler Hat', the enemy treated us to a very neat little artillery shoot. His guns were cunningly sited out to a flank, in such a way that they could almost reach right round behind each Pimple. I felt very like a small boy at school again, curled up under a table, just out of reach of a much larger boy, who was trying to get at me with a stick. Not only did the guns seem to be trying to reach me personally, but they also showed, quite clearly, how well they could cover all the approaches I wanted to use during the attack. The railway bridge in particular rattled and clanged with shell splinters, and it was obvious that if machine-gun fire was added to this it would become a very dangerous route, and I decided to ask Brigade for some alternative bridging elsewhere. In between the salvoes, I exchanged ruderies with some of the officers of the 3rd Battalion, who were fairly comfortably underground by the bank of the river. We could hear the shells coming and I thought that some predictions as to their final destinations showed a very warped sense of humour. Finally one round landed in the river only a matter of feet from David Dobie, and drenched him deservedly from head to foot.

The evening before we left the mine, we held a service in the big machine shed. The men sat on shelves, in tiers round the sides of the building, and Padre Watkins officiated from a table in the middle. Everyone who could, went, and everybody sang, led by a small harmonium. Now that the hour of fresh battle approached, there were many amongst us who wondered what really happened if our number came up. Death in battle was apt to come so suddenly that it seemed wrong to be completely unprepared, and yet, with very few exceptions, none anticipated it. Whenever it seemed that Death's finger was near enough to give us a sudden prod, we found ourselves thinking of the effect it would have on others and what bad luck it was for them to be deprived, so prematurely, of our company, but our most serious regrets were on the effect it would have on our parents, for we felt that they were the people who would grieve the most. Only a very few of us were married.

We were fortunate in being as well served by our padres as we were by our doctors, for they all felt dedicated to their task. When guidance and comfort were required they were not found wanting and moreover they understood the unfortunate fact that the majority of our young British soldiers were ignorant of the simple fundamentals of their own professed religion. The padres never had sufficient time to rectify that state of affairs, but when assurance and inspiration were required, they gave them.

After the service was over I felt constrained to speak. It is never easy to find the right words on such occasions for any form of exhortation usually leaves the experienced soldier quite unmoved, while the recruit will forget all that has been said as soon as the battle begins. Nevertheless, it was the first time the battalion had been formally assembled for several weeks and a great deal had happened during that time. It was the right occasion. I do not suppose

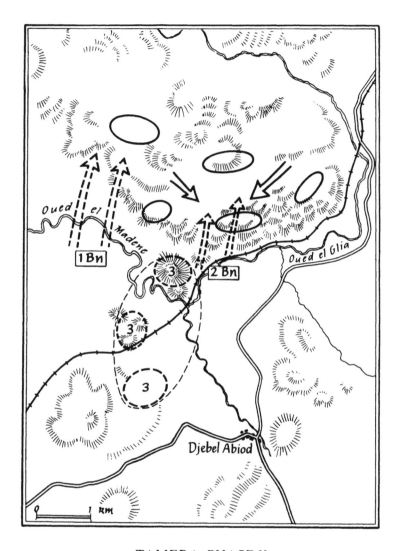

Oued el Madene

1 Bn

2 Bn

Oued el Glia

3

3

3

Djebel Abiod

0   1 km

TAMERA: PHASE II

I shall ever speak to an audience quite like that again. I remember ending: 'I don't know what you think of us, but I know I speak for all my officers when I say we have nothing but the highest possible regard for every single one of you.'

At 10 p.m. on the night of the 27th, the divisional artillery opened up. The leading companies crossed the start line and all the preliminary arrangements had gone without a hitch. None of us had heard a heavy artillery programme before, especially with all the guns pointed in the right direction, and we felt urged onwards in a strange and mystic way. It was a perfect night with the air warm and still and the noise of the shells moving above us was orchestral in infinite variation. Behind us, the flashes from the gun-lines kept the sky alight, while the shell-bursts on the hill ahead of us showed us where we had to go. To begin with there was no answer from the enemy and there was nothing to bar our way. The two forward companies disappeared into the darkness of the woods on the hill, hurrying to keep as close as possible to the fire-plan moving on in front.

I went behind the forward companies with a small navigating party. We were laying a thick white tape which would mark the battalion main axis of advance up the hill. This was meant to be roughly equidistant from the axes of the two forward companies and would guide the reserve company and the rest of the battalion coming up behind.

Unfortunately, I had underestimated the time it took to lay the tape in the darkness, over difficult country, and before long we were far behind the leading companies, being unable either to see or to hear them. I could talk to them by wireless, but it was not possible for them to describe their exact whereabouts, and meanwhile they had to follow the guns. The barrage was steadily climbing the hill and, long before we were ready, it lifted over the top to deal with suspected enemy positions on the reverse slope. Owing to the steepness of the going I had not got the means of communicating with the artillery with me, and so could do nothing to slow down or alter their programme in any way. The noise from the gun-lines still echoed back from the hills and the flashes still helped us to keep our bearings.

Gradually the enemy began to come to life on the

forward slopes, and before long we were able to hear the companies fighting their way up to the top. As our gunfire died away, we realized how dark the night was, with no moon at all and just a faint glow from the stars. The enemy's first reaction was to fire a series of light signals and illuminating flares. Each time, we froze where we were as the glare lit up our surroundings. Immediately it died away, we hurried on.

After clambering up one particularly steep place we found ourselves on a gently sloping plateau, and suddenly I realized that we were in the middle of a German defensive position. We could hear muffled German voices all round us and see the odd figure moving among the trees. Then one of these blundered into our group and he was promptly seized by Sergeant Cloves, our Signals sergeant. Our small group was certainly not equipped to assault and capture an enemy position; there were only ten of us and our *raison d'être* was the tape and two wireless sets. I decided to move out smartly and summon 'C' Company to deal with the Germans we had stumbled upon. Sergeant Cloves had a firm grip on our captive, but could not resist twisting his arm, and as we slithered down the hill I was very much afraid that the prisoner's shrieks of pain would give us away. While we waited for 'C' Company, the enemy brought some light mortars into play and their bombs landed all round us. None of us was hit but the thumps of the bombs jarred disturbingly, and one was reminded of the effectiveness of the mere shock of high explosive at close quarters.

'C' Company, led by John Ross, soon came puffing up the tape and cleaned up the enemy position very quickly. Several prisoners were passed back and these carried our wounded down as well. This small plateau we had chanced on was not marked on the map, nor could it be seen from the valley below. I got the impression that it was very near the top of the hill and that therefore it would make an excellent fire base. The ground fell away steeply on three sides and it seemed that the crest of the hill, which was our first objective, was straight ahead and not very far.

I now tried to discover the exact positions of the two leading companies. 'A' on the right were easy to trace for they had made disappointing progress, and I decided to bring them close in to our immediate right. 'A' Company had only one officer left by this time and could not be counted on to do any difficult movement in the dark on their own. 'B' Company, on the other hand, had gone well ahead, but had been checked by an unsuspected minefield.

They had come under heavy fire while trying to find a way round, and both Mickey Wardle, the Company Commander, and Victor Dover had been wounded. I was able to talk to Douglas Crawley, who had taken over the company, but we were unable to tell each other exactly where we were. I asked him to put up Very lights from his position, but when he did so, the Germans immediately followed suit from other places and succeeded in confusing the issue.

While this was going on, 'A' Company arrived through the woods on our right and took up positions on that flank. We now had most of the battalion together on what I considered to be a good firm base. We were able to make considerable use of the enemy defences with which the area abounded, and I felt that we could also secure the route to our rear. Time was getting on, and I began to think of the German counter-attack, which we could expect to be mounted soon after dawn. I thought that we were very close to the top of the hill which was our first objective, and I considered that it would only require one good heave from the whole battalion to complete the job, and this would best be done when it got a bit lighter. I reckoned that we should all be much better poised if we could gather in 'B' Company as well, and therefore told Douglas to make towards us. Thereupon, he disengaged and managed to steer the right course, bringing the wounded with the company. We did our best to guide him by using different combinations of light signals, concentrating on red, white, and blue, but the going was by no means easy or unopposed, and in one encounter, Douglas, the last remaining officer of the company, was wounded too.

However, I now had the battalion together and there was nothing more to do but wait for more light. We had been lent a young sapper officer called Simpson for emergencies and I told him to take command of 'B' Company.

With the eagerly awaited first faint light of dawn, I realized with growing horror that the battalion was very closely bunched indeed. The position which we had built up in the darkness, to what, I felt, was one of strength, was now shown to be dangerously overcrowded and therefore extremely vulnerable to any enemy shelling or mortaring.

Much worse was to come. As soon as we could see more than a few score yards, it was plain that we were still a long way from the top of the hill and that I had been completely taken in by a false crest. Beyond this crest the ground went on rising, and there could be no doubt that I had failed dismally to take the first objective.

Fortunately, at this desperately depressing moment, the Germans provided some light relief, for despite all that had happened during the night some of them had slept on in their dug-outs and holes in the ground. These were dull and stupid types, who have their counterparts in any army, and the expression of amazement on their faces as they emerged to stretch themselves in the open, or blundered into one of our posts, made for much ribaldry.

It was essential to restart the attack before the enemy commander discovered where we were. While I was discussing alternative plans with John Marshall and the acting Adjutant, there was a sudden clatter in the branches of the tree under which were standing, and an unexploded medium mortar bomb slithered down to land at our feet. Deciding that on no account must we all become casualties together, we scattered and continued our conversation by shouting. However, a few minutes later, we were all drawn together again to look at a map, and almost immediately another dud bomb thudded into the ground less than two yards away.

John Ross attacked straight up the hill with his company. With the coming of daylight we could use our own guns and mortars again and by this time our mortar platoon had moved up the hill close behind us. Our mortarmen and machine-gunners, in addition to their normal duties, were fully trained as riflemen and they were always available to provide a reserve in emergency. They also played a full part in any patrolling programme, so they were by no means 'lost' to the battalion as forward fighting troops. 'B' Com-

pany, under the command of our young sapper, went back
over some of the ground they already knew, as a left
flanking hook. 'A' Company remained to hold the firm
base and all who were here got on with their digging.

For a time both 'B' and 'C' Companies made good
progress, but before long 'C' began to meet strong opposition. This opposition stiffened quickly as more Germans
were moved to meet their threat, and then built up into a
properly mounted counter-attack. Closely packed groups
of well-drilled men advanced through the trees, many firing from the hip as they came, using the slope of the hill to
keep momentum and gradually gathering speed. At one
moment a party almost enveloped the company's right
flank and Dicky Spender charged to push them back. In so
doing he fell, riddled with bullets, but took four Germans
out of this world with him. John Ross now had to pull back.
He was the only officer left and casualties had been heavy.
Some prisoners had been taken in the course of this savage
little clash and they were Witzig's men. We knew they
would come again as soon as they had sorted out their
ammunition. The Germans were much more liberally supplied with automatic weapons than we were. Their rifles
were self-loading and their L.M.G.s were belt-fed. This
meant that they could produce a tremendous volume of fire
for a given period, but in this difficult, hilly country, where
supply was a constant problem, they often found they used
their ammunition up too quickly, as indeed did we all.

The Brigadier, realizing that we were having a difficult
passage, sent David Dobie with 'B' Company of the 3rd
Battalion to our aid.

On our left, the 1st Battalion had come up against the
Italians. After a fairly brief exchange of shots, some twelve
hundred Bersaglieri surrendered en masse. Still farther
left, the Tabor of Goumières were to all intents and purposes unopposed.

Soon after David Dobie arrived, the Witzig men drew
near again. There was no room to manoeuvre and, if we
became too hard pressed, I considered that we should have
to charge, and so all were ordered to fix bayonets and get
ready. The very act of fixing bayonets struck a wonderful
note among all ranks and morale reached a peak. At this

juncture, one of our brighter characters picked up a tray of Italian hand-grenades, and as he handed them round he cried: 'Cigarettes, chocolates.'

Shells and bombs poured down towards us, but nearly all went over our heads. The enemy must have been having trouble with crest clearance and with bringing his guns to bear, neither did he have good opportunity of observing his fire. Our own guns joined in to help us and, as the Germans closed in, our mortars caught them at minimum range. It was not easy to discern the enemy among the trees, which provided such excellent cover, and we knew them by the volume of their fire rather than by seeing their bodies. This time it was 'A' Company who bore the brunt and I moved the gunner O.P. to them. This officer had his work cut out to conform with all the requests made, for the Company Commander continually shouted: 'Swing it about, boy, swing it.'

At about this time, 'B' Company were making excellent progress with their left hook and had made contact with part of the 1st Battalion near the top of the hill. They began to punch into the right and rear of the Witzig and this had an immediate effect on that regiment's counter-attack on us. Unfortunately the 1st Battalion were called upon to switch their axis just when there was this opportunity to help us and to deal the Witzig a surprise blow. Left to themselves, the remnants of battered 'B' Company called for artillery fire to support them on. It was almost impossible for the gunners to observe, and although effective fire was brought to bear, a number of shells landed among 'B' Company and the resulting casualties left them too weak and stunned to do more. However, the Witzig had shot their bolt too, and the men of 'A' Company caught glimpses of them flitting back up the hill as the counter-attack faded away.

It was tempting to chase after them and many were eager to do so, but we badly needed reorganizing before we were capable of any but the most limited movement. I had been told that I was not to use David Dobie's company in an offensive role, and if we went forward on our own and blundered into serious trouble, the enemy might still gain the day. We had a number of wounded and prisoners to evacuate, but were waiting for a break in the shelling before sending them down. If one looked backwards one could catch fleeting glimpses of enemy shells as they plunged from the sky.

The Witzig prisoners were a lively lot and the wounded among them made the minimum of fuss. One, with a large wound in his backside, made a great joke of it, and though offered a ride on a mule or a stretcher back to the rear, insisted on walking and helping another man. Among those waiting was Mickey Wardle, and we were delighted to see him being carried off by four hefty Germans, for it was he who had seemed to feel so depressed before the battle. All the greater was the shock when we learned later that he and the four Germans were all killed when a shell landed on a small hut in which they were sheltering on the way down.

Early in the afternoon, the remnants of 'B' Company came back to the main battalion position, but altogether we mustered no more than one hundred and sixty. A staff officer at Brigade Headquarters expressed surprise at our slowness compared to the 1st Battalion. Our patrols discovered that although their counter-attack had failed, the enemy were still firmly holding positions farther up the hill. To attempt to push on in daylight, while the Germans were fully prepared and waiting for us, would be to incur quite unnecessary casualties. Fortunately the Brigadier himself fully realized this, for he silenced the mewing of his inexperienced subordinate, and sent Stephen Terrell – my old competitor when we were adjutants – up to us with another company of the 3rd Battalion, while agreeing with me that we should not attempt another attack until the latter part of the night.

I now formed one rifle company out of the remnants of our three and called it Number 1 Company. John Ross took over command of it. The two companies of the 3rd were also temporarily rechristened Number 2 and Number 3. As darkness fell it began to pour with rain and before long we were all drenched to the skin. The rain made the night absolutely pitch-black, the ground underfoot waterlogged, and I began to wonder if we should ever be able to move at all. Soon after midnight, the enemy unloosed a lot of ammunition in our general direction, and David Dobie reckoned that this betokened their imminent withdrawal. At three o'clock in the morning we moved forward with Number 1 Company leading and from then on encountered very little opposition. We rounded up several Germans from the Tunisian Regiment who had got lost or left behind by mistake, and by the time we reached our old positions in Cork Wood, we had collected no less than fifty, together with a great deal of booty. We patrolled forward on to the slopes of the Djebel Bel and rounded up a few more Germans, who were retreating in front of an infantry brigade which had been attacking south of the road.

This was the end of the Battle of Tamera. We had been in action as a Brigade from the 7th to the 29th of March. It was a classic in that we had withstood every attack until, through the failure of others, we had been called to withdraw to prepare and execute the counter-stroke, which was, in effect, the start of the whole successful offensive to clear North Africa. Nobody except the enemy and we ourselves knew that we were fighting. Our presence in the forefront of the battle was not divulged and no reporters were allowed in our area. We did not realize this at the time, nor would we have cared, but it did hurt a bit when parents and friends said: 'And what have you been doing?'

The main road leading back to Djebel Abiod had been heavily mined and no transport could come up to us. I was very surprised therefore to see a motorcycle come up from behind carrying an outsize passenger on the pillion. It was the Corps Commander, General Allfrey. The driver had managed to thread his way between the mines. It was a very sporting gesture, for it is never possible to see exactly where all such mines are laid, and they could easily have come to grief. The General was most anxious about the demolition we had blown to block the road in the defile ahead, and was afraid that now it might delay his pursuit of the enemy who, he reckoned, had gone right back to the positions they had held before they began the original offensive in February. Fortunately, the Germans had repaired most of the damage themselves, and the road could already be used for single-lane traffic. I was rather disturbed to discover that the Corps Commander was under the impression that I ordered the demolition without reference to Brigade. As it happened, Alastair Pearson had overheard Brigade telling me to blow it, as he had been listening in on Brigade wireless net at the time. There always seems to be trouble over the simplest of demolition, for whatever is done is sure to be wrong in someone's eyes, and as the umbrellas go up all round, it may be difficult for the most innocent to avoid being made 'Mr. Scapegoat'.

On this occasion, General Charles Allfrey was prepared to forgive us anything. Before coming up he had seen some of the interrogation reports, and he reckoned that the 2nd Battalion had borne the brunt of the one counter-attack that really mattered and that this had been led by the redoubtable Colonel Witzig himself. Once this was defeated the enemy had little left, and from now on it would be a case of regrouping and rolling up. So the General left us feeling in great heart. We had had a very sticky and expensive battle, but now it all seemed to have been so well worth while. It was time to relax.

Although we were unlikely to get any hot food up through the minefields, I reckoned that if the Corps Commander could come up on the back of a motorcycle, so could the ration of rum and a double one at that. We still had fifty German prisoners with us and the 1st Battalion had asked to keep fifty of their Italians as well. While we were all waiting beside the road during the late afternoon, the Goumières, who had been operating out on the left flank, came past. On sighting our prisoners they made blood-curdling noises and drew their fingers across their throats in the accepted style. Some of the prisoners became very alarmed and so, when the rum arrived, we let them have some too.

That evening we had an impromptu concert. The Germans and Italians sang magnificently, but in contrast our contributions were pretty horrible. It seems that the unpractised production of vocal harmony is not one of our national gifts. Later we received a mild rebuke on account of this party. A German Feldwebel arrived at the Corps Interrogation Centre in tremendous form, having had more than his fair share of rum, and when asked where he had spent the previous night, he said: 'Singing and drinking with my comrades of the English Fallschirmjäger.'

The following day I went back to the ground we had fought over, and it was most interesting to trace the German defensive layout, for although we had found the main feature difficult to attack, it was certainly not easy to hold either. The forward slopes had been held with a comparatively thin screen of machine-gunners and O.P.s, but there were many alternative positions prepared so that the defenders could concentrate wherever a threat developed. The screen was thickest at all the most likely approaches, and all such positions were fully stocked with ammunition, water and whatever else was required. There was another series of positions on the top of the hill, but these seemed to be more in the nature of staging-posts, and routes were marked from them to the forward positions, to the flanking positions, and also to the rear. To the rear, on the reverse slope, there were deep dug-outs surrounded by fire trenches, barbed wire, and in some cases mines. They were almost miniature fortresses, very comfortably fitted up with electric light and wireless sets. I presumed these held a series of reserve units who could be moved and concentrated quickly on any part of the sector. It was very well thought out and carefully planned. There was no doubt that we had been opposed by very professional soldiers, and it may have been that we were fortunate to fight our main battle against them on the edge of, rather than in the middle of, their spider's web.

When I got back to Battalion Headquarters I found a huge crater no less than thirty feet across just beside it. A German aircraft had suddenly swooped over the hill and unloosed his missile at almost exactly the right place. Fortunately everyone escaped serious damage, though John Marshall and Father Egan were severely bruised by great chunks of falling mud.

After a few more days of holding the front we were relieved by a complete American Division, and, rather sadly, now that the time had actually come, we moved back in easy stages to our base at Boufarik, near Algiers. It seemed rather galling to be missing the glorious end after having been at the front almost from the beginning, but

Algiers promised to be fun. It had all the ingredients.

Our small brigade consisted of the equivalent of only ten rifle companies, totalling about one thousand officers and men, and added to this there were approximately two hundred machine-gunners, mortarmen and signallers at the sharp end. We had suffered one thousand seven hundred casualties during just over four months, so we had got through one and a third of our true front-line strength, and it would obviously take some time to get properly parachute-minded again, for such figures were high even by First World War standards.

Our Brigadier received many splendid messages from all the Generals under whom we had served. They made very pleasant reading and we all began to feel quite prima-donna-ish. General Alexander drew attention to the fact that we had earned the name of 'Red Devils' from the Germans, and best of all, I liked General 'Boy' Browning's message which ended: 'Such distinctions are seldom given in war and then only to the finest fighting troops.'

Three thousand six hundred prisoners had passed through the Brigade's cage during these four months and they had all been taken in hard fighting long before the mass surrenders which came later on in the campaign. In addition to this, we could fairly claim to have killed or wounded another five thousand of our foes. These figures were largely substantiated from enemy sources as well as our own, and also our supporting gunners' observations. On the way back to Algiers, the railway passed round two sides of one of the biggest prisoner-of-war camps in North Africa and, as the train, full of our red berets, approached this camp, we wondered if we had captured any of this particular lot. The word that our train was passing very soon got round the camp, and as it drew slowly by, scores of Germans came tumbling out of their tents. They ran towards us, throwing their hats in the air, and cheered us to the echo. This was the tribute that I liked most.

CHAPTER 12

Sicily

When things had been particularly uncomfortable up in Tunisia, Jack Parker, our Quartermaster, was apt to say, 'Ah, you wait till we get back to Boufarik, it's nice there; very comfortable it is, everybody likes it there.' Boufarik was the Brigade rear main base where the reinforcements, heavy baggage and spare equipment were kept. Each unit had been allotted a fine French farm with its outbuildings for its own use. These farms were surrounded by vineyards and orange groves. Food was plentiful and apparently the sun shone a great deal more than it did in Tunisia. Now that we had finally reached the promised land we were able to enjoy it to the full.

Algiers, about thirty miles away, had come to life since the early days of the campaign. Restaurants and hotels of all kinds were doing a roaring trade and there were amusements to suit all tastes. Soldiers from the armies of France, the U.S.A. and the British Empire put on their smartest uniforms and one often saw jeeps, which had become the most popular vehicle for all purposes, more full of cheerful young women than of men in khaki. Some elements made life extremely difficult for the military police, but these were in the minority and on the whole the 'Red Caps' of all three nations kept a firm measure of control.

Meanwhile, up in Tunisia the final stages of the campaign were being reached and when General Alexander brought the fighting to a brilliant end we felt out of it and jealous of those who were in at the finish. Perhaps this made us all the more determined to try to excel in whatever our next assignment might be.

General Eisenhower, the Supreme Commander, inspected the Brigade during this time and he left us all feeling very pleased with ourselves. He had a wonderful knack of saying the right thing to the right man and he thoroughly enjoyed the occasional quick answer which he seemed to go out of his way to invite. General 'Boy' Browning, who had been completing the task of forming the Airborne Corps, spent a few days in Algiers. The veritable father of airborne forces, he had set us very high standards which had not been easy to achieve. I think he had sometimes felt that our rough and ready ways could never produce the results required, but now he could relax amongst us and feel that his faith had been justified.

One morning when I happened to be driving with him on the outskirts of Boufarik, passing soldiers from the various units of the Brigade, he said: 'You know that whatever happens to these battalions in the future, and however much they are renumbered, amalgamated, or absorbed, they will always, somehow or other, retain characteristics put into them by their first commanding officers.'

Now, all these years later, I believe that there is much in what he said. The battalions at this particular time, although made up from much the same material, had already developed quite distinctive characteristics. I was glad that my 2nd Battalion looked different with their brilliant yellow lanyards and was pleased to see that they were as good as any at recognizing the 'Boy's' Flag car. He was most interested in my telling him what we thought about the Germans, especially their 4th Parachute Regiment and the Witzig. He told me that the Guards Division had had much the same respect for some of their opponents in the First War. He said that on one occasion, Alex, with the 1st Irish Guards, had fought a great battle with the Prussian Guard and on being relieved had said, 'We won't crawl down a communication trench. We are going to march out. They won't shoot.'

They didn't.

We took the opportunity of visiting our wounded in the base hospitals around Algiers. The nursing sisters said,

'You will have no trouble finding your men because they wear their berets all the time.' So indeed they did. Even in bed with pyjamas on. In fact I heard that one tried to keep his on en route to the operating theatre.

Brigadier Ted Flavell, our brigade commander for over a year, left us to take up another appointment at home. He was considerably older than most of us, having fought with distinction in the 1914–18 war. He had not had an easy row to hoe, for nobody in the higher headquarters knew how airborne forces should be used and it had been difficult to get suitable airborne tasks. Then when it was realized how our parachutists could perform as infantry, it had been equally difficult to prevent their being used in that way, to such an extent that we might never have been able to parachute again.

In his place came Brigadier Gerald Lathbury who had been the original commander of the 3rd Battalion. He was very much a regular officer, having qualified at the Staff College before the war. He also served in the War Office in the directorate which deals with airborne affairs and he now brought to the task of commanding 1st Parachute Brigade the latest ideas and outlook on this particular form of warfare.

It was soon confirmed to a very limited number of us that our next mission was to be the invasion of Sicily. This event had seemed fairly certain and had been forecast by several newspapers. The problem of maintaining security as to our detailed tasks was obvious from the start. We now had to receive large numbers of reinforcements of both officers and men, also equipment, vehicles and weapons. Most important of all, we should have to re-learn to parachute. John Marshall, who had been Second-in-Command during most of the fighting in Tunisia, now left us for an appointment on the Planning Staff in Cairo. In his place I was given John Lane who had been with the battalion before and was well known to all of us. Two new company commanders in the shape of Dickie Lonsdale and Tony Fitch also arrived at this time. Victor Dover became the Adjutant, having recovered from his wounds.

Having reorganized as much as possible, we moved westwards to the plateau south of Oran and into camp round the airfields near a town called Mascara. This plateau was hot, dry and dusty after the nice fertile land round Boufarik, but we were at least as close to our aircraft as we possibly could be. Too close in some ways, for when aircraft took off, they raised enormous clouds of red dust which covered every part of the camp in which we lived. For the operation we were again to be flown by the United States Air Transport Command. Many of the pilots were old hands by now and had covered thousands of miles during the last few months. They were very keen to learn to drop us in exactly the right place by night in the light of the moon, but this was easier said than done. At Mascara we found the remainder of the 1st Airborne Division which had flown out from Salisbury Plain. The division was now under the command of General Hopkinson, who was by way of being a glider enthusiast and was determined to show that gliderborne assault was as effective as any other.

Really hard, prolonged training was now the order of the day. We didn't attempt anything very fancy, but concentrated on moving across country by day and by night, and in ensuring that everybody had as much practice as they possibly could at using their weapons. Parachute training was soon in full swing and parachute exercises were designed so as to coincide as nearly as might be with the task we were to undertake in Sicily. Two of these exercises were done by night and the battalion learned extremely quickly. We developed a system of rallying at the end of our dropping-zone to a series of sound signals and in the still African night we found this far quicker than rallying to light or smoke.

We developed a method of parachutists dropping with their weapons actually attached to the man. Until this time all weapons, except stens and pistols which were tucked underneath the parachute harness, were packed in containers which were hung underneath the aircraft or carried in the bomb bays. The drill was that the weapon containers were dropped either in front of the parachutists, or in the middle of a stick of parachutists, or at the end. This meant that before the parachutist could be effective he had to find the weapon containers in the dark, sort them out and extract the weapons. We had found that this was extremely difficult in practice and took a lot of valuable time. Indeed some containers were never found at all. John Ross suggested that we would do very much better if we dropped with our brens and rifles actually attached to our legs, and I decided that that was what we would do.

From our own resources we found materials to protect the more delicate parts of the weapons from damage and we used unserviceable parachute rigging lines to attach the weapons to our bodies. Although we had some failures, we proved that we could drop in this way and be off the dropping-zone very very much quicker than any battalion which used the normal containers. I believe that the battalions in the Middle East had also stumbled on this solution, but the 2nd Battalion was certainly the first to make it work and actually use this system in action.

Strange things could happen to the parachutist in the prevailing atmosphere. There were sudden eddies and up-currents so that on occasions a man might remain aloft for far longer than the normal time. Such events incurred ribaldry such as:

'Going up to heaven already, Joe?'

'That is what comes from being on American rations.'

'Stop muckin' abaht up there then.'

When I was examining the maps of Sicily on a small hillock where I had my tent, a sudden whirlwind tore them away and up into the sky, past the wheeling hawks and vultures, which seemed to peer at them until they were right out of sight. Fortunately the maps were unmarked and not graded secret.

At this time, my personal life was rather lonely. So many friends had gone. There had been several changes of Second-in-Command and Adjutant and each new incumbent was inclined to be more diffident. Only the doctor and padre bore the same relationship and they had a wider choice of company. Without the immediate penalties that breaches of discipline in the line imposed, there was need for me to wield a heavier hand; so one had to learn to find consolation in one's own company, anyway until the next battle was done.

Early in July, having satisfied everyone that the Brigade

could parachute as a Brigade, we were flown to the other
end of French North Africa eastwards to Tunisia. This time
we camped in the shade of olive trees several miles to the
east of the holy city of Kairouan and not very far from the
port of Sousse. Our airfields were farther away, but still
within easy range. Training continued while final plans
were made and on 7 July I briefed the company commanders for the operation which went by the code name of
Fustian. The brigade had been given the task of seizing the
Primosole bridge on the road between Syracuse and
Catania. We were to establish positions on the high ground
to the south of the River Simeto and also establish bridge-
heads on the plain to the north. It was considered vital to
capture the bridge intact, because at this early stage of the
campaign, very little spare bridging was available, and the
ground troops needed a clear run to the Catania plain.

On 9 July the 1st Landing Brigade flew off for their task
of capturing the Ponte Grande near Syracuse. In addition
to this task they had various subsidiary ones, but the bridge
was their main assignment. This venture turned out to be a
disaster. Many of the gliders were cast off by their tug
aircraft too early in the face of an offshore wind, and came
down into the sea, with the result that many of the soldiers
were drowned and those who made the shore were without
weapons and ammunition. Other gliders were released
over a very wide area and the troops they carried were
unable to meet up during the operation. The landing-zone
which had been chosen was very unsuitable for a gliderborne operation in that it consisted mainly of small fields
which were bounded by solid banks or walls. Many of the
gliders which arrived approximately at their appointed
places hit these obstructions and severe casualties resulted
to their cargoes. All was confusion and a bitter disappointment.

The net result was that only some eighty men were
available to take the main target. After capturing it and
holding off repeated counter-attacks with limited
resources and ammunition, they were finally forced to
relinquish the bridge, which was soon afterwards retaken
by our own ground troops. The widely scattered soldiers
did, of course, have some impact on the local defence

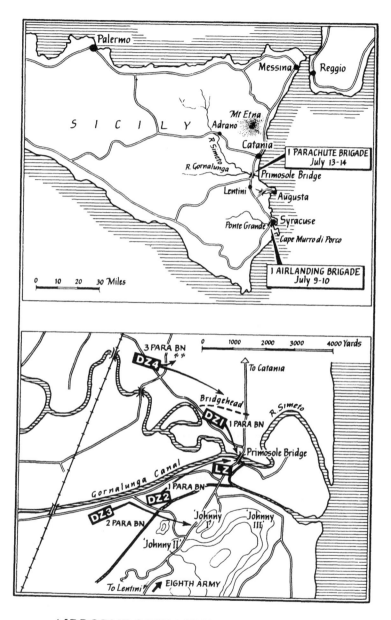

AIRBORNE OPERATIONS IN SICILY: 1943

which was almost entirely Italian, and they did give the Italians many excuses for surrendering, which was the one thing that many of them longed to do. The 1st Air Landing Brigade no longer existed as a fighting formation and could take no further part in the campaign. It is questionable whether the outcome wouldn't have been more successful if the Ponte Grande task had been allotted to a company group, who should have been able to land reasonably near with sufficient stocks of ammunition to see the battle through.

This was a severe blow to the division. Although the press at the time was complimentary and made out that many wonderful feats of arms had been achieved, it is doubtful whether this airborne operation had any effect on the success achieved by the initial landing from the sea. The operation planned for the 2nd Parachute Brigade never took place. Their task was another bridge near Augusta, but this was captured by the ground troops before the brigade were able to leave Africa. This was perhaps fortunate because the dropping-zones were almost non-existent and, if the brigade had arrived, their casualties on landing would have been very heavy. Moreover, because the zones would have been hard to find from the air, another brigade would have been scattered far and wide over the rocky, hilly ground.

On 12 July we of 1st Parachute Brigade left our base camps and drove to the airfields, but before we were able to emplane our operation was postponed for twenty-four hours and back we all came. However this gave us a little extra valuable time to tee-up our plans and to make final arrangements.

I was very happy with the task given to the 2nd Battalion, which was to capture and hold the high ground to the south of the River Simeto. This consisted of three definite features controlling the road running up from the south which were given the code names of 'Johnny I', 'II' and 'III'. The remainder of the brigade were given tasks either at the bridge or beyond it. General Lathbury's orders had been crystal-clear and I felt therefore that there was no doubt in anyone's mind as to what had to be done. Our dropping-zone was clear of and beyond those allotted to the rest of

2nd Battalion Parachute Regiment, 1944. *Back row:* Lieut. J. H. A. Monsell; Lieut. J. A. Russell; Lieut. A. Roberts; Lieut. A. L. Tannenbaum; Lieut. D. M. Douglass; Lieut. J. G. Blunt; Lieut. J. T. Ainslie; Lieut. J. G. Purdy; Lieut. A. J. McDermont; Lieut. R. A. Vlasto; Lieut. C. M. Stanford; Lieut. D. E. C. Russell; Lieut. G. F. W. Ellum, *Middle row:* Lieut. P. H. Cane; Capt. J. W. Logan, D.S.O., R.A.M.C.; Capt. A. Frank, M.C.; Lieut. J. H. Grayburn, V.C.; Lieut. W. N. Dormer; Lieut. P. H. Barry; Lieut. R. B. Woods; Capt. R. E. Morton; Lieut. R. H. Levien; Capt. J. Timothy, M.C.; Capt. A. J. Rutherford; Lieut. P. B. Jessop; Lieut. C. D. Brieux-Buchanan, M.C. *Front row:* Rev. B. M. Egan, M.C., C.F.(R.C.); Capt. D. McLean; Major V. Dover, M.C.; Major P. J. Albury; Major D. W. Wallis; Lieut.-Colonel J. D. Frost, D.S.O., M.C.; Major A. D. Tatham-Warter; Major D. E. Crawley, M.C.; Capt. F. K. Hoyer-Millar; Capt. S. C. Panter, M.C.; Lieut. (Qmr) J. T. Parker.

Emplanement. Most soldiers, whatever their feelings, managed to look enthusiastic and cheerful at this stage

Men dropping on to their D.Z.s eight miles from the objective at Arnhem. This distance ensured that the element of surprise was lost

Six-pounder anti-tank guns on the way in. The nearby country was ideal for the enemy to lay ambushes. Later the guns moved into the vanguard to meet sudden armoured attack

Tough-looking S.S. Panzer Grenadiers who were our main opponents in the battle; here they are our prisoners

Above: This photograph of Arnhem Bridge was taken by a Spitfire pilot on the first day, soon after we had destroyed most of the 9th S.S. Panzer Division's Recce Squadron as they tried to cross from the south

Opposite: Lieut.-General Willi Bittrich, the debonair and gifted G.O.C. of the 2nd S.S. Panzer Corps which happened to be refitting in the Arnhem area when we arrived

Opposite below: Field-Marshal Walter Model, the C.-in-C. of the German Armies in the West. He was surprised by our arrival, but in the ideal position to galvanize their defensive arrangements

The ruins of the building, near the bridge, from which H.Q. of the 1st
Parachute Brigade operated throughout the battle. This was a keypoint,
and, as it burnt, the continued defence of the north end became
impossible

Addressing the people of Arnhem in 1945 at the unveiling of a monument to commemorate the battle at the bridge

The bridge at Deventer which was used by United Artists to represent
Arnhem Bridge in the film *A Bridge Too Far* many years after the battle

the brigade and our pilots should have no difficulty in finding the right run-in and the landmarks in the shape of the river, the road and the main bridge itself. After dropping and assembling we had a ready-made, unmistakable axis to our objective in the shape firstly of a bund (a high bank), south of the river, and thence the main road to the 'Johnny' features.

I planned to bring the battalion from the dropping-zone in one long column along this well-defined route. I wanted to produce the battalion intact on their objectives under my own control. However, just in case the Italians, whom we knew to be holding the 'Johnny' features, panicked when they saw our aircraft arriving, I detailed one platoon under Tony Franks to make straight for one of the features and to seize and hold it if they could. This particular one was called 'Johnny II' and from it a determined enemy could cause quite a lot of trouble to our assembly and subsequent movement. 'Johnny II' was the nearest feature to our dropping-zone. 'Johnny I' was the central and most important of the three and possession of it gave absolute control of the main road leading to the bridge. This was the keypoint on which I planned to put most of the battalion. 'Johnny III' was away to the east towards the coast and not as important as the other two features.

On the 13th we again embussed and drove to the airfield. There were no hitches, delays or troubles. We had had such excellent relationships with the Americans that one felt nothing could go wrong. The weather was perfect and at 7.30 p.m. the battalion began to take off. 'A' Company and part of Battalion Headquarters were being flown by one of the best squadrons. This squadron had always managed to drop us accurately on the exercises we had done before, and their commander was confident that he could do likewise in Sicily.

Our flight went exactly according to plan. Later I learned that some of the other squadrons had flown over the Navy and been fired upon. This had caused considerable confusion so that several aircraft became dispersed and a number were actually shot down. We, however, saw none of this. At the expected time we turned westwards towards Sicily and headed to what was obviously a fully alerted defence. From the door and the windows of the aircraft we could see streams of tracer moving upwards. A number of fires were burning on the ground and smoke was rising from several other places. I could glimpse the mouth of the river and the high ground to the south of it. Our aircraft flew steadily on. The gum-chewing crew chief ordered us to our various states of readiness, the aircraft throttled back to the recognized best parachuting speed, and despite all the distractions from the ground we were all duly dispatched to our duties down below.

I landed in a shallow, empty ditch. The sides were sun-baked hard and my left leg took most of my weight at an awkward angle. My knee ligament scrunched and the pain came later.

My stick and I were quite close to our pre-arranged rendezvous. We could see the bund and the high ground comprising the 'Johnny' features. Most of the fires we had seen from the air were stooks of corn burning and not crashed aircraft, as we had feared. However the streams of tracer were there and enemy weapons of various calibres were being fired at all approaching aircraft. Enemy artillery were firing air bursts in our general direction.

The effect of this was alarming and annoying rather than dangerous, for whenever I tried to say something important to my entourage, my words were blotted out by a peremptory 'crack' from above.

Meanwhile, although the entourage was growing, it soon became obvious that all was far from well. Long after the time had passed when we should have assembled, only a handful of my headquarters had arrived. Most of Dickie Lonsdale's 'A' Company were present, but otherwise just odd bits and pieces of the battalion. There could be no doubt that few of the other squadrons had flown in as staunchly as ours had done. In fact we saw no other aircraft flying in formation anywhere. Some Dakotas flew over the general area at varying heights. Most of these were going flat out and some were weaving through the air in desperate evasive action. On one occasion two of them approached each other from opposite ends of the dropping-zone. We watched with bated breath, for a really sickening crash seemed inevitable. However, they tore past each other, perhaps not even knowing how near they had been to disaster.

Some aircraft had static lines streaming behind them from the door, showing that they had unleashed their sticks somewhere. In the doorway of others one could just see the shape of a man. The odd glider came in almost silently. One caught in a searchlight was riddled with machine-gun fire and crashed against the bund.

It was bitterly disappointing. There was no sign of Victor Dover, my Adjutant, or of Johnnie Lane, my Second-in-Command, the two officers with whom I had made detailed plans for the operation. Dicky Lonsdale was confident that he could take and hold 'Johnny I' with just his own company and so, having waited until there were no more aircraft about and therefore little possibility of any more of the battalion arriving, I moved off with few more than a hundred men towards the objective. By this time my knee was really painful, but I was able to pole myself along quite well. We passed Brigade Headquarters on the way. I remembered that it was General Lathbury's birthday and wished him many happy returns. He had been dropped in the wrong place and had only just arrived. His communication network was practically nil so he had little idea of what had happened so far, but from the noises off he gleaned that the 1st Battalion were dealing with the bridge and he ordered me to continue towards my planned objective.

On the way I met Mervyn Dennison, with a small party of the 3rd Battalion, who was vigorously destroying all the telephone lines he could find near the main road. Small parties of Italians were moving about in the dark looking for someone to surrender to, and the difficulty was to know which parties wanted to surrender and which might want to fight on. At this stage we had other things to think about, for once we cleared the river area and were on the main road our objectives loomed up clearly before us. At the bottom of the hill we met Tony Franks who had come across country with as many stragglers as he had been able to find. He had gone over the top of 'Johnny II' and found it virtually unoccupied. From there he had gone straight to the main objective on 'Johnny I', capturing one hundred and thirty Italians en route, and was firmly in position.

Dickie Lonsdale moved up with 'A' Company and deployed his force without further ado.

By this time my knee had seized up and so I left Dickie in command of 'Johnny I'. I remained with a small party in a dug-out where we had originally planned that the Battalion Headquarters would be. By 5.30 a.m. one hundred and forty men of the 2nd Battalion were in position on 'Johnny I' with no supporting weapons or communications, but poised for all-round offence. At six the enemy opened the proceedings. The noise emanating from 'Johnny II' was unmistakably that of German machine-guns. During the night some of our soldiers who had been dropped wide of the correct place had become mixed up with German parachutists and some men had picked up German equipment which had been found lying undamaged on the ground. We later discovered that German parachutists had actually dropped on almost the same D.Z. earlier in the evening. Their task, like ours, had been to capture the high ground and take control of the main road from the south. Fortunately for us they had remained on the low ground during the night, contenting themselves with firing at the aircraft. This allowed us to forestall them and now they had to try to make up for it.

By 6.30 a mortar bombardment was added to the machine-gun fire. The battalion had nothing with which to reply effectively and the enemy fire became more and more accurate. Their mortar fire was all the more deadly on the rocky ground and the number of our casualties began to grow. Nevertheless it was the German machine-gun fire from 'Johnny II' which seemed the more dangerous, so at 7.30 a.m. a fighting patrol moved off to try to put them out of action. Unfortunately this patrol was spotted by enemy armoured cars which caught our patrol in the open and drove it back with further casualties. Meanwhile the long dry grass to the south of the positions caught fire. Soon the smoke from this became an effective screen behind which the Germans were able to improve their positions and the intense heat from the flames forced our own forward elements back to a smaller and dangerously constricted perimeter. The casualty rate continued to increase. The machine-guns from 'Johnny II', the mortar bombardment, the smoke and the flames made life for anyone lying in the open hazardous in the extreme. There had been no time to dig before the attack commenced and most of the men were lying behind and among rocks and stones. There was still no support of any kind available, but we did have a gunner officer, Captain Vere Hodge, who was acting as Forward Observation Officer for the 6-inch guns of a cruiser lying out to sea.

Ever since the enemy had been located on 'Johnny II', Vere Hodge had been trying to get in touch with his naval counterparts. We had been told not to expect a great deal from this source as it was said that naval support of this kind was inclined to be inaccurate, erratic and, because of the extensive danger area of the comparatively large missiles, unemployable for any form of close support. But about nine o'clock Vere Hodge was tuned in and almost immediately the high-velocity medicine began to arrive with a suddenness and efficiency that completely turned the scales. The principles of surprise, economy of effort, concentration of force and flexibility were amply demonstrated by one young officer, a signaller and a wireless set. What seemed like imminent defeat was staved off and from then on the danger receded. By ten o'clock enemy infantry had ceased to move forward, though he maintained spasmodic strafing of the positions until well into the afternoon.

Once the easement came it was possible for our posts to move forward again and 'Bombs' Panter discovered a deserted, but fully operational, Italian howitzer battery concealed in the valley next to 'Johnny I'. He and his 3-inch mortar crews, whose weapons had failed to arrive, soon had the Italian guns in action and to such effect that they began to attract enemy counter battery fire. Not having valid targets within sight, they were ordered to cease firing as being more likely to bring unwelcome retribution than any harm to the enemy.

Meanwhile more and more Italian prisoners were coming in and it could have been a considerable problem. However as their one wish was to get out of danger and take no further part in the war, they were herded together under cover and left to their own devices.

During the course of the morning, though suffering from

painful wounds received during the night, Gerald Lathbury
walked up from his headquarters near the bridge. He confirmed what I had suspected about the drop of the remainder of the brigade: less than a third had finally arrived and
nearly all the vital equipment was missing. Nevertheless
the bridge and the bridgehead had been firmly secured and
so far the enemy had made no attempts to retake them. He
still had no wireless links with his battalions or the advancing ground troops who were expected to reach us during
the day. No support of any kind was available so it was
arranged that Vere Hodge would bring the cruiser's guns to
bear in defence of the bridgehead when that became necessary. There had been no sign of the R.A.F., but one or two
German aircraft came in to attack the bridge from time to
time. Fortunately they wasted most of their effort on the
empty gliders which by this time were conspicuous but
quite innocent targets. We wondered why no form of
friendly reconnaissance was flown. In the absence of
information from our own non-existent wireless, one
would have thought that Army Headquarters would spare
no effort to find out what the form was. Incidentally, it
would have encouraged us to see one of our own aircraft if
only just to know that we were not out of sight and out of
mind.

As the afternoon wore on all the enemy's efforts were
switched to the bridge and bridgehead. We had a grand-
stand view of their trials. I was able to hobble out of our
dug-out whenever there was something to see, and gradually the pain was lessening. The guns of the cruiser were
brought to bear effectively against an enemy battery which
was shelling the bridge, and a direct hit was scored on an
ammunition dump which blew up. It was difficult to see the
attacking enemy infantry because there was a considerable
amount of cover leading right up to the bridge in the shape
of trees, bushes and undergrowth. It was therefore almost
impossible to give the cruiser targets in this area without
seriously endangering our own troops. The afternoon was
hot and the atmosphere sultry. Smoke and fumes hung
about for a long time.

Meanwhile the 2nd Battalion had had time to consolidate their positions and count the cost. During the morning

two officers and forty other ranks had been killed and roughly the same number wounded. All through the day small numbers of stragglers continued to arrive in dribs and drabs, but the effective fighting strength remained at about sixty men. The whole scene was dominated by the great mass of Mount Etna to the north which almost seemed to be taking part under its own moving cloudy mantle.

As the evening approached, that old parachutist's bugbear, acute shortage of ammunition, began to make itself felt. Full use had been made of all the captured Italian weapons, but there was still insufficient fire-power to prevent the steady pressure from the Germans having effect on the 1st and 3rd Battalions behind the bridge. Before long there was an acute danger of enemy infiltrating behind the forward positions and this caused the bridgehead to be given up. With the bridgehead gone, the Germans were able to bring up assault guns with which they pulverized the blockhouse and other defences controlling the bridge. While this was happening reports reached me to the effect that a fresh attack against our positions on 'Johnny I' was imminent. On hearing this I moved up to join Dickie Lonsdale, but although we could see considerable enemy movement in the distance and hear the sound of enemy vehicles, no active measures were resumed against us.

Brigade Headquarters had been sited very close to the bridge and they had had their full share of continuous pounding from the enemy. They had been out of touch with us since the battle began, apart from a visit from the Brigade Commander, and had the impression that we had been overrun. Accordingly the 1st and 3rd Battalions were told to split up into small parties and make their way south, and this is what we now saw happening from our position on the top of 'Johnny I'.

We did all we could to collect as many of these small parties as possible by waving and shouting and sending out patrols. It wasn't altogether easy to persuade some of them that we were still firmly established, but by the time it got dark we had been considerably reinforced and were in a much stronger position than before. So much so that we no longer had room for the five hundred Italian prisoners within our perimeter and they were ordered to fall out for the night, but to make quite sure they reported again at first light in the morning.

At 7.30 p.m., rather to my amazement, a troop of Sherman tanks, the leading element of the 8th Army, rumbled down the road followed by a company of the 6th Battalion Durham Light Infantry on foot. The D.L.I. had covered some twenty miles during the heat of the day and were in no shape for offensive operations for the time being. We understood that plans were going to be made for an attack in the early hours of the morning. There was still no sign of Gerald Lathbury or Brigade Headquarters, but Alastair Pearson, the redoubtable 1st Battalion C.O., joined me before midnight.

Early the next morning Alastair and I watched the preparations and execution of a full-scale daylight infantry assault supported by tanks and artillery. We had never taken part in such an operation, and having seen this were determined never to do so. It all went according to plan. There was massive expenditure of ammunition on suspected enemy positions. Medium machine-guns kept up continuous pressure and tanks were interspersed with the infantry. There was a smoke-screen to cover the last and most dangerous stretch. The infantry plodded remorselessly on with bayonets fixed for the final assault across the river. The Germans held their fire until the Durhams were within some fifty yards, more or less point-blank range, then mowed the leading platoons down. Then they engaged the follow-up platoons. They fired burst after burst of machine-gun fire at the tanks, which had the effect of forcing them to remain closed down and therefore unable to identify enemy targets. The enemy anti-tank fire appeared nevertheless to be ineffective, but, without protection, the infantry attack just faded away and both Durhams and tanks came back.

While all this had been happening Gerald Lathbury and his headquarters came up the hill. They had spent the night below our positions and near the advance dressing-station which had been visited several times by German patrols during the night. Gerald met there the Fourth Armoured Brigade commander who intended to order another daylight battalion assault which was to use exactly the same axis and method during the afternoon. Alastair Pearson, who had been listening to this informal conference, said loud enough for all to hear: 'I suppose you want to see another battalion written off too.'

There was a hurried and scandalized little sub-conference during which Gerald persuaded all to listen to Alastair's advice. The net result was that the daylight attack was cancelled and Alastair led a fresh D.L.I. battalion across the river during the night. This time surprise was achieved, the enemy were taken in the flank and the gallant Durhams retook the Primosole bridge with very few casualties to themselves.

The next day we left our hill which looked across the plain of Catania, which in its turn was dominated by Mount Etna to the north. During the planning it had been thought that having taken, held and handed over the Primosole bridge, we of the 1st Parachute Brigade would advance on Catania as part of the 8th Army. Now we, like the 1st Air Landing Brigade, were to be shipped back to Africa useless and unused for the remainder of the campaign. It was yet another humiliating disaster for airborne forces and almost enough to destroy even the most ardent believer's faith. However it was to be many days before Catania fell. The Germans fully realized the importance of denying the easy run across the plain to the narrow route between Mount Etna and the sea, which was the key to the defence of Sicily. In fact Catania was never taken, but was outflanked as a result of very hard fighting elsewhere. The Catanian plain was an ideal D.Z., and with the whole of it in our hands, Catania and the key would have quickly been at our mercy. I consider that if the whole of the 1st Airborne Division had been put down on the Catania plain, from the Primosole bridge to Catania, the whole campaign in Sicily would have been won within ten days.

CHAPTER 13

Italy

A flotilla of tank landing ships carried the remnants of the brigade back to Sousse in North Africa. We were an attenuated and somewhat dispirited party, having lost many old friends. From the 2nd Battalion John Ross, John Lane, Keith Mountford and Victor Dover were all missing, with several other officers and one hundred and forty men. Gerald Lathbury went off to hospital in Tripoli, leaving me to take over the brigade in his absence, and I set about the business of reporting, making recommendations and rebuilding. It seemed to me that the first thing to do was to try to find out what had gone wrong with the air transportation. Almost every day stragglers from Sicily got back and they all told us how they had been bundled out of their aircraft all over the place, some even being dropped on the slopes of Mount Etna twenty or thirty miles away from the correct D.Z. Gradually we were able to build up a picture of what had happened and our findings were totally different to the debriefing reports which had been put in by the pilots when they returned. A considerable number of aircraft had returned to base without having dropped their sticks at all, the pilots claiming that they couldn't find the way.One or two had been forced to fly in at the pistol-points of the more determined parachutists. It was difficult to claim that the fireworks round the Primosole bridge were invisible from anywhere out over the sea.

Divisional Headquarters were against a distasteful and awkward *post mortem*, but I felt that the Americans' short-comings would jeopardize all future operations by night, and that it was essential that they be invited to make good their navigational deficiences. As soon as my map was as complete as could be, I invited the Americans to a presentation. In order to sweeten the pill, I had managed to collect adequate stocks of Scotch for all of us, and then when the pilots and my senior officers sat down at 1st Brigade Headquarters, the Brigade Intelligence Officer unfolded the tale. The Americans received it with barely a comment. At the end I made none either, but asked the Commander if he and his officers would now join us in the mess. He asked if they could stay with the map for a few minutes on their own, so with my officers I went on ahead. It was at least three-quarters of an hour before the Americans rejoined us and by then they were in no mood for a party. It was obvious that their Commander had had no idea of the extent of the fiasco. We all knew that they would do their best to ensure that it would never happen again.

Nearly a month after the operation Victor Dover and a brigade signaller suddenly arrived. His stick had been dropped on the slopes of Mount Etna and most of them had been rounded up. However he and the signaller had managed to hold out for twenty-three days, their only food being apples and scraps. They successfully dealt with the odd dispatch rider and managed to make a considerable nuisance of themselves to the enemy in several other ways.

This somewhat amazing performance was rather different to that put up by another officer who had previously been decorated for gallantry. He had been dropped quite close to the correct D.Z. and when he reported with some half-dozen men, just after the battle was over, noticing that they all seemed to be fresh, clean and untroubled I said: 'Hullo, and where have you been?'

He pointed to an area just beyond the D.Z. and said: 'Things seemed to be rather boisterous between where we were and where you were so I decided to wait till things quietened down.'

The officer left the battalion, prospered very greatly and became a byword in more ways than one.

I was delighted to have Victor back and asked him to reassume the duties of adjutant which he had carried out so well before. He was a great enthusiast and a very fine member of a team. Perhaps rather noisy and rumbustious, one always knew when he was about, and therefore missed him, more than a little, when he was not there. He had lost a lot of weight as a result of his diet of apples while on the run and as it was a quiet period I sent him off to Algiers for a few days at the fleshpots soon after. He was in fine shape when he returned.

Meanwhile reinforcements arrived and the wounded began to come back. Training was put into full swing and we revisited our old battle-fields in Tunisia. This last was a labour of love. It was a tremendous pleasure for those of us who had taken part to revisit and wander about on the ground over which we had fought so long and so hard. It was most instructive to look at our positions from the enemy's point of view and to examine the routes we and they had used. It was revealing and salutary to hear some of the comments of other members of the division, who were often amazed at the extent to which we had had to extemporize, and were horrified at the frontages we had been forced to hold. We were able to take presents to some of the French people who had helped us in those difficult days and so make amends for some of the damage that had been done.

It was hot during the daytime and the sun shone continually. The nights were always cool and restful. In a very short time all three battalions were back to full strength, fit and ready for whatever might come. The reinforcements soon found their feet. Among them as Regimental Sergeant-Major came Strachan, my old Company Sergeant-Major from Bruneval, now completely recovered from his stomach wounds.

The sea bathing at Sousse was great fun. The only hazard was occasional shoals of jellyfish, which, if one wasn't careful, would sting any protuberance, and, as we swam in the raw, this could be most uncomfortable.

Within the 8th Army all bars, clubs and other institutions selling alcohol had to stop doing so at 6 p.m. Sousse, the little seaside resort and port nearby, had a number of such places which of course attracted the soldiers when they had time off. The limitation to the drinking hours meant that the soldiery poured Vino in against the clock, and by the time they reached camp they were in a fairly parlous condition. No amount of normal punishment stopped the main offenders, and it was difficult to know what to do. Eventually I stationed the photographer by the guard-room, and he was able to produce accurate and picturesque records of what our topers looked like when they got back. I found that threats to send copies of these pictures back to mothers or girl-friends at home provided the most effective deterrent.

Perhaps the most irritating thing that happened at this time was that the Divisional Commander, Major-General Hopkinson, convinced in his own mind that the only sensible way to go to war was in a glider, despite the utter failure of the Air Landing Brigade's operation in Sicily, used to call conferences of his three brigade commanders after dinner. At these meetings he would try to persuade us that our brigades should consist of mixed gliderborne and parachute units. I used to call in on Eric Down, the commander of the 2nd Parachute Brigade, on my way to the meeting. Whereas we agreed that the glider was probably the best means of introducing the supporting and heavier weapons and equipment, we still felt that the parachute was the best, and least vulnerable, means of bringing in the men. Shan Hackett, who commanded the 4th Parachute Brigade, was, on the whole, neutral. So the discussions were apt to continue far into the night. As an inducement to an agreement, General Hoppy even suggested that some of my beloved Assyrians, who by this time had been trained as parachutists, should become part of 1st Parachute Brigade.

It was rather idle and useless talk and probably I was the only one who gave Hoppy any encouragement for I at least enjoyed the whisky with which we were tempted. Nothing was ever decided but I was reproached by Gerald Lathbury when he came back during our battlefield tour, for he almost snarled at me: 'I hear that you have been conniving at the break-up of 1st Parachute Brigade.' I forebore to comment.

Gerald was away for nearly six weeks. The Italian armistice was signed shortly after his return and the whole division was whipped off to Taranto in the south of Italy at short notice. This was almost exactly two months after the operation in Sicily. 1st Parachute Brigade were given very little to do, for the 8th Army was moving slowly in those days and while the 5th Army fought desperately for its beach-head at Salerno, the 8th was maintaining its balance. We spent four days digging in at Taranto in case the Germans produced a sudden riposte which might force us back into the sea.

The 4th Parachute Brigade had seen quite stiff fighting during which poor General Hoppy was killed and Eric Down took over the division. The Divisional Reconnaissance Regiment and other elements followed up the retreating enemy and at one stage 1st Para Brigade were in the van. After various moves, we ended up at Barletta on the Adriatic coast, practising amphibious landings from naval craft based at this port. Tim Timothy dropped with a small party near Pescara, more than a hundred miles to the north, with the task of finding, marshalling and guiding escaped British prisoners-of-war. He had some measure of success, but a part of his force were themselves rounded up. Some of our own old members who had been captured in Africa managed to rejoin us, including a party who had spent three weeks on active service with the 2nd German Parachute Battalion. During the whole of this time they had been treated as honoured guests and had managed to escape during an excellent evening's carousal. We also provided boarding parties for the destroyer flotilla which was rounding up Axis shipping in the Adriatic. Our parachutists grew very fond of their cutlasses and became formidable swordsmen with them.

Other rather odd things happened during this period. There was no exact front line and some people, adventurously inclined, were able to make deep incursions into areas that might well be held by the enemy. The general uncertainty was complicated by the state of the Italian Army, which by this time was supposed to be firmly on our side as a co-belligerent. However, dedicated fascist elements sometimes continued to support Nazi ideals and clandestine forces on either side could stand a good chance of achieving their ends when wearing Italian uniform.

Tony Deane, commanding the 4th Battalion, was

determined not to be caught out in any ambush. He had armed his personal jeep with two L.M.G.s facing forwards and two sten guns facing to the rear. All could be fired by the driver by pulling a string. When one of his patrols, which had been detailed to report on the state of a bridge, came back with an indeterminate answer, he set off in high dudgeon to see for himself. Unfortunately while actually on the bridge he dismounted to have a really close look and German soldiers debouched from both sides and poor Tony was marched off to captivity without being able to prove the efficacy or otherwise of his somewhat strangely accoutred vehicle.

Freddie Gough's Reconnaissance Squadron could always be counted on to be active and venturesome though perhaps not always punctual or precise. One day one of their vehicles was patrolling through an olive grove when, at a corner, it nearly ran into the front of a German armoured car. The driver backed away hastily to find another track which jinked and turned to such an extent that it was hard to keep any sense of direction. Suddenly, to the driver's horror, he nearly rammed the rear end of the same German A.F.V. that he had met just before. This time, before he had had time to reverse, a beetle-helmeted figure arose from the turret to say, in perfect English: 'For goodness' sake make up your mind as to whose side you are on.'

'Very sorry,' said the driver, making good his escape.

A staff officer, who had been captured as a result of a similar incident, was asked to stay and dine with Major-General Heydrich, the G.O.C. of the 1st German Parachute Division. The General evinced much interest in all the senior officers of the British 1st Airborne Division and spent much of the time questioning his guest about their more intimate characteristics. Anyway they passed an amusing and pleasant evening. Early the next morning, the General arose in his pyjamas to see his guest depart in a truck driven by two of his parachutists. These both sat in the front and as they seemed to have great difficulty with their map-reading they took very little notice of their passenger in the rear. So much so, that when the vehicle stopped at a cross-roads and while the Germans pored over their map, our gallant Staff Officer jumped out, ran into some woods beside the road and eventually made his way back to the division.

While the Irish Brigade were at Termoli on the coast, they could not fathom how it was that the Germans were able to strafe their vital communications with quite uncanny accuracy, until the resourceful foe were caught in the act of relieving their artillery observation party which was functioning from a church tower right in the middle of Termoli.

Duncan McLean took over as adjutant from Victor Dover before we left Italy. Like me and all his predecessors Victor felt quite lost after relinquishing an appointment which, though it entailed long hours and hard work, meant that one was the C.O.'s right-hand man and always knew exactly what was going on. Being promoted to command a company was rather like being banished to outer darkness and Victor, like those before him, was apt to haunt the orderly room, hoping to be able to sneak a view of the 'In' tray so as to be in the picture again. As always the newly appointed would guard his information like a tigress her cubs and drive off the previous incumbent with ribaldry, even abuse.

The short days and cold nights of November gave us a foretaste of what an Italian winter could be like. The Germans were fighing hard for very inch and the rain was no friend to offensive mobile operations. We knew that we were probably being saved for the coming operations in north-west Europe so when we were finally ordered back to Taranto on the first stage of our journey to the U.K. there were no regrets.

CHAPTER 14

U.K. Interlude

What bliss it was to lean over the rail of a troopship newly docked at a U.K. port in war-time. To start with the quay was deserted, then cat-calls and groans marked the arrival of a couple of Military Police who stood, imperturbably, affecting to take no notice. In contrast members of H.M. Customs and Excise appeared to be very annoyed at the volume of abuse they drew. There were cries of joy for some very smart W.R.A.C., or A.T.S. as they were then called. It was nice to think that they were part of our army. Finally cheers of derision for a Flag car bearing a general from the War Office, whose task it was to make a welcoming speech over a Tannoy to all of us on our return to the homeland.

No evidence of more austerity, grey skies or rain could dampen our spirits. No relative or friend could know we were back or even coming back, so there was no need to hurry to a telephone or worry at the absence of welcome. The newspapers were even smaller, cigarettes scarcer, beer even weaker, spirits almost unobtainable, but on the other hand skirts were shorter and we again had good solid silver coins to buy things with. Lincolnshire became our base for the next few months. The battalion was spread about the country south of Grantham. Each company was allotted a large country house or its equivalent. My headquarters were initially at Hungerton Hall and moved later to Stoke Rochford Hall. After leave, which included Christmas, we forgathered to make ourselves ready for battle again.

An old friend of mine from pre-war days called David

Wallis joined us to be Second-in-Command. He was a most
gifted man and ideal in the appointment from my point of
view. He brought a new look to our headquarters and
relieved me from all worries regarding the details of parachute and weapon training. Digby Tatham-Warter was a
comparatively new company commander, having joined us
in Italy shortly before we left. He was lusting for action at
this time having so far failed to get into the war. There was
much of 'Prince Rupert' about Digby and he was worth a
bet with anybody's money. The other company commanders were Douglas Crawley, lanky, ginger-haired, quietish,
absolutely reliable and steady in action; Victor Dover of
'apples in Sicily' fame, and finally 'Bombs' Panter, now in
charge of the support company, who had been with the
battalion from the very beginning. There was scarcely one
weak link among the other officers, and I was particularly
fortunate to have Duncan McLean as adjutant. Father
Egan remained firmly attached, one eye cocked critically at
all the proceedings.

Early in the year 1944 Eric Down was taken away to
command the Indian Airborne Division and Major-
General R.E. Urquhart, presumably Monty's nominee,
was appointed as his successor. He had had no previous
airborne experience, though considerable battle experience, which few of the senior airborne officers could claim.
The snag of bringing in a complete newcomer was that
however good they might be, they were inclined to think
that airborne was just another way of going into battle,
whereas in fact the physical, mental and indeed spiritual
problems were, when the battle might have to be fought
without support from the normal army resources, very
different. Two of the most important basic problems were
ammunition supply and care of the wounded, about which
the British Army is notoriously cavalier when it comes to
making adequate arrangements. Failure to ensure that
these two essentials are properly covered, just for a start,
could make all the difference between defeat and victory.

In all our previous battles, both airborne and conventional, perhaps because we were so lightly equipped, we
had found ourselves running short of ammunition at the
most critical times, and had been much embarrassed by our

inability to evacuate our wounded from the thick of the fighting. It needed constant reiteration, even within one's own mind, to ensure that these aspects were remembered.

It obviously takes time for anyone to adjust to different circumstances and one of the greatest was the realization of utter dependence on another service in the shape of the R.A.F.

Roy Urquhart was not a man to court popularity and, largely owing to the way the division was dispersed all over Lincolnshire, we did not see him as much as we would have liked, but he very soon earned our complete respect and trust. In fact few generals have ever been so sorely tested and have yet prevailed.

I now had time and opportunity to put my convictions on training essentials into effect. Firstly skill-at-arms. Efforts to achieve the highest possible standards were relentless. Those who failed to shoot well were kept practising until they could, or else they were discarded. Secondly, immaculate communications. The wireless links had to be working whenever they were required and there was no food on exercises or leave afterwards for those responsible unless they were. Thirdly, physical fitness. There was P.T. for everyone each day before breakfast and the required marching standard was thirty miles per day carrying half a hundredweight. Once the standards were achieved we found it not too difficult to maintain them.

Commanding a Parachute Battalion was by no means a sinecure at this time for all of them contained a number of hard cases who did not set much store on obeying regulations, particularly as regards returning from leave on time. After every weekend there were several absentees. This adversely affected the administration and training and brought a sense of embarrassment, even shame, to those who did their duty. Any weakness shown in the way of accepting excuses resulted in more subsequent offences, and the very fact that they were being committed tended to weaken discipline throughout. Within the brigade there was much unrest in one battalion, and another was found to be incapable of marching on a test exercise. In each case there had to be change of commanding officer before the battalion settled down.

We were by no means the only formation to have problems: we knew of famous divisions that were reduced to a fraction of their normal complement by absenteeism. It was not that the soldiers had any intention of avoiding action: indeed, as soon as an operation impended, the grapevine brought all the miscreants back. Indeed, one party is said to have arrived for the Arnhem take-off in a London taxi.

We did several noteworthy exercises which included acting as enemy to the 6th Airborne Division to test them for their landings in Normandy, and also a prolonged divisional exercise ending in Yorkshire, during the course of which we out-spearheaded the divisional Reconnaissance Regiment and distinguished ourselves in many ways. Writing after the exercise Gerald Lathbury described us as 'a most formidable battalion.'

We had a lot of fun too; the people nearby were kind and we made many friends. There were several weekends in London, with evenings at the '400' and the 'Embassy' and the 'Senior', and the Berkeley, the May Fair and Rosa's were good for a party at almost any time. It was now or never to make hay, or so most of us felt.

It may seem to be a terrible thing to say that we found London to be more attractive when the enemy turned their attention to it than otherwise. When there were no raids, London was packed and it was difficult to get rooms in the club, tables in restaurants, seats at the theatre or the services of taxis. A sudden blitz in the spring and then the coming of the flying bomb in the late summer had the most noticeable effect of clearing the environment we needed and it was great to be able to pick and choose again. Some of our number were horrified to learn about the attempt on the life of Hitler in case it should bring a premature end to the war; I had already seen enough of what war was like to wish to share their fears.

A distinct change had come about in our attitude towards the Germans since we had been away and this sometimes caused trouble. By now the least we felt was a wholesome respect for German soldiery; mutual sufferings and memories of being close to them on rain-soaked tops of lonely hills persisted. There had been times when stretcher-bearers of both nations could move the wounded unharmed, and sometimes even helped by friend and foe. Once at a tea party when I had been inveigled into talking about our experiences I was almost ostracized for telling tales of chivalry. It was sometimes difficult to remember that hatred is harshest on the home front.

The battalion H.Q., the H.Q. and Support Companies were all housed in Stoke Rochford Hall, which was owned by the Turnor family. We did our best to keep damage to a minimum, to keep the grounds and gardens tidy, and to discourage poaching. Major Herbert Turnor, an old 17th Lancer, when he realized how much we appreciated living in his lovely house, gradually opened up many more of the gracious rooms than he need have done for our use and enjoyment. Some of us were asked to shoot and permission to fish in their waters followed. There was a nine-hole golf course in the grounds. David, Digby, I and a few others could play in the long summer evenings when off duty. Golf balls were extremely scarce and I found that my immediate military subordinates were the most unprincipled competitors when given the slightest possible chance of winning by nefarious means. Suddenly calling a dog, or treading in an opponent's ball, were two of the least of these measures, but we all had the greatest of fun and when we had to leave Stoke Rochford, it was with the happiest possible memories.

The friendliness of the townspeople of Grantham and the surrounding villages, the understanding and forbearance of all the publicans, most particularly of the Blue Horse at Ponton, made such a great difference to our happiness. We can only hope that they enjoyed us a little bit as much as we enjoyed them.

On 6 June the Allies invaded Normandy. We were not included in the assault and this was a great blow to some. However we were very nearly called upon in the early stages and some of the tasks envisaged were hazardous in the extreme. On one occasion we were to drop virtually on top of one of the Panzer divisions attacking the beachhead. During the rest of June, July, August and the beginning of September, many possible tasks were considered, worked on and discarded. There were further possibilities in dropping behind the German counter-attacking forces, or flying in to reinforce the beach-head. Greater dividends might have ensued from dropping ahead of a breakout. The problem was where and when. In the event the armies moved so fast that our targets were overrun before we could become airborne. So finally we remained inactive until the momentum had been exhausted on the Albert Canal. On the credit side it could be said that the 1st Airborne Division had provided a continuous and effective threat. In conjunction with an imaginative wireless campaign it had kept German defences tied down in the Pas de Calais when they were urgently needed to batter against the beach-head in Normandy.

On 15 September Brigadier Gerald Lathbury briefed his subordinate commanders of 1st Parachute Brigade. We were to take part in a great offensive which had the ultimate aim of surrounding the Ruhr and making it impossible for the Germans to continue the war. In the first phase the Allied airborne army was to lay an airborne 'carpet' over which XXX Corps of the 2nd British Army would ride at great speed. The vital points which had to be assured by the airborne troops were the road bridges over the major obstacles provided by the rivers Maas, Waal and Lower Rhine. 1st Airborne Division was assigned the bridgehead and the bridges at Arnhem over the Rhine. This was a very long way from XXX Corps' starting-point, but it was considered that if the other bridges were captured intact, leading elements could reach Arnhem within twenty-four hours.

We were highly delighted to be given a really worthwhile task at last. This was the genuine airborne thrust that we had been awaiting and we felt that if things went according to plan, we should be truly instrumental in bringing the war to an end in 1944.

There were, however, some glaring snags. First, the D.Z.s selected by the air forces were several miles from the objectives and on the north side of the great main river obstacle only. This entailed a long approach on foot, through enclosed country and built-up areas, which meant that if there was anything in the way of opposition, surprise would be lost and the enemy would have plenty of time and opportunity to destroy the bridges. Furthermore, capturing bridges, which are in fact narrow defiles, is extremely difficult and hazardous if you are on one side of the obstacle only, because the defender can concentrate his fire on all the approaches to and on the defile itself from the comparative security of the other side. Therefore you require to be on both sides of the obstacle if you hope to capture the defile without heavy casualties. One advantageous characteristic of airborne troops is that they can be put on both sides of an obstacle before the battle commences, yet now that this was paramount, the air forces still would not conform.

The reason for this seemingly unreasonable attitude was that there were A.A. guns specially sited to protect the bridges and also an airfield at Deelen, some miles to the north, near which the aircraft would have to pass if they dropped us anywhere near the bridges.

However, at this stage, our air forces could achieve complete ascendancy over the Luftwaffe and there were hundreds of fighter and fighter-bomber aircraft available to act as advance guard or escort. Given the A.A. guns as their priority targets one would have thought that they could have destroyed or neutralized them to such an extent that the transport fleets would have little to fear. Certainly it would have immeasurably better for the airborne troops to have been exposed to a slightly more hazardous airborne access to their objectives than the long and doubtful approach on foot that they had to accept.

Then, again, the Air Force planners contended that the farmland to the south of the river was unusable for gliders and not really suitable for paratroops. The last was not said with much conviction for it was planned to drop the Polish Brigade south of the main bridge on D-Day plus 2. In the event they landed successfully south of the railway bridge on D plus 3. They had to make do without their glider element which was directed to L.Z.s north of the river. It was almost impossible for our superior commanders to query these decisions for they were made at Army and Airborne Corps H.Q.s several hours distant and it was not the sort of thing that could be discussed on the telephone.

Even then, this unsatisfactory selection of D.Z.s might

not have mattered so much if the Air Forces had been willing to fly two sorties on D-Day. It was a comparatively short haul from the U.K. airfields we were using to the middle of Holland and with good staff-work aircraft would have needed no more than five hours from take-off to landing. Thus if the first sortie had left at dawn on D-Day, their initial missions could have been completed by noon, leaving the rest of the day to take the second lift which could have been ready and waiting. As it was, the great air armada stayed put for nearly twenty-four hours, for the two-sortie day was thought to be too much to ask of the crews.

Uncertain weather adds weight to the argument. As every farmer knows, you make hay while the sun shines, and there is a price to pay for those who fail to make full use of it. D-Day was lovely but D plus 1 was not. This delayed the arrival of the second lift with all the attendant disadvantages, not only on the ground but also to the airmen who had a far more hazardous run-in than they would have faced on D-Day evening.

The net effect of all this was that there was enough lift for about half of the division on D-Day and of this proportion only half could go for the objectives because the other half would have to safeguard the D.Z.s for the subsequent lift. Thus on D-Day, only one brigade, the 1st, was available to carry out the divisional task. Much the same handicap was imposed on the American Divisions which were dropped to the south by the other rivers.

However the information about the enemy was such that we were assured there was nothing to worry about. There were said to be some S.S. recruits in the Arnhem area without guns or armour and it was anticipated that Luftwaffe personnel from the airfield at Deelen together with those manning other installations could be assembled in due course. The German Army was thought to have taken such a beating in Normandy that all remaining availability was facing XXX Corps on the Albert canal and that there was nothing else in reserve.

We were not told much about the Dutch underground. It was said to have been penetrated by the Germans who had planted their own adherents so it was not to be relied upon.

Here was yet another implement that could have been used to our advantage denied to those who were going to need every possible aid.

Our own Army was on the crest of the wave. After the long hard slogging-match in the summer, they and their allies had won an epic victory, driving all before them till forced to stop for administrative needs. Now they had had time to rest, reorganize and get poised for the final run-in and we had every confidence in their ability finish it off. We were told that XXX Corps would effect the breakout towards us and we knew all about their commander, General Horrocks. Affectionately known as Jorrocks, he was the Beau Sabreur of the 8th Army. The Guards Armoured Division would be in the van and who could be better than they to bash their way through to us should we be beleaguered, particularly with the 'Boy' directing things from Nijmegen where we thought he would be.

The 1st Parachute Brigade plan was affected by the aircraft shortage because instead of being able to put maximum effort on to the bridge objective, the Brigadier had to maintain touch between the troops allotted to this and to the rest of the division who had to remain in the D.Z. area. Eight miles of very enclosed, built-up area separated the two parts. The 3rd Parachute Battalion were given the task of taking and holding the western part of the town and to do this they were allotted the main road as their axis. The 1st Parachute Battalion were to move round towards the north of the town, but were in fact the brigade commander's reserve. Finally the 2nd Battalion were given the task of taking the bridges and forming close bridgehead garrisons. The Divisional Reconnaissance Regiment under Freddie Gough were to attempt to motor in in front of the parachute battalions in order to seize the main bridge by *coup de main*.

I was allotted the most southerly route near the river for the 2nd Battalion. Shortly before giving out my final orders I was told that a pontoon bridge which had been functioning west of, and close to, the main bridge had now been dismantled. However I supposed that it might still be possible to make some use of it. There was also a railway bridge about two miles west of the town. I was ordered to seize this as well as taking the main bridge at Arnhem.

This main bridge was my real task and the *raison d'être* of the divisional operation. I had every confidence in being able to take and hold the north end, but realized that we were on the wrong side of the river for taking the south end. My plan was for 'A' Company under Digby Tatham-Warter to move off from the D.Z. first and make straight for the main bridge. Having consolidated on this end he was to pass one platoon across to the south side. I and my headquarters would follow immediately behind him with Victor Dover's 'C' Company, which was to capture the railway bridge near Oosterbeek, and then pass across it so as to reach the south end of the main bridge. This action would be supported by the battalion's mortars and machine-guns. Last in the column was Douglas Crawley's 'B' Company, which was my reserve for any eventuality.

CHAPTER 15

Arnhem

I got up with mixed feelings on the 17 September 1944, the day for which we had planned and trained so long. Like most soldiers, when well dug-in I was inclined to be against moves in any direction, and this promised to be a most decisive one. Stoke Rochford was a pleasant place and we had had such a good time there that I was very sorry to think that I might never see it again.

Owing to the reasonable hour fixed for our take-off there was no need to hurry over breakfast and I read the papers as usual while eating the last plate of eggs and bacon I was to have for some time to come. My equipment, weapons, food and parachute were all ready, so having fed, I wandered along to the mess to find everyone else reading and smoking, all in the best of spirits and no worries anywhere. Quite a contrast to some of the operations we had done before! Here was no dashing off to find transport, no last-minute changes, no meals at extraordinary hours. Just the normal beginning to an ordinary day. One had the sense of perfect arrangement, the feeling that everything would be so well conducted, that having dined well, slept well and breakfasted well, we would make our leisurely way to the airfield, and from there, having wished each other well, we would fly across the sea undisturbed and gather again some three hundred miles away in Holland and then proceed to do battle for a bridge that Montgomery urgently required.

I don't think any of us had any doubts as to the ability of any part of the forces engaged to fulfil their role. I certainly did not anticipate much difficulty as far as our task was concerned and was thinking ahead to the time when we would fight as infantry again, well supported by adequate artillery, with our own tanks never far away and the comforts that are always at hand when the heavy transport is available. Once more I checked the kit with my batman, Wicks – gun, cartridges and golf clubs to follow in the staff car, heavier baggage to be stacked in such and such a place and so on. I went up to the Orderly Room to see if there was anything to do there. The place was nearly empty. A solitary clerk was typing some orders for the rear party and the scene of so much feverish activity in the past was strangely forlorn. From the window came the noise of Headquarter Company embussing and I watched them for a while. When they had gone, complete silence settled over the building. Time dragged on as it does on these occasions. It was still too early for me to leave and so I went down for a last look at the garden.

A light mist was drifting across from the golf course, but the sun would soon deal with this. There would be no weather problem this day. As I expected, there was quite a lot of rubbish, which had been flung out of the windows on to the grass below. I thought of the fatigue party from rear details cursing when they were ordered to clear up the mess and of how they themselves would have flung similar rubbish out of the windows had they been going. I wondered if Wicks had left my room fairly tidy and I found that he had; in fact he was all packed up, ready to go.

With the good wishes of a few old campaigners, who would campaign no more, ringing in our ears, we moved slowly down the drive. The old cock pheasants were proudly strutting about the park. We had always left them severely alone and they took not even a passing interest in us. Two coveys of partridges were not so bold and whirred away over the stream to the golf course beyond as we came upon them. Then we were out and on the main road to Saltby.

The huge airfield swarmed with Dakotas, and convoys of lorries were moving slowly round the perimeter track. A group of men were busy by each aircraft checking containers and readjusting parachutes. Officers in jeeps were driving in all directions. I went to the Air Liaison Officer's place.

'Nothing to worry about, sir,' he said. 'Met report couldn't be better, and everyone seems to have arrived on time. Your plane is No 16. You'll find a mark on the tarmac beside it. Times for emplanement and take-off unchanged. Tea and sandwiches will be round shortly.'

I drove round to our particular aircraft to make sure. To say that everything went like clockwork would be an exaggeration, because the human brain does not work like a clock, and sure enough it wasn't very long before an N.C.O. of the airfield staff came round to say that the time of take-off had been put forward twenty minutes and arrangements were made accordingly. But when the air-crews arrived they denied the alteration and so we were back where we started. In the meantime the tea lorry was not to be found, and then when it came, it had nothing to serve tea with. However these were small troubles, almost welcome in that they helped to speed the time of waiting.

My pilot was a reassuring type of man who exuded confidence, and his crew were feeling fine. Colonel Styles, the American Group Commander, drove up to wish us good luck. I went down the column to have a last look at everyone. The zero time to emplane caught some sticks unprepared as it always did, but there was no delay and true to schedule we were taxi-ing down the perimeter to our take-off positions.

The time of waiting for the aircraft to take off is, for the parachutist, the transition from peace to war. For him there is no gradual, growing consciousness of battle that other Arms must feel. There are no enemy positions to study with binoculars. No preliminary bombardment to wait for, no careful moving up in dark or wet with fingers crossed against the enemy's defensive fire. While planning the discomfiture of an enemy so many miles away it is hard to picture him exactly and to consider what his reaction will be. The enemy is rather impersonal and one is perhaps apt to underrate him and even have a little compassion for him. One seems to have such advantage in initiative that his potential does not find quite as important a place in one's calculations as it should.

This time, in the light of our past experiences, I felt that we had trained, prepared and planned well, and was sure that the battalion had reached its highest peak of readiness. We had been chosen for the most important task, but I was sure we should succeed. In fact, I found that I was happier at this stage of going into action than I had ever been before.

There came a roar from the engines as we started to move, and now my thoughts turned to the pilot, the navigator, the men in the plane, the escort, the glider pilots and the troops on the ground in Holland moving inward to conform with our landing. Our lives and our future lay in their hands and we had nothing to do but trust in their gumption. As we climbed and circled, plane after plane could be seen leaving the runway down below to join us. Our machine seemed superior to those lumbering along down there and not until other planes appeared in formation with us did it lose its advantage and become just an ordinary aircraft after all. From the door, formations of other aircraft could be seen climbing up from several other airfields nearby and the whole lot formed a very big fleet indeed.

I wondered if the people down below realized what was on. It was difficult to hide the imminence of an operation from our friends. We often got invitations to parties when confined to camp for security reasons and we had to think up valid excuses to refuse them, which was never easy. Gradually our friends had come to know that periods of intensive preparation meant our seclusion from the rest of the world. Few people of Grantham could have failed to notice our absence from their town on Saturday night and now this tremendous Sunday morning activity must surely signify 'Der Tag'. Anyway, I felt sure that those who realized would wish us well and hoped that those who might pray for our return would do so successfully.

We circled over the country we knew so well for nearly an hour and then headed for the coast. The air was exceptionally calm and the aircraft comfortably warm, and before reaching the sea we flew over extensive mud flats, gleaming in the sunlight, which ended in muddy water with not a ripple showing until far out. Even there the wind was practically nil, which augured happy landings later on. Small coastal patrol boats and rescue launches were moving slowly across the water. I saw one aircraft from our formation turn back for home and hoped it carried no vitally important part of the battalion. We had all the Sunday papers to read, sandwiches for those who could eat them, and cigarettes, so the time passed pleasantly enough.

Mud flats and floods were the first sign of land. Small farms surrounded by water, then areas of dry cultivation. We became more conscious of our vast escort the deeper in we flew, but only once was the peaceful scene disturbed by the sound of cannon. Fighters were flying all round us and overhead other large formations of transports were going home having completed their missions. At ten minutes to H-Hour I stood in the doorway and tried to compare the country with my memory of the map. I was surprised to see no sign of any activity on the ground and thankful for the lack of opposition of any kind. The Maas river was easy to recognize and, as we crossed it, we got our pilot's warning to be ready. The stick had travelled well, but as usual one could feel the tension among them all. The transparent insincerity of their smiles and the furious last-minute puffing at their cigarettes reminded me that the flight and prospect of jumping far behind the enemy lines was no small test for anyone's nervous system and I remembered that this was my first jump since Sicily some fourteen months ago.

We passed the Waal, and finally the Lek, for whose bridges we were to do battle, while the red light glowed. I peered anxiously ahead at the D.Z. for any signs of trouble. In front and below parachutes were falling and then I was out. Once again the thrill of falling, the great relief of feeling the harness pulling and that highly satisfactory bounce as the canopy filled with air. The rigging lines were slightly twisted, needing a vigorous pull on the lift webs to bring me round and leave me free to enjoy the feeling of floating down. Following this came the fear of injury on hitting the ground; a last feverish pull as I touched down and then a resounding bang on the back of my helmet told me that all was well.

There was no sound of enemy action, just the steady

continual drone of aircraft approaching, leaving rows and clusters of parachutes in the air, followed by the fiercer note of their engines as they wheeled for home at increased speed. I felt grateful for the way they had done their task. A few kitbags broke away from the men as they were released, making it wise to keep a good look-out. This fault was a serious one as it meant that the contents of the kitbags, weapons, ammunition or wireless sets were apt to be damaged.

The battalion landed with practically no other trouble, however, and there was no difficulty in finding the way to the rendezvous. En route some Dutch people greeted us. There was no doubt as to the sincerity of their welcome and they told us what they knew of the enemy. The Germans were in Arnhem, but not in any great strength. Some were using the roads between Arnhem and the coast, so that we would probably meet them on our way into the town. This was most satisfactory as the difficulty of maintaining security at home had made us feel that if the German Intelligence was functioning efficiently, they must by now have gleaned some intimation of our mission.

Digby Tatham-Warter was setting up his lights and yellow smoke signals at the rendezvous to guide the battalion in. To the north we could hear the Americans bombing the airfield at Ede. Some nameless idiot released yellow smoke at the wrong end of the D.Z., but this misled nobody and gradually the sections, platoons and companies began to take form. It was by now about half-past two in the afternoon and quite hot. The sweat was pouring off the cheerful faces of the men as they filed past me into the wood. Wireless sets seemed to be the only casualties from the drop, among them the brigade set, but fortunately a spare was available. Just as I was beginning to feel that on the whole things could not be going better, the sound of firing broke out in the woods not more than three hundred yards from where I was standing and I moved to a track junction in the middle of the wood, which was where we had planned to set up Battalion Headquarters. A battle at our rendezvous in the woods was one of the things to be feared most of all. It was vital that we should be able to move off without delay and equally vital that our ammunition should not be expended unduly early when we had so much to do.

At first it was hard to tell what the trouble was, but we didn't let it interfere with the process of forming up and getting ready to move. The troops and anti-tank guns allotted to us arrived punctually, also most of our airborne transport, consisting of five jeeps and a bren carrier. I passed some anxious moments while they were being sorted out. All army drivers have a predilection for driving into the middle of a headquarters, thereby causing the utmost confusion, and our drivers were no exception to the rule. To the tune of vigorous cursing, order was restored. The companies reported in over ninety-five per cent, and the firing turned out to be caused by a small party of Germans who had driven up in a lorry with one armoured car as escort. By the time I thought of moving off, the armoured car had fled, leaving the lorry and several prisoners.

Soon after three o'clock a message came from Brigade Headquarters telling us to move on with all possible speed, without waiting for stragglers, and just as the message went to 'A' Company, who were the vanguard, firing broke out afresh from their area. However, there was no delay, and as we passed their old positions we found two lorries and three motor-cars in various stages of destruction, also an untidy little bunch of dead and wounded Germans. It seemed a pity that the vehicles were now unusable, but there had been no time to arrange a road-block. It was however a very encouraging start. Approximately thirty Germans, including officers among them, and valuable transport, accounted for without loss to ourselves.

We marched towards Arnhem. A man and a woman on bicycles made as if to ride on past the column and seemed quite surprised at being ordered to turn back. The road led through dense undergrowth of gorse and birch, ideal cover for an enemy to lay an ambush. We had no time to spare for flank guards, so trusting everyone to do the right thing if attacked, we pressed on *ventre à terre*, merely leaving very small parties to cover the more important roads leading into our own. A few more prisoners were passed down the line. From one of them I learned that a company of S.S. had been in Arnhem that morning and were now thought to be covering the entrances to the town from the west. I went forward in a jeep to see Digby in order to arrange a lift for his leading platoon in the available transport. He was fairly enthusiastic about this plan, but as I was waiting for Battalion Headquarters to catch me up, the noise of firing broke out again from in front and the column ceased to move. There was no mistaking the rattle of German machine-guns. A few bursts passing harmlessly well above our heads had the much-desired effect of making everyone realize that they might expect the enemy's attention from then onwards.

There was nothing to be done for the time being. The last thing the vanguard commander wants is to have his immediate superior breathing over his shoulder. Digby was a thruster if ever there was, and if it was possible to deal with or circumvent the enemy, I knew that we should be on the move again as soon as could be. Gradually his company began to slide away once more. Bren guns added to the Germans' noise. We heard two-inch mortars open up and saw smoke rising round a small densely covered hillock, then heard a bugler sound 'The Charge'. A little later they wirelessed back to say the enemy had gone, leaving casualties, and that their own were very slight.

The brigadier came up at this stage and was glad to know that all was well. On our left we could hear a bit of a battle and he said he thought that the 3rd Battalion were having a difficult time getting through. We were to spare no pains and Brigade Headquarters would follow us into the town. By the time he left us, we were halted once more, but not for long. Soon we passed through the small village of Heveadorp. The Dutch gave us a great welcome; apples, pears and jugs of milk appeared, orange flowers were pressed upon us to wear and one old gentleman asked me if I would like to use his car. Knowing well what its fate would be I declined, pointing to the jeep which was moving ten yards behind me. Quite a few of the people spoke English fairly well, many being anxious to know if we had come to stay and were in sufficient strength to beat the Germans.

The country was rather like that round Aldershot, and the people seemed familiar rather than foreign. Certainly they impressed us very favourably by their bearing and generosity. The houses and gardens were neat, tidy and workmanlike. I only hoped that they would have no cause to suffer on our account and that the ravages of war would pass them by. From Heveadorp we passed into Oosterbeek. Occasionally we heard the leaders of the vanguard in action, but we were not really checked again until the outskirts of Arnhem itself.

As we moved on through Oosterbeek, Victor Dover took 'C' Company down towards the river in order to capture the railway bridge over the Lek. I had planned that our machine-guns and mortars would support this attack as air photographs had shown a considerable number of flak positions in this area, but as these offered no resistance, the company swept on. During the morning Typhoons and bombers had given this particular part a very effective strafing. However I do not think there were any guns there that day. Most of the battalion were in a position to be able to watch 'C' Company at work. As their forward elements came near the bridge, enemy opened fire from the southern bank, but there was hardly a pause while our own men laid a smoke-screen and in next to no time little figures appeared on the bridge. Then we saw a general surge forward of those who had been supplying the covering fire during the first phase. Bren guns were set up on the embankment to deal with the Germans on the other side of the river and men began to cross.

Our impression that the bridge had been captured intact was a little premature, however, for just as I received the message to this effect there was a mighty explosion, and when the smoke from this had cleared away, we could see the southernmost span lying half in and half out of the water. This meant that we would now have to cross either using part of the pontoon bridge or the main bridge, but I did not underestimate the difficulty of taking the big main bridge intact from one side only, if the other side was firmly defended.

The fundamental mistake of dropping airborne troops on the far side of a large water obstacle when you actually require them on both sides appears altogether too obvious now. The whole idea of parachutists was that they should land behind the enemy and not be forced to cross rivers in the face of intense fire which can always be counted on to defend the enemy's vitals. We had had the D.Z.s selected by the Air Force and after so many postponements and disappointments we were anxious to get into action at any price, rather than to add difficulties to the task of the people who had to fly us there by challenging their plan.

It was no fault of Victor and his Company that the railway bridge went up. No body of men could have been more skilful and vigorous in action than they. Peter Barry, the commander of the leading platoon, and some of his men had been wounded when the charge was blown. By this time a party of divisional sappers were waiting on the embankment above the bridge and I sent a runner down to tell them to take over responsibility for what remained. Victor was to follow the battalion into Arnhem and capture the German headquarter building there.

Meanwhile 'A' Company were temporarily stuck. There was a prominent feature behind the railway line from the railway bridge, called Den Brink. The railway line itself curled round the western outskirts of the town, and this formed a logical barrier for any local defence plan, with Den Brink dominating it from behind. All attempts to move forward along the roads were met by fire from patrolling armoured cars, while anyone appearing on the railway line was hailed by machine-gun fire and sniping. Digby called for an anti-tank gun to keep the armoured cars in order while he tried his luck through the back gardens of the houses. I told Douglas Crawley to see what he could do with his company by trying to the left under cover of the railway embankment. A map taken from a prisoner showed us the patrolling routes of the enemy armoured car unit. From this it looked as though they might suddenly appear behind us and I made arrangements to deal with them in good measure if they did.

During the late afternoon a squadron of Spitfires had flown over the town unmolested, so it looked as though the flak had been adequately dealt with by the morning's strafing, or else it had moved. The inhabitants of Oosterbeek continued to press good things upon us, paying very little attention to the bullets cracking in the air above their heads. As darkness began to fall the accuracy of the

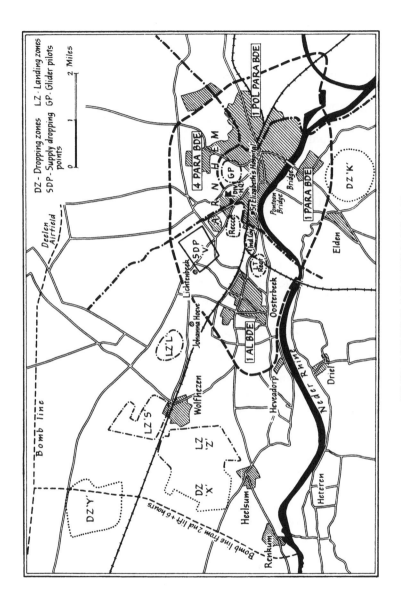

THE ARNHEM BATTLE PLAN

enemy's fire decreased, though in places it grew heavier, and Peter Cane was killed at this time.

Suddenly I realized that the hindermost parts of 'A' Company had disappeared. Everyone in the area by the railway was engaged, so I went on ahead with 'Bucky' Buchanan, our Intelligence Officer, to find out what had happened. Some three hundred yards beyond the railway I found a party of ten German prisoners guarded by one of 'A' Company's men, who wasn't sure what the situation was, but had seen the company moving on fast. I surmised that Digby's back-garden manoeuvre had been completely successful and that he had rushed on again as the way was open, leaving the information to reach me by wireless. We ran back to the railway and soon had the battalion on the move again.

It was now getting dark and though at times bursts of fire swept across the road, we could afford to ignore them. Up to this time we had had very few casualties and our progress had been highly satisfactory. The enemy were obviously still in position on Den Brink to our left, but they harmed us no more. 'A' Company had another satisfactory brush with them at a road junction in the town, where we found several dead and wounded lying round damaged motor vehicles. An empty ambulance was captured intact, also a river barge with a number of Germans on it. I never did discover what happened to the barge, which might have been useful later on.

'The night is the friend of no man,' say the Germans, but often we had welcomed darkness in our previous battles. Twice in Africa we had been surrounded, desperately short of ammunition, and weary beyond imagination. Yet when all seemed lost, as darkness fell, the German fire had faltered, paused, then broken out again in one last clattering hate, before ceasing altogether, leaving us to seize our chance of breaking out and moving on. Our patrols seldom returned without prisoners and our night attacks had nearly always succeeded. In Sicily the German parachutists might have wrecked our plans if they had moved as we did, in the dark, but as before they had preferred to wait for dawn.

So now I knew that we were not to be prevented from

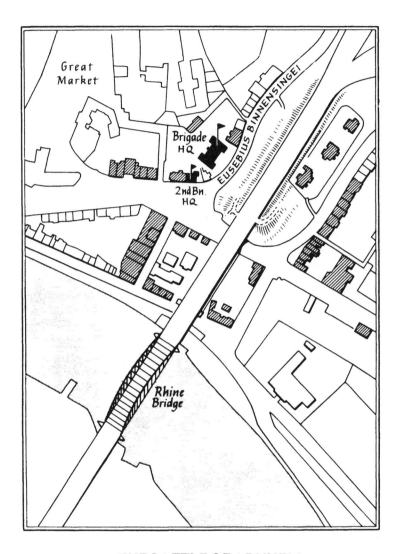

THE BATTLE OF ARNHEM

reaching our objectives. At increased speed we swept on through the streets of Arnhem to reach the pontoon bridge. We found the centre portion dismantled and useless to us for the time. Leaving part of the support group to wait for 'B' Company there, we marched on for the main Rhine crossing. When I arrived 'A' Company were already taking up positions on the embankment leading up to it from the town. They were still allowing what little traffic there was to use the bridge, as they did not want to give the alarm until they were ready to rush the other side. Meanwhile David and I looked for a suitable building in the area for Battalion Headquarters. We found a house on the corner overlooking the bridge and we roused the owner, who spoke very good English. He was not at all happy at the prospect of billeting soldiers of any sort. The Germans, he said, had gone and he would much prefer us to chase on after them. When I convinced him that the Germans were still very much there and furthermore that we didn't merely want billets, but proposed to fortify the house in readiness for a battle, he retired to the cellar quite horrified, leaving us to our own devices.

Headquarters company took over a government building next door, where there was room to park the transport in a yard behind it. Shortly after this Brigade Headquarters arrived in force, but without the brigadier. With them were Freddie Gough with a few more of his reconnaissance squadron. David Clarke of the Divisional R.A.S.C., a platoon of R.A.S.C. and, best of all, a captured lorry full of ammunition from the D.Z. Also some engineers. Brigade Headquarters established themselves in the attic of the government building, and all the available fighting men were put in houses on either side of the road leading to the bridge. Freddie Gough's jeep-mounted squadron had planned to by-pass the town from the north and come in to the bridge from the east, but this proved to be impossible and several jeeps had been shot up in the attempt. So, leaving the squadron with divisional headquarters, he had followed us by the route we had cleared. It was unfortunate that more use of this route could not be made on this, the first night of the battle. Both the 1st and 3rd Battalions were held up on other routes, and earlier on I had been warned that they would remain outside the town during the night. This pause gave the Germans valuable time to close the gap, which eventually resulted in sealing us in and the rest of the division out.

Meanwhile 'A' Company were having trouble at the bridge itself. As they started to move across they were met by withering fire from a pillbox and an armoured fighting vehicle sited on the bridge. It was obvious that there was no future in the direct approach, so one platoon with a detachment of sappers carrying a flame-thrower moved round through the houses to deal with the enemy from the side. While this manoeuvre was taking place the enemy counter-attacked the embankment positions. After putting up illuminating flares of various colours, then lobbing over a few mortar bombs, they attempted to rush straight in, but this cost them dearly and that particular lot retired into the darkness to lick their wounds. Robin Vlasto's platoon succeeded in getting into position by mouseholing through the buildings. We heard the crash of his P.I.A.T. bombs smashing into the side of the pillbox, then the sky was lit as the flame-thrower came into action. All hell seemed to be let loose after that. Amid the noise of machine-gun fire, a succession of explosions, the crackling of burning ammunition and the thump of a cannon, came screams of agony and fear. A wooden building nearby was wreathed in flame and soon German soldiers came staggering towards our edge. The north end of the bridge was now clear, but just as we were prepared to carry on across, a column of four lorries approached from the other side. We halted them near the burning pillbox, but unfortunately they caught fire before we could call them our own. The Germans with them became our prisoners and swelled the number of enemy in our hands to well over one hundred. Keeping and feeding them all was to become a fairly acute problem.

The fires on the bridge lit up the whole area like daylight and the heat from them made the bridge impassable for that night at any rate. Anyone attempting to move to the other side now would be silhouetted against the flames in a way that would turn such a gamble into suicide. Now it was impossible even to try. Our only hope of getting across, therefore, was to find and use some boats farther up the river. We had seen various types of river craft in a small bay near the pontoon bridge. It seemed conceivable that we might find one or two there to suit our purpose. By this time our wireless communication with 'B' and 'C' Companies had broken down.

I planned to get 'B' and the brigade defence platoon across. 'B' Company would then move down and attack the south end of the main bridge. The defence platoon would hold a bridgehead in the crossing area, while 'C' Company would leave the German headquarters and take over 'B' Company's commitments. George Murray, our senior sapper officer, would be responsible for getting a boat to go. But this plan was of no avail. No usable boat or barge could be found. The enemy were in position on the other side. A battle was already being fought in this area and 'C' Company were hotly engaged near the German Headquarters, so that the patrol with the message destined for them could not get through.

There was nothing more to be done for the present but snatch what rest we could before the battle, which I knew would start in the morning. At least we had the important end of the Rhine bridge from the point of view of the ground forces, who were due to reach us at lunch-time the next day, and provided we could hold what we had and the bridge remained intact, all should be well. The possibility of the bridge being blown was a continual worry. It was, however, the opinion of the sappers that the heat of the fires would destroy any fuses already laid from the bridge to the town, and we cut all the cables we could find, but the fires prevented even one man from being able to get on to the bridge itself to remove any charges that might be there.

The rest of the night was fairly quiet. Every now and then the comparative stillness was disturbed by the flames near the bridge discovering fresh boxes of ammunition to destroy. There was a great flash as each petrol tank flared up and we were warmed and very comfortable. I visited various people, among them 'A' Company, who were in great heart, as indeed they had every reason to be. They had fought their way in for eight miles, through very close difficult country, to capture their objective within seven hours of landing in Holland, accounting for one hundred and fifty Germans and several vehicles en route. A very fine feat of arms. Most of the prisoners were S.S. men, fighting soldiers of great repute.

It was pleasant to settle down for an hour or so when all was done. The R.S.M. made sure that a mug of tea was available when wanted, but it was hard to sleep. There were many things to think about and many details that one thought should perhaps be altered. The wireless operators were continually calling, but throughout the night no answers were received.

At dawn we stood to our arms and we didn't have long to wait. During the night we had heard a certain amount of enemy movement and we suspected that they would have a fairly good picture of the situation at the bridge. However our first visitors were some truckloads of Germans, who drove slowly into the area dominated by the buildings in which we lay. One could see by the hesitant look on the faces of our foes that they sensed some unknown danger. As at a signal, a stream of bullets tore into their crowded ranks. Too late, their drivers tried to accelerate away or reverse back the way they had come. By the time they thought to surrender, few were left alive. We carried their wounded into the R.A.P.

'Armoured car coming across the bridge!' came the cry from the signaller at the top of the house. For one moment I and many others wondered if this was the vanguard of XXX Corps. From the general air of optimism in high circles which flourished in the planning days, this well might be the case. We were not left long in doubt. These vehicles were obviously German and malignant. Behind the leader a whole column was reported. The anti-tank gunner whose gun was sited on to the bridge made ready, as also did the P.I.A.T. men in the buildings above. I had thought that the burning lorries would prove an obstacle to anything except a tank, but by now their fires were almost out and the leading armoured car was able to nose its way successfully through a gap between them and accelerate away, undamaged, even by the necklace of mines we had laid during the night. The explosion of one mine seriously disturbed the crew, but three more managed to pass our

ambush and move away at speed into the town. By the time
the fourth one appeared, our anti-tank weapon crews had
found the range and seven were soon disabled and burning
before our eyes.

Meanwhile German infantry were on us from the landward side. All round the battle raged. Mortar bombs and
shells were landing. Behind each window and on every
rooftop snipers and machine-gunners lay. To show ourselves for more than a second or two brought immediate
attention and we were by no means untouched in this
respect, as the calls for stretcher-bearers showed. There
were no exceptions from the fighting line, all ranks and
trades were in it. Staff officers, signallers, batmen, drivers
and clerks all lent a hand. We were content. Amid the din
of continuous fire and crash of falling burning buildings,
laughter was often heard. For a while I couldn't understand
how what sounded like German machine-guns were firing
from immediately below our windows. By craning out, one
could just see Freddie Gough in action behind the twin
K-guns mounted on his jeep, grinning like a wicked uncle.
Four more enemy A.F.V.s were hit, more prisoners taken
and the dead lay where they had fallen.

After what seemed like several hours, but was in reality
no more than two, the battle died away and gave us some
breathing space. Battalion Headquarters had not suffered
much. Two men had been killed on the landing of the first
floor and considerable damage had been done to the
house. 'A' Company and Brigade Headquarters were still
secure. It was not possible to get really accurate news of
casualties as snipers still made any movement between
buildings extremely dangerous. We were feeling very
pleased with ourselves and were rather hoping that we
would have the honour of welcoming the army into
Arnhem all to ourselves. By this time we knew that the rest
of the brigade would be on their way in from the west, but
so far we had received no message either from them or the
division. David Wallis wrote out a report on what had
happened so far, and this we dispatched by a pigeon, which
should have flown to London. The pigeon wasn't very
anxious to start at first, but took to the air after some round
abuse from the R.S.M. The supporting battery commander

of the Light Regiment R.A., which had been landed by glider at the same time as we had, was with us. He had found an excellent observation post on the roof of one of our buildings and his guns had already done yeoman service in helping to persuade German infantry that all the bridge belonged to us.

The signallers picked up a message from the leading elements of XXX Corps, which added to our feeling of satisfaction. It meant that they were well on their way towards us and though we didn't actually know how far they were, the signals were so strong that we felt we should see them arriving before very long.

Meanwhile there was by no means a reign of peace in the town. Shelling and mortaring became continuous and in between short periods of comparative quiet, bursts of machine-gun fire came from every direction. At last wireless communication was established with 'B' Company and Doug Crawley was asking if he should remain where he was by the now useless pontoon bridge or join us at the main bridge. I decided to strengthen our position at the important place, where we were always liable to be attacked again, so told him to disengage and move towards us. Doug didn't find this manoeuvre any too simple and had to fight a fairly hearty little battle before he arrived. On the way half a platoon was cut off in a side street. This had to be left to its own devices, for the time being, until the approach of the remainder of the brigade, which I expected some time during the day.

I began to realize that things were not going according to plan in this direction, and though we could hear no sounds of conflict from the west it was obvious that something solid was delaying them or they would have joined us very much earlier. The first message we got from them stated that they had reached the pontoon bridge and could we do anything to help. I was somewhat surprised at this, but told Doug to send a strong patrol back to his old area to see what they could do. He decided to go himself with this patrol, but as soon as he had got well on his way, we heard a correction to the original message which now gave the position of the 1st Battalion as not far beyond the railway on the outskirts of the town, and there was nothing we could do to help them there. We still had no news of 'C' Company in the area of the German headquarters.

Throughout the rest of the day small bodies of enemy continued to attack the edge of our positions and shortage of ammunition began to tell. This close-quarter fighting had made a heavy call on what we carried with us and we had become badly in need of resupply. The reserve which the R.A.S.C. had brought had been distributed, and we couldn't expect any more until some part of the remainder of the division joined up with us, thus opening the route between us and the divisional dumps. We had no men to spare for this. The whole object of the operation was to seize and hold the main bridge. It would have been extremely dangerous to weaken our garrison and to risk losing the bridge. The enemy shelling was taking a steady toll of our numbers. I gave orders that to save ammunition our men would cease sniping, keeping what they had for beating off assaults at close quarters. This was an advantage to the enemy, in that he could risk a certain amount of movement, and it enabled him to improve his positions in some respects. It also misled him into thinking we had lost heart, which supposition cost him dearly before the battle was over.

Movement from one building to another was strictly limited, for to cross a street in daylight was to draw fire from the Germans and, at night, the indiscriminate attention of both friend and foe. The fires from burning buildings lit up the whole area so that there was no real darkness. I managed to visit all our positions to the west of the bridge and the ramp leading up to it, but to move under the bridge to see people on the eastern side was suicidal. Here were most of the sappers, some of whom under the staunch leadership of Eric McKay shared a building with part of 'C' Company of the 3rd Battalion, which had joined us by coming up the railway line into the town under the highly skilled direction of Peter 'Pongo' Lewis.

Digby had put the various detachments into position as they arrived that first night. Key buildings had been allotted to Bernard Briggs and a party of Brigade H.Q. and also Pat Barnet with the Brigade Defence Platoon. Once there, they were literally sealed in as daylight showed that the enemy had occupied all the adjacent houses. There was no way we could support our people to the east of the bridge except that the gunner O.P. on the roof of the H.Q. building could bring some defensive fire to bear.

There were still a few Dutch civilians in our area, but most had been wise enough to leave for safer places during the night. It was distressing to see the chaos and destruction in the houses we were occupying. All the windows had been shattered, furniture had been hastily built into barricades and all inflammable material got rid of as far as possible. One could imagine the despair of the owners, returning to enjoy the fruits of liberation and finding their much-prized possessions lying pathetically scattered, broken and spoiled. The total destruction of their homes which followed was perhaps a mercy.

At the request of Tony Hibbert, the Brigade Major, I left David in command of the battalion and moved across to Brigade Headquarters, so as to be able to direct relieving troops to their positions when they arrived.

We searched for and took what food we could find for ourselves and our prisoners, but there was nothing much beyond apples and some particularly juicy pears. We carried with us only a light ration for forty-eight hours and food might now become as important to us as ammunition. During the afternoon our machine-gunners, who were covering the south bank, had an unpleasant time. The enemy brought up some 40 mm. flak guns, and methodically proceeded to demolish the rather flimsy houses in which our machine-guns lay. Before long these houses caught fire, and the crews had to scramble vigorously to find new places from which to reply. The Germans were not allowed to set foot on the bridge. At each endeavour, sometimes with small numbers and sometimes with large, our mortars, artillery and machine-guns hit them hard and accurately.

Towards the end of the day the enemy made some penetration into what we called our own part of the town. I arranged to form a mobile storming party with Freddie Gough. He had two jeeps mounting K-guns and I could bring our bren carrier. Volunteers were called for and we decided to make a detour and come in from behind against

them, going as fast as we could make it, but the situation
was restored before we had to show our hand. The next
rude shock in store was the arrival of a 150 mm. gun, firing
a shell weighing nearly 100 lb. from point-blank range at
our building. Each hit seemed to pulverize the masonry
and the appalling crash of these missiles against our walls
scared the daylights out of Headquarters. Just as I made up
my mind that something drastic would have to be done, our
mortars got the range, one direct hit killing the entire crew
and apparently disabling the gun. We saw it being towed
away round a corner and it troubled us no more.

'Bucky' Buchanan brought disturbing news during the
afternoon. He had been interrogating prisoners in our
cellars and found that among them were several from the
9th S.S. Panzer Division. They had come in during the
morning. On the previous day the prisoners had been from
various units of no particular renown. It had been thought
that the well-known 9th and 10th S.S. Panzer Division had
been written off in the Falaise battle on the far bank of the
Seine in France. I told Bucky to find me one of them who
spoke English. He produced a captain. 'What are you
doing in these parts'? I asked.

'We have been resting, re-equipping and getting reinforcements between here and Apeldoorn for several days.'

Well, there it was. Further questions elicited the fact that
most of the key personnel of the 2nd S.S. Panzer Corps,
which made up the two fine divisions, had got back across
the Seine, and now they would soon be able to put ever-
increasing pressure against our lightly equipped 1st Airborne Division, which had its back to the Rhine. We had
been given absolutely no inkling of this possibility. The
odds against an outcome in our favour were heavy indeed.

As night fell there was still no sign of relief or ammunition arriving. I visited as many of our garrison as I could,
telling them all that I confidently expected reinforcements
during the night and that we could count on XXX Corps
arriving the next day. They were all in high spirits. There
was barely one who could not claim to have killed an
opponent. 'Our most enjoyable battle,' they said, and, 'Let
us always fight from houses,' or 'The more they come the
merrier,' and so on. Not that there was anything extra-

ordinary in this; all the way through, however hard or dangerous the going, they were always cheerful and always ready to give more than one thought it possible to ask.

We set fire to a small building near the bridge to light it up during the darkness. We need not have bothered as our own caught fire, and then the one next door. We managed to stop our own, but all night long various fires were raging and we could see to shoot at two hundred yards. David Wallis was killed during the night when another attack developed in 'A' Company's sector. The Germans in considerable strength overwhelmed two outlying positions and he was shot while going forward to see what needed putting right. Shortly before he had been with me at Headquarters. We had been friends for many years and he had been all that one could wish for as a Second-in-Command. Nothing was funny now. Digby came in to take over his job.

Tuesday morning came and with it we expected to see the Polish Parachute Brigade arrive. In the original plan they were to drop south of the bridge. I dreaded to think of the reception they would have. Our mobile storming party again stood ready. This time, in the confusion we hoped would be caused by the arrival of more parachutists, Freddie Gough's suicide squad would try to rush the bridge, so that if they did succeed in crossing and getting through the built-up area on the far side, the Poles would at least find a handful of friends to meet them. But the Poles did not arrive.

There was still no sign or encouragement from XXX Corps. During the night I was informed by wireless that two battalions from other brigades of the division were on their way, inside Arnhem, towards us, but there was still no sign or portent from them. The great flaw in the divisional plan was that there were not sufficient aircraft available to land the whole Division at the same time. This meant that only half the force landed on the first day could take advantage of the enemy's surprise and move to Arnhem, while the remaining half had to stay where they were, in the landing area, to cover the rest of the Division on the next day. This gave the enemy, who were in far greater strength than had been expected, the opportunity of cutting the inter-divisional communications and concentrating against each part in turn. By now, on Tuesday morning, the Division was in three main parts. We, who were by the bridge, our objective, were firmly sealed in unless more ammunition arrived. Approximately four battalions were trying to batter their way in towards us, with the enemy besetting them from all sides, and the remainder were stretched from Oosterbeek, the village outside Arnhem, to the area of the original landing. The abundance of cover provided by the woods and buildings made the whole area ideal for ambush, so that quite small bodies of enemy, armed with machine-guns and supported by tanks, could interfere with and even paralyse movement along the roads leading into Arnhem.

We fed from the small ration packs that we had brought with us as and when we could. My faithful batman Wicks was never far away and at suitable moments he would brew up something from our combined resources and we would hope for a few moments of respite while we gobbled it down. The batman plays an essential part in keeping his officer going in battle. Like any good groom who regards his horse as his own property, the good batman reckons that he owns his officer – something to be watched over, guarded, fed, kept clean, tidy and free from all minor personal worries.

All through the day the enemy pounded away at us. We parried their thrusts and we countered their moves. The water supply suddenly failed and our doctors had cause to worry about the wounded. The medical supplies they had brought with them were obviously limited and some of the earlier wounded should have been operated on before this. I knew that something would have to be done about them soon and I feared that that something would mean a temporary truce with the enemy while we evacuated them to our own M.D.S. outside the town. It was unlikely that they would lend us transport for this purpose and most probable that they would capture ours if we used it.

During the day the Germans had sent back to us one of our sappers whom they had captured earlier. The German commander wished me to meet him, unarmed, under the bridge at midday to discuss terms for our surrender. It was quite pointless that we should continue to fight, he had said, but the sapper reported the enemy to be most disheartened at their heavy losses and I felt that if only more ammunition would arrive, we would soon have our S.S. opponent in the bag. New weapons came to harry us and all the buildings by the bridge were set on fire. It became increasingly difficult to find new positions while keeping the bridge under our control. Towards evening heavy tanks appeared, incredibly menacing and sinister in the half-light, as their guns swung from target to target. Shells burst through our walls. The dust and settling debris following their explosions filled the passages and rooms. The acrid reek and smell of burning together with the noise bemused us. We had to stay prepared to meet the rush of infantry I knew would follow if we wavered for a moment. The battalion Headquarters building suffered badly. Digby, Father Egan and others were hit. Then our gunners man-handled a six-pounder round to the front under the very noses of the enemy, while the P.I.A.T. crews climbed to new positions, and our bold reply drove them back, but one remained and could not move again.

All the way through the gunners of the 1st Air Landing Anti-Tank Battery excited our admiration and respect. No one was exposed to greater danger than they. They never hesitated for a moment to engage enemy armour whenever it approached without thought for themselves. They were a fine example of the Royal Regiment giving their all to their guns.

As usual the men of the Parachute Royal Engineer Squadrons fought through to the end. Throughout the war we of the Parachute Regiment thought that it was almost a waste to use them as sappers when they were so good at killing the enemy. Shock troops in the full sublime sense of the words.

The Brigade Staff and their signallers never ceased in their efforts to establish communication. The attic in which they laboured was hit repeatedly, but they never flagged. Tony Hibbert, the Brigade Major, and Rex Byng-Maddock, the D.A.A. & Q.M.G., had to sit it out with as much cheerful resignation as they could muster, filling in time by taking turns at sniping whenever they had a chance.

This last onslaught had left us weary. As we prepared for yet another night Arnhem was burning. Two great churches were flaming fiercely and for a while the shadow of the cross which hung between two towers was silhouetted against the clouds of smoke rising far into the sky. The patrols we sent to probe the ring about us made no progress. It was like daylight in the streets. An enamel, metallic daylight. The crackle of burning wood and strange echo of falling buildings was almost continuous. I climbed the stairs to the attic with Freddie Gough to watch the flames and to discuss our movements should we in turn be driven out by fire. If the wind changed to the west we were certain to be burnt out, as showers of sparks and burning material flowed from the churches and other large buildings in the area. A mortar bomb had landed in the attic during the day and though it had burst amongst the signallers' wireless sets, not a man had been wounded. The roof no longer provided cover, so from the top we could see all round us.

'Well, Freddie, I'm afraid it's not been a very healthy party and it don't look like getting any healthier as time goes by,' I said.

'In other words, there may not be much future in it,' he laughed back at me.

'What's worrying me,' I went on, 'is that if we take fire here, we can't fight it out to the last minute and then go and leave our wounded to be roasted. We'll have to leave them time to carry the bad cases up and out of it. The trouble is that I can't see where else we can go to. What do you think about going north?'

Freddie thought it would be better to go westward towards the river bend and we left it at that for the time being.

This night was fairly peaceful. I prowled about occasionally, sleeping in between whiles amongst the litter in one of the rooms. Sometimes a light rain fell. I saw two hatless figures down the road and took a shot at them with a borrowed rifle, but neither moved. During the day we had taken it in turns to wait with a sniper's rifle for a German officer to show himself in a window of the house which we presumed was their headquarters, some four hundred yards away. I had spent an hour watching in vain, but others had been more successful and our guns had strafed it from time to time, when sounds of movement came to us from the gardens surrounding it. When I looked up after reloading, the figures I had fired at were gone.

Soon after first light on Wednesday morning the shelling began again. This was to be our third day of holding on under continuous enemy pressure, after three long nights of suspense and alarms. It was all the more exacting for our patience in that it followed on after that exhilarating journey from England and our successful thrust into Arnhem of the Sunday afternoon before. Now that the buildings on either side of the bridge had been destroyed and their rubble was still smouldering, the bulk of what remained of the force were concentrated round the headquarters buildings. From here we could still control the bridge. We had found a limited water supply in one of the houses, sufficient for one more day at any rate.

At last divisional headquarters came on the air and I was able to speak to the General. He had been missing for two days and there had been various rumours as to his fate. It was very cheering to hear him, but he could tell me nothing more than I knew already about XXX Corps, and not anything really encouraging about the ability of the Division to get through to us. They were obviously having great difficulties themselves.

The wounded in the cellars were now lying crowded almost on top of each other, making it difficult for the doctors and orderlies to get round to attend them. I walked round the perimeter to see our defences which, though fairly secure, included some very weak places, where a determined rush by the enemy could carry them into our midst. The Luftwaffe had reappeared in considerable strength. We removed the British identification marks which we had formerly displayed all over the area as there was no sign of the R.A.F. except for one defenceless Dakota which forlornly ran the gauntlet. We held our breath as we watched it forge its way through the puffs of black smoke.

As I was talking to Doug Crawley outside his headquarters about arranging a fighting patrol to give us more elbow-room to the north, there was a sudden savage crash beside us. I was thrown several feet and I found myself lying face downwards on the ground with pain in both legs. Doug was lying on his back not far away and he started to drag himself into the house. Stunned and bemused I did likewise and Wicks my batman came to drag me in under cover. Before long strecher-bearers carried me to the R.A.P. where Jimmy Logan made light of my wounds and I felt that after a rest I should be able to carry on. I sat on a box in the doorway of headquarters and vainly tried to pull myself together. I tried to swallow the whisky that remained in my flask, but this made me feel like vomiting. After a bit I got some men to carry me on to a litter in one of the cellars and tried to rest. By now the pain had localized itself to my left ankle and right shinbone.

I lay there rather dazed, hoping that the worst of the pain would lessen. Several people came to see me, but I don't remember much. The news went from bad to worse. Digby was brought in to sit beside me for a while and he told me about Jack Grayburn. Though hit several times, he refused to leave his men and died in action with them.

I told Digby that my ankle was the trouble and before long one of the M.O.s came in to dress it, as this had not been done before. Now I was given morphia and most of the pain went, enabling me to sleep. When I woke some bomb-happy cases were gibbering in the room. In the evening the Germans began to pound the building again. The doctors came to see me about the evacuation of the building in case of fire. I remembered discussing this with Freddie Gough on the evening before and now I sent for him. The doctors said it would take an hour to get everybody out from the cellars and so I told him to be prepared to move with all those still able to fight from new positions. The building took fire several times, and they fought the flames as best they could, but gradually the fire began to spread. One of the doctors came again to say that we would have to do something fairly quickly. I sent for Freddie once more and told him to move. I gave him my own belt with revolver and compass and we wished each other luck. Down below where I lay it was pitch black and we had to use our torches continuously.

Later I heard shouts from above of: 'Don't shoot! Only

wounded are here.' George Murray suddenly appeared, wanting to know what on earth was happening. Scarcely had he gone when I heard German voices in the passage outside and sounds of the stretcher cases being moved out. Then Wicks came in. He said he was going to stay with me till they took me out and I was very glad to see him. He went away to get a stretcher, but while he was gone a German N.C.O. rushed in intimating that we must get out as soon as possible. With the help of one of the bomb-happy cases he dragged me up the stairs to the door. We had to move quickly outside to avoid burning debris from the house. I sat down among the stretcher-cases on the embankment leading to the bridge.

All our buildings were burning fiercely and, as I watched, the old Battalion Headquarters collapsed into a heap of smouldering rubble. The whole scene was brilliantly lit up by the flames. Both sides laboured together to bring the wounded out and I saw that the Germans were driving off in our jeeps full of bandaged men. The prisoners we had taken were standing in a group nearby, not seemingly overjoyed at their liberation. Wicks found me again and put me on a stretcher, at the same time moving me alongside Doug Crawley. As one of the orderlies was giving me an injection of morphia for the journey, I said good-bye to Wicks and thanked him for all he had done for me. He was going to get back to our people as soon as the opportunity arose.

The S.S. men were very polite and complimentary about the battle we had fought, but the bitterness I felt was unassuaged. No living enemy had beaten us. The battalion was unbeaten yet, but they could not have much chance with no ammunition, no rest and with no positions from which to fight. No body of men could have fought more courageously and tenaciously than the officers and men of the 1st Parachute Brigade at Arnhem bridge.

Suddenly the Germans rushed away to take up positions for battle again. Their medical orderlies carried us down to the far side of the embankment. As we went I heard weapons being loaded and orders being given. Though the bridge was now lost our men would fight on till all hope had gone, but I knew that their hours were numbered.

On the back of one of the trailers towed by the jeeps and being driven away by the Germans was a set of bagpipes that had been presented to the battalion by the Lord Provost of Glasgow to replace the set that had disappeared on the back of a mule-cart at Oudna in 1942.

I decided that if I commanded the 2nd Parachute Battalion in battle again I would leave the pipes at home in the bank.   .

Some of my old soldiers and I had had many narrow shaves and been so nearly overwhelmed, but each time, fate or the God of Battles had intervened in our favour, but not this time and verily for us, Arnhem had been 'a drop too many'.

CHAPTER 16

Prisoner

Once all the wounded and rescued German prisoners had been got out of the way, the battle began again. There was no more mortaring or gunfire because our own side's positions were so intermingled with the enemy's. However, buildings were still burning, and now German tanks could rumble across the bridge. I remember saying to Douglas:

'Well, Doug, I'm afraid we haven't got away with it this time.'

'No, sir,' he replied. 'But we gave 'em a damn good run for their money.'

We could still not believe that XXX Corps would fail to come to our rescue. It was difficult to feel that there was enough genuine opposition to stop them. It was desperately disappointing that having done everything we had been asked to do we were now prisoners. It was shaming, like being a malefactor, no longer free. For the moment all this was alleviated by the sympathy and even admiration of our captors. I could remember saying to someone when it did seem inevitable that we would fall into the hands of Hitler's S.S., 'I don't think that this is going to be much of a pleasure.'

We had all heard stories of them shooting their prisoners or herding them into burning buildings, but these men were kind, chivalrous and even comforting.

A little later our stretchers were put on to a half-track and we were taken to the St. Elisabeth Hospital where many wounded from other elements of the division had already been taken. We had removed our badges of rank, hoping that it might be easier to get away as private soldiers than as officers. As I was brought in a padre, whom I did not know, greeted me as 'Colonel' just in front of a German officer who was taking down names. However it didn't seem to make any difference as I was put into a bed on the ground floor, but now my great trouble was that I could not manage to urinate and I was caused much inconvenience thereby.

Still hoping for the arrival of XXX Corps, it was very galling to be put into an ambulance on the Thursday morning. The jolting on the journey caused me more and more acute discomfort in my bladder, so much so that I could almost forget about the pain from my wounds, the worst of which was from a gash across the shinbone. The ambulance dumped its occupants at a railway siding and we were loaded into a cattle truck where we lay side by side on the floor. Here at last I was able to pee into an empty bottle that was handy and I felt more comfortable and relaxed than at any time since I had been hit.

A very young S.S. man was the sentry by the doorway in our truck. He had a smattering of English and he did his best for us by shouting to railway people to fetch water for us to drink. When an engine was brought up, it was coupled on to the train so roughly that we were all shaken up and he was catapulted out of the door on to the line. We heard him setting about the engine driver, at any rate verbally, in full volume, and from then on the shunting was decorous.

The man lying beside me was in agony. Someone produced a phial of morphia which I tried to inject, but the needle was malformed and it was impossible to put it into even the most fleshy parts, nor could we find means to sharpen it. We were taken to a prison hospital which had been hastily prepared as if for this emergency. I think the place was Lingen, not far inside Germany, and here I was operated on.

It was rather primitive. I took my turn to have my bandages ripped off. There were linguistic difficulties and the German doctor in charge attempted only one word which was put in the form of a question: 'Kaput?' Not knowing quite what this meant, I nodded. Whereupon he waggled each leg in turn and said, 'Nein'.

I was then laid down on an operating table and a nurse

clamped a mask on my face on which she poured some ether. Before I went under, a man in French officer's uniform showing under a white coat advanced to the side of the table with a knife in his hand and began to probe about in the wound in my ankle. I then remember no more till coming to in a cell with bars which had two other beds and a lavatory pan.

The terrible thing was to wake in the morning. So often in normal life one wakens after a nightmare or unpleasant dream to find oneself in one's own comfortable surroundings, and one can pinch oneself and say: 'Thank goodness for all the blessings I now enjoy.'

Now I woke in discomfort, hunger, fear and uncertainty after what was often quite a pleasant dream. It was dreadful to come back to stark reality.

I rather lost track of the hours or days. The lights were kept on all the time, and food consisted of a couple of slices of heavy brown bread and some soup, I think twice per day. There was nothing to read and I cannot remember much in the way of medical attention. Our wounds had been bandaged with paper dressings which soon came loose and fell off if not actually held on. The most worrying thing was not being able to discover what was going to happen. I was still without badges of rank and I cannot remember that any of our captors were the least bit interested. The sudden influx of so many unexpected wounded prisoners, added to the large number of German wounded, completely swamped their resources, so that perhaps it was a wonder that we were tended as well as we were.

At last we were on our way again, this time in third-class passenger coaches. There were no stretchers, so the cases who were unable to walk had to be dragged along the railway platform on sacking. This was treated as rather a joke, even by the sufferers. Quite a number of German wounded were also on the move and we noticed that they were not much better off and also had to make do with paper bandages. We all clung to our red berets as our most precious possessions. The German civilians who saw us nodded knowingly to each other, for our battle had been written up as a great German victory and we were living proof.

This leg of our journey took us to a huge P.W. camp, where the officers were separated from the men, and after one night a small group of a dozen or so were on our way to Spangenburg, which was an established Oflag, not far from Kassel. We nearly got into trouble while waiting for a connection on one railway station. We were sitting in a group in the middle of the platform and gradually civilians gathered round us. Their curiosity soon got the better of any animosity and before long badinage and miming became of almost *entente cordiale* dimensions and our sentries so far forgot themselves as to start smoking, and acted as though we were prize exhibits of which they were really rather proud. Then a train drew up at the platform and close to us were the first-class carriages. One was full of German officers who took a very poor view of what was going on. One of them leaped out of the carriage window, bellowing with rage at our escort for allowing us, 'Verdammt' Gefangener', to show off in the Reich in such a manner. In no time our erstwhile friendly audience was transformed into hostile, even threatening master-race types and we were banished to a far corner of the platform with our much chastened sentries.

All we could say to each other was, 'Phew!'

Anyway, we arrived safely and once we were in the hands of the staff of the well-established Oflag, we were properly sorted out, searched, documented, fed, given cigarettes, and I was put to bed in the camp lazarette where I remained for about three weeks.

The camp was in two parts. One was the old castle at the top of a hill and the other the stable block down below, adjacent to the village. This was where I was and there was much to be said for it, for from the windows one could watch the villagers going about their daily business and this made one feel less cut off. People were most kind in supplying items from their own precious savings and were, of course, avid for news. David Clarke of the R.A.S.C. was another wounded officer with me in the lazarette. It was he who had come through to the bridge with his platoon and the truck full of ammunition. It was largely because of this that we had been able to go on fighting for as long as we did.

Many of the officers at Spangenburg had been in for

several years. A large proportion had been captured at the time of Dunkirk and there were a considerable number of the 51st Highland Division who were taken at St. Valéry. The doctor was one of these and I think that he was quite glad to have some wounded to look after again. We had a lot of visitors. People came to play backgammon, picquet or poker dice games and we got much more than our fair share of rations. The old 'Kriegies', as the experienced prisoners were called, had got camp life fairly well buttoned up. Once a man had made up his mind to make the best of things and use the time with a purpose, all sorts of activities became available: all the arts and crafts, languages and literature, religions and selfless good works, games and gambling, not to mention military studies (officially forbidden), keeping fit and preparing to escape.

My wounds, comparatively light, took some time to heal and even after I was discharged from the lazarette I could still only hobble. I moved into a room with five other lieutenant-colonels, all some twenty years older than me. The winter was now coming on and I began to feel the cold acutely, especially at night. We were short of bedding and we stuffed newspapers between our blankets to reinforce them so that there was much rustling every time anyone turned over. We didn't get much sympathy from the Germans owing to the British predilection for fresh air. They reckoned that if we insisted on opening windows and letting cold air in, we could only blame ourselves for the waste of what heating fuel there was, and that was precious little. I always thought that the Germans had a point there.

I was hungry all the time and I am sure that all the other newly captured were, too. One did not like to mention it because the old inhabitants had taken such infinite pains to ensure fair shares and to improve and embellish wherever possible. They had got used to the deprivations and had learnt to live with them. They ate their helpings of food very slowly, savouring each mouthful. I found that my mouth watered readily at the sight, sound, smell or thought of food and I couldn't help bolting my helpings, possibly in the hope that there might be some more somewhere and one ought to be ready in case. It was difficult to settle to anything. I enjoyed the gramophone and other concerts, and the carefully rehearsed plays or discussions.

I could so well echo the remark of the famous suffragette who, when asked what was the worst thing about being in prison, said: 'Couldn't get out.'

Although the average age of most of the prisoners was high there were a fair number of fit and active men, including our airborne contingent. Among us were some of the Polish officers who had been dropped to the south of the river at Arnhem and had made valiant efforts to come to our aid. Genuine attempts to escape had by now become difficult and as Hitler had recently declared that all who were caught while trying to do so would be shot, the senior officers in the camps did not exactly encourage anyone to volunteer.

However there was a general feeling that when faced with absolutely certain defeat Hitler and his Nazis might retreat to a redoubt in the mountains, where they could hold out for a long time using prisoners as slave labour and hostages. If that were the case then senior officers' camps might be high on the list and it seemed possible that, as soon as there was a chance of our camp being relieved by our own people, we would be marched off towards the mountain keep and this would be very unpleasant for all concerned.

As there was no plan for such a contingency, I worked on one which envisaged the doping of our guards, an assault on the guard-room under cover of smoke-bombs by men armed with hockey sticks, the seizure of the guards' weapons and the subsequent move of a column of small parties towards our own relieving forces. We did in fact have all the necessary items to put this into effect. I had a very small party of co-planners, among them, I think, 'Sheriff' Thompson who later became military correspondent of the *Daily Telegraph*, and when ready I expounded my plan to the Senior British Officer. He was frankly horrified and said that he had orders direct from Eisenhower that all prisoners were to continue to obey the German orders to the end. I pointed out that these were the same stupid unimaginative orders that had condemned so many to remain prisoner in Italy after the collapse there when so many could have been freed, and in fact many who disobeyed the order were now free. I also said that any marching columns might be mistaken for columns of troops by the Air Forces of either side, but to no avail. My plan was burned.

Shortly after this my ankle wound broke open and the camp doctor arranged for me to be sent to the big P.W. hospital at Obermassfeldt. Late in the evening before I left, the Senior British Officer sent a message which ordered me not to attempt to escape while on the journey, while at the hospital, or on the way back. I tried to see him to reject his order, but lights out came before I could find him.

I was to go by normal passenger train and my escort consisted of a lance-corporal and a private. Perhaps I should have insisted on something more appropriate for my rank, but I was too anxious to get to the hospital to worry about protocol, if such existed. It was just before Christmas 1944, very cold with ice and snow everywhere. We had one change and while waiting for our connection the lance-corporal took us into a troops canteen for coffee. I was still wearing the clothes I had during the battle, pretty scruffy, but still looking like a British officer. Anyway my little corporal was obviously quite proud of me. He spoke no English and we communicated with nods and jerks.

Suddenly the door burst open and in came a Hauptmann of the German Military Police. There was a tremendous roaring, cursing and damning at my presence there. My corporal stood up to him well. I could tell that he was insistent that I was an Oberst and had to be looked after and there was nowhere else to take me. Anyway, we were expelled, but I could not help sensing that most of the soldiers in the canteen were on our side and that the Military Police were no more popular with the German soldiery than they are apt to be with ours.

Arrived at the hospital, I found other old friends. Arthur Marrable, one of the Airborne Division's Field Ambulance Commanders, was the Senior British Medical Officer, and he gave me a great welcome. I found Padre Egan in the next bed. He had been wounded in the Battalion H.Q. at the bridge. The food was marvellous after the Oflag and I was soon in great shape for an operation to extract bits of mortar bomb from my ankle. Then there was the long business of lying in bed waiting for the thing to heal. The daily dressings were always an ordeal. We were looked after by the British Army nursing orderlies with just as much devoted care as we were accustomed to have from the females of the species.

Most of the patients were American and then mostly Air Force. Severe burns were the most common injury and some men were in great pain for much of the time. Some shattering cases came in towards the end. These were Americans wounded in the German offensive in the Ardennes which had taken place in December. For some reason they had been starved and their debility was only matched by that of some of the living skeletons which is what our own servicemen had become while being marched away from the advancing Russians. The sheer magnitude of suffering everywhere weighed down upon us. When our own aircraft attacked the railway station, inevitably German civilians were killed, and sometimes the guards would intimate that the local population might take revenge upon us. It was not always easy to keep a semblance of good cheer in the circumstances. I found considerable solace in playing bridge.

One of the German staff, who spoke good English, told me that when I was fit to leave, I was not going back to Spangenburg, but to the Straflager at Colditz. However, my ankle was still a long time healing and I knew that Arthur Marrable would keep me as long as he could.

We were able to get the latest news from the B.B.C. and as March drew on, we heard that Patton's Sixth US Army was approaching. Then came the day when the German guards moved off and soon after an example of what was the once invincible German army went past below our windows. Old men and boys, Tiger tanks and horse-drawn farm-carts, captured jeeps and bicycles, with a motley collection of motor vehicles of all kinds. One could not help wondering why they went on fighting, for if ever there was now a hopeless cause, it was this. I suppose that, like their leader they hoped for some miracle. I felt pity.

Then, almost as if by magic, the American spearheads were down below. Highly professional, tanks and half-tracks, always covered by fire, all under control. There was a small river running past the hospital and through the town and here the Germans caused delay. I could see where their snipers had positions on the rooftops and I went down into the street to pass the information on. Knowing that I was safe I put a bold face on it, but some of the American soldiers were doing the crouchy-wouchy act and taking their time. A sergeant, noting this, gave one of his crouchers a kick in the backside, saying: 'Stand up. Don't you see that there is a British officer watching?'

The enemy were soon winkled out. Patton's men were then on their way. They had had no idea that our hospital was there, but before long administrative staffs had all the walking cases out and beamed towards home. I was teamed up with Jimmy Cleminson from the 3rd Battalion and two Canadian officers, George Comper and Peter Clegg. We were passed back from Squadron to Corps and all the way the soldiers were singing the praises of 'Old Blood and Guts', their Army Commander, George S. Patton. If ever an army developed a peak of efficiency, this was it. Everything worked. There were no delays. If something was going to happen at a certain time, happen it did. Their equipment was in first-class working order for if anything even looked like failing, it was immediately replaced. The four of us found ourselves at a medical establishment near the Army H.Q. on a Sunday. Invited to a church service, we found that we were the only takers apart from the padre and harmonium player, everyone else being too busy. The service was brief but among the hymns was 'God Bless America', which we the congregation sang with all might and main.

All ranks of this army, when they saw our red berets, would say: 'Arnhem. Aye. We'd have gotten through. Yes, sir. We'd have gotten through.'

I could not help believing that they would have. There was nothing slow or ponderous about them and they didn't stop for tea or the night for that matter. This set me thinking about what had gone wrong with the mission on which we had set out with such high hopes.

One thing that had puzzled me was that during the lulls in the fighting, there was no noise or any sound of battle from Nijmegen only seventeen miles to the south, nor were

there any flames lighting up the sky as there were at
Arnhem. It seemed that either the bridge had been taken
with a walk-over or else its capture had not yet been
attempted. Surely, the Corps Commander, having laid so
much stress on the need to capture Arnhem bridge, would
have put the same degree of priority on the taking of the
Nijmegen bridge, for without that we were in jeopardy
however weak the immediate opposition.

But, in fact, it turned out that he had not. The same voice
that had so firmly said to Roy Urquhart:

'Arnhem Bridge. And hold it,' said to James Gavin,
G.O.C. of the U.S. 82nd Airborne Division, 'The Groesbeek Heights. Nijmegen Bridge later.'

Nijmegen bridge was there for the walk-over on D-Day.
The Groesbeek Heights, so called, are several miles from
Nijmegen. They do not constitute a noticeable tactical
feature and their occupation or otherwise has little or no
bearing on what happens in Nijmegen or at Nijmegen
Bridge. The Guards had expected to be able to motor on
and over, but when they arrived, late as it was, the bridge
was still firmly in German hands. Now the 82nd, trained at
vast trouble and expense to drop by parachute over obstacles, had to cross the river in the teeth of intense opposition
in flimsy canvas folding boats that they had never seen
before. When so bravely it was done, it was too late.

Perhaps our singing at the service had been reported to
the right quarter for soon after we were on a Dakota
heading for the U.K. As we approached, the captain called
me forward to look over his shoulder:

'There, Kunnel, there's yer white cliffs. There's yer
white cliffs of Dover.'

CHAPTER 17

Rehabilitation

The aircraft landed at Lyneham. Our joy at being back in England was soon dispelled, however, when we found ourselves aboard a train for a hospital in Wales. We were so used to doing what we were told that it was not until we arrived that we felt a sense of outrage—captivity must be the most unrewarding type of service that any soldier can experience, and having tried it his one firm resolve is to be free. The Wing Commander in charge of the hospital told us that there were strict instructions as to how wounded ex-POWs were to be handled, and that we had been delivered into his charge, presumably to undergo such handling. I cannot now remember how we got away, but after one night in Wales we were back on a train, this time determined that London was our terminus.

We were an odd-looking quartet in the West End, still wearing the battledress in which we had been captured, which was sown up where it had been slit to allow our wounds to be dressed. Jimmy Cleminson was an arm case, George Comper and Peter Clegg were both throats, and I was still a hobbler. We had one celebratory meal together, rather marred by the effects of laughter on George and Peter, which sometimes forced unswallowed food to spout from holes below their jaws. Then, having contacted our next of kin, we departed on our ways.

My parents were living with my sister and her R.A.F. husband in an old rectory in Rutland, and there with them I once more enjoyed all the good things of life. My old battalion had been reformed, and was now stationed only a

few miles away. John Marshall, our second-in-command
from Tunisian days, was now commanding and Digby
Tatham-Warter was with them. He had escaped from the
hospital in Arnhem, was picked up by the Dutch Underground and, after an amazing series of escapades through
which he sauntered with his customary sangfroid, helped to
organize a mass evacuation of British prisoners from
enemy-occupied Holland to our own lines. On his return he
had written a report about the action at the bridge, in which
he told the story which had gained, rightly, the award of the
Victoria Cross to Jack Grayburn for his quite incredible
guts and devotion to duty during our battle. Tony Franks
was another survivor who had made his escape, and in
doing so helped many others. Gradually one picked up
other people's stories and discovered what had happened
to the rest of the division; I had only had gleanings and
rumours up till now.

I could not help twinges of jealousy at seeing someone
else commanding that which for so long had been mine, but
it was going to be some time before I was fit for duty. There
was, however, one thing I had to try, and that was to get
Airborne Forces to gather up their unfortunate members
who had been taken prisoner and whose one abiding desire
was to get back to their units again for active operations. It
is really quite easy to let things slip in captivity. The
Germans, when taking prisoners, were apt to say 'For you
the war is over', and many people took this literally. However, nearly all our 'Red Beret' men kept up their standards
throughout their time as prisoners, and I was now rather
disappointed that we were all just passed through the
normal machine. At Airborne Corps Headquarters I found
that fine old Airborne soldier, Lieutenant-General
Richard Gale, in command. But he and his staff were now
working night and day on operational matters which were
directly concerned with ending the war as soon as possible,
and I soon realized that no one was going to be able to form
a welcoming party for the rather battered prisoners arriving in dribs and drabs.

In order to be passed fit again, I had to go back to
hospital for further treatment, galling though it was. Fortunately I was sent to Lincoln, which was quite near the 1st

Airborne Division's Rear Headquarters. Major-General Roy Urquhart, with his main headquarters and one brigade, was part of the force charged with liberating Norway, and I was offered command of the divisional Battle School there provided I could pass the medical. This was just the boost I needed, and in a remarkably short space of time I got a clean bill of health, reconnoitred in Norway, came back to gather a staff and set up the school at Trandum, some sixty miles north of Oslo.

1945 produced one of the loveliest summers for several years, and Norway was to be a most wonderful country to spend it in. The Norwegians did all in their power to make us welcome; most of them had a fair knowledge of English, and the social side of life could be almost overwhelming at times. Food and good liquor had been scarce for several years and, since we were now able to have liberal shares of the German Army spoils, our parties were more than popular. The Battle School was a great success. We had the use of a former German Army training ground, set in a quite lovely countryside of lakes and gentle hills. There were German prisoners to do all the hard work, which in fact they seemed to enjoy, performing their duties with all might and main. At first, our 'customers' at the school were mostly from the division, but soon we had Americans and Norwegians attending.

In this new job I was lucky enough to have Francis Hoyer-Millar as my adjutant. One of the old hands of the 2nd Battalion, with Tunisia, Sicily, Italy and Arnhem under his boots, he had Foreign Office inclinations and languages came to him easily. As our Intelligence Officer, he had been able to interrogate any Germans we caught in Tunisia; Italian was soon mastered in Italy, and now he must have been one of the very few British soldiers to try Norwegian. Pat Barnet, another Arnhem survivor, was our Quartermaster.

This idyllic phase came to an end in autumn, when we sailed home with the rest of 1st Airborne Division to be told that disbandment was the next item on the programme. The 1st Parachute Brigade was to remain intact and be transferred to the 6th Airborne Division, currently earmarked for Palestine (as Israel was then called before the ending of the British mandate there), where there was considerable civil disorder. I was suddenly called back to reassume command of my old 2nd Battalion, then stationed at Bulford, and shortly after this met Jean, my wife-to-be who, as a member of the Y.M.C.A., was driving tea vans around the units of the division.

I found many wartime survivors with the battalion, which was in excellent shape. Peacetime accounting was by now in force, bringing with it many long-forgotten procedures of a bygone age; one wondered how we would settle down after the excitements of the last few years. It had often been said that a wartime soldier was not always so good in peace, but we were determined to reach and maintain the best possible standards. In any case, Palestine was not going to be exactly peaceful. By 1946 two Jewish terrorist organizations, the Stern Gang and the Irgun Zvai Leumi, had been raiding British installations and perpetrating atrocities on Arabs and British soldiers, with the aim of forcing a relaxation of restrictions on Jewish immigration, and of preventing an Arab/Jewish partition of the country. These activities, on the whole, were supported by the rest of the Jewish population, and a most unpleasant atmosphere prevailed. British soldiers came in for their full share of disfavour, and the Airborne Division, in particular, was labelled as fascist. The rights of the indigenous Arab population were considered irrelevant by the terrorists and their supporters, and elsewhere in the world we, the peacekeepers, were vilified. Anyway, as usual in such circumstances, British soldiers grinned and bore it. Their traditional good humour often succeeded in breaking through the wall of hatred surrounding them.

1st Parachute Brigade was the last element of the division to leave the U.K., in the early spring of 1946, and by then Jean and her Y.M.C.A. unit had already left with the Divisional Headquarters. From her letters back to me, it all sounded as though it was great fun. Then one morning I was listening to the wireless and heard that the Irgun had carried out a raid on our base at Sarafand, and that a British woman welfare worker had been very seriously wounded. No name was given, but somehow I knew only too well who it was—a call to her parents confirmed my fears. Apparently, Jean had been looking out of a window on hearing the firing and a bullet had come through the wooden wall of the house she was in and pierced her stomach. Fortunately Sarafand contained the major hospital for the area, and she was brought into intensive care without delay, but there were many anxious days ahead. The face I saw when I arrived several days later was very different to the one that had left England, but there was no question of defeat and every day brought strength, even though another operation had to be borne.

When properly fit to travel, Jean sailed home while I remained for a few months of that rather tedious activity known in the Army as Internal Security. By now I had been selected for the Staff College and so, in the late autumn of 1946, I handed over command of the battalion with which I had been so intimately concerned for so long. At any rate, I could look back with much pride and pleasure on having served at such times with such men, and nothing that could happen in the future could ever take that away.

The year at the Staff College went by in a flash, not easy to describe even if one wished to. It is enough to say that I emerged as keen to be a staff officer as I had been to be a commanding officer, and I now embarked on a series of staff and command appointments which kept me busy and contented for the rest of my career. Now at last Jean and I were able to marry, and it so happened that the only suitable day was the last day of December 1947, my thirty-fifth birthday. My ankle wound had been giving trouble for some time, and the first day of the honeymoon found me in the Millbank hospital for yet another operation—I think that at that time I was the first patient to go in and out on the same day as his operation.

CHAPTER 18

Representation

Arnhem has become almost a spiritual home to many of those who fought there, and to the relatives of those who died. Many people attend the Annual Pilgrimage, and now visitors come from all over the world throughout the year.

The first official act of remembrance, in 1945, was the erection of a monument by the Dutch at the north end of the bridge. This is a part of a stone column taken from the ruins of the Palace of Justice, bearing the simple inscription '17 September 1944'. I was very proud to be asked to speak at this ceremony and now each year, during the pilgrimage, a procession forms up at the Main Provincial Government Building and marches silently to the monument, where wreaths are laid whilst honours and respects are paid. Since that first occasion, a plaque describing the battle in outline has been installed on the bridge in a small building similar to the pillbox, and more recently, since the bridge has been renamed the 'John Frost Bridge', another plaque has been placed above the steps which lead pedestrians on to the bridge.

The noise from the volume of traffic now using the bridge makes it difficult for anyone to describe the battle from either place, while the rebuilding of the ruins at the north end in forms different from those we remember makes it hard to visualize the scene during those hectic days of September 1944. Perhaps the picture painted by David Shepherd, which now hangs in the Officers' Mess of the 2nd Battalion, the Parachute Regiment, conveys the actuality as well as could be. I was able to help the artist by revisiting the site with him while he was painting, and we have to be eternally grateful to the R.A.F. Spitfire pilot who photographed the bridge during the battle (see illustration section following p. 206) to bring back proof of our success against the German Recce Squadron in the early stages. The ground immediately to the south of the bridge, which is today heavily built up, was typical Dutch farmland in 1944.

The focal point of the divisional battle was the Divisional Headquarters at Hartenstein in Oosterbeek. It was from this solitary, medium-sized, yet in many ways imposing hotel that Major-General R. E. Urquhart conducted his classic defensive action for several days, before withdrawing back across the river with 2,000 soldiers. This building is now the Dutch Airborne Museum, which has a wealth of relics, photographs, tableaux and models. Quite near, across a stretch of grass, is the memorial to mark the division's battle, but this is overshadowed—perhaps rightly—by the war cemetery some few hundred yards away.

It is here that the main event of the annual pilgrimage takes place. The site and its surroundings have been most carefully chosen, and the whole precinct is kept immaculate and treated with devoted care. Every year the crowds increase. The traffic has become so dense that most vehicles have to be stopped a considerable distance from the gates, and if one loses one's companions for a moment it is very hard to find them again. However, all in good time the leaders are assembled near the dais, from which the padres conduct the services alternately in Dutch and in English. The ambassadors of Great Britain and Poland arrive just before the representative of H.M. the Queen of the Netherlands.

And so to the service, short but very moving. The hymn music is the same for all three nations, and the lesson is read in English by the ex-Airborne officer leading the pilgrimage. He is usually one who played a fairly prominent part in the battle, and some have reached high rank in the Army since then. On the thirtieth and thirty-fifth anniversaries General Roy Urquhart officiated, and it is much to be hoped that he and other veterans will still be here for the

fiftieth in 1994. On the thirty-fifth, H.R.H. Prince
Bernhardt represented the Queen of the Netherlands, and
charmed everyone with his gracious and easy manner.

At the end of the service, Dutch children from the local
schools lay flowers on each individual grave. There is something very moving about this simple act that those who have
seen it never forget. Finally, after the National Anthems,
wreaths are laid on the memorial, and then, slowly and
quietly, everyone moves away.

There are many other events during the pilgrimage
weekend and each year our friendships with the people of
Arnhem and of Oosterbeek are re-cemented. We can
never cease to marvel that there should be no resentment at
all the damage that was done to the lovely riverside towns
we were unable to hold. Having so suddenly raised their
hopes of liberation, we had to abandon these people to
suffer eviction from their homes with the subsequent loss of
all their much-prized possessions. Those who willingly
risked so much to help us stood in constant fear of savage
reprisals from a ruthless foe, and yet each year they meet
us, the cause of so much misfortune, with loving welcome
and comfort still.

There came a time when difficulties arose over the
attendance and representation of our Polish allies. Those
who had fought with us were mainly U.K.-based, and the
attendance of the present-day communist hierarchy from
Warsaw hardly seemed consistent with the presence of
those who had fought for freedom alongside us. Indeed,
this difficulty almost brought the pilgrimage to an end, and
for a year or two official British Airborne support was
minimal. This, however, was quite unacceptable to Dutch
people, British veterans and the next of kin of all concerned. Support or no, large numbers were determined
that they wanted a pilgrimage and that a pilgrimage there
would be. A 'Lest We Forget' Society was formed to boost
and galvanize where necessary, and all the branches of the
Old Comrades' Association found ways and means of
having members in that place where they would always
want to be on the weekend around 17 September.

Down by the river stands the old Dutch Reform
Church of Oosterbeek, which was a bastion in the defence

of the perimeter. It was near this that the route of the retreating remnants of the division lay as they passed in the darkness and the rain. The building has been restored to the similarity it has borne for centuries, and each year the sharing of the services with our Dutch brethren brings warmth. Next door is the home of the Ter Horst family, used as a dressing station during the battle until it was completely destroyed. It seems invidious to mention any Dutch names, for there are so many who have done so much for us for so long that it would be heinous to omit any of them. In those few square miles live people who will have a place for ever in many British hearts.

Many accounts have been written about the battle of Arnhem and, on the whole, the authors tell the same story. Some have gone into considerable detail, with maps purporting to show the exact positions held by sub-units during their various actions. There has been time enough for people to check these, though the original operations maps, which never were very accurate, may have misled the writers in some instances. However, it was the publication, in 1974, of Cornelius Ryan's *A Bridge Too Far* that really brought the battle to the notice of a worldwide readership.

Connie Ryan had already produced two bestsellers when he began work on 'The Bridge'. He never claimed to be a meticulous historian, but made history come to life by combining the memories of as many participants as was reasonably possible so as to provide a vivid and immediate picture of a battle. The detailed research involved was fantastic, and wherever possible stories were checked and counter-checked; individuals, however, often have a very limited view of a battle at the time but very firm convictions afterwards. Inevitably inaccuracies and exaggerations creep in, yet most of the participants would accept the Ryan version. For the first time, the British public was made aware of the supremely important part played by the two American airborne divisions, for this had been given scant attention in our press reports at the time, as well as in later British accounts, and it now appeared that the American press had been denied the facilities given other journalists. We had been given to understand that the key

Nijmegen Bridge had been captured by the Guards
Armoured Division, and the saga of the river crossing by
U.S. 82nd Airborne in daylight against most formidable
opposition was left untold.

Sadly, Connie Ryan was to die of cancer soon after his
book was published, but by then both he and his wife,
Kathie, had become well known to many in Airborne
Forces, for they had exactly the right approach. In September 1975 Jean and I, with a number of Dutch people,
were invited to New York to help in publicising the arrival
of 'The Bridge' in paperback form. There were many
parties, and we had great fun. The key item was the press
reception at the Waldorf, where the Ryan organization had
pulled out all the stops. They waited with bated breath for
the outcome. It turned out to be a huge success, for there in
pride of place in the *New York Times* was the article which
made the whole expensive exercise well worthwhile.

By this time Joe E. Levine, one of the great American
film producers, had decided to tackle 'The Bridge'. He had
engaged a host of super stars, a crack script writer, William
Goldman, and Richard Attenborough as the director. On
20 September 1975 we were invited to Joe Levine's seven-
tieth birthday party at his house at Greenwich, which I can
only describe as fabulous (Jean wrote down a description
while it was fresh in her memory and has been able to give
talks about it since). I was just left with the impression that
nothing was too much trouble and there would never be a
party quite like it again.

Before long Joe was in Europe. He came to lunch at my
club, and produced a most fantastic list of equipment
wanted. I was able to put him in touch with the Ministry of
Defence, who were extremely helpful throughout. Then he
set off in a helicopter to find a bridge over a river in Holland
that would resemble the Arnhem bridge, which could not
be available for filming because of the traffic load. He spied
the bridge over the Ijssel at Deventer, some twenty miles
north of Arnhem, decided that this would just about do,
and then set about fixing things. There was considerable
discussion as to who should be the military adviser, a job
that meant being involved with the film for six months. In
the event, Colonel John Waddy was given the necessary

leave by his firm, Westland, the helicopter makers. He was an ideal choice: a dedicated Airborne soldier who had been the Parachute Regimental Colonel and had also commanded the S.A.S., he was infinitely painstaking and patient. He earned and deserved the confidence of all concerned while doing a job which produced unimaginable difficulties as day followed day.

As I knew that I would be involved as a consultant for the bridge sequences, I was most anxious to see the script before it was finalized. I had been told that the script was the film maker's bible and that once it was fixed it could not be undone. As the time of filming approached and I was still uninformed, I became more and more anxious. It then so happened that, in February 1976, I was invited to lunch by the Prime Minister, Harold Wilson, at No. 10 Downing Street—the Dutch Cabinet were visiting and it was thought that I could help to amuse them. After lunch Lady Falkender, the Prime Minister's famous press secretary, approached me and said, 'I hear that you will be concerned with the film *A Bridge Too Far*. The Prime Minister is very keen that we should do all we can to help. Have you anything to suggest?'

I then told her about our difficulties in getting a look at the script and she said she was sure that she could arrange things. Two days later, my copy arrived.

Well knowing how the views of American script writers and film producers differ from our own more mundane outlook, I was agreeably surprised as far as the bridge chapters went. I had only one adamant objection—to the treatment given to an incident when the Germans sent one of our own captured sappers back to me with a message to the effect that, as we were in such a hopeless position, would I personally meet the German commander, under a flag of truce, to discuss surrender.

I said, 'Tell them to go to hell.'

Sergeant Halliwell, the sapper, replied, 'Do I really have to go back to tell them?'

I answered, 'No. It is up to you. If you would like to stay and continue fighting, they will get the message anyway.' He stayed.

The film script, however, demanded that I (or rather the

actor playing me) should actually meet the German general
and tell him that I had no room for him or his soldiers as
prisoners, and so he would have to continue fighting. Mag-
nificent cinema, perhaps, but so divorced from reality that
it was laughable.

In the end a very unsatisfactory and most unrealistic
compromise was reached, in which one of 'my' officers
sarcastically informed the Germans that 'we' could not
accept their surrender. A few years later, when I asked
Major-General Heinz Harmel, the G.O.C. of the 10th S.S.
Panzer Division, what he and the Germans thought of the
film, he mentioned this particular episode as being quite
ridiculous.

I went to Deventer in Holland for my stint as a consultant
during the lovely month of May 1976. When I arrived on
the set, Anthony Hopkins was dressed up to look like me
and was commanding my battalion with cameras and arc
lights in full support. It was an odd feeling, not at all
pleasant. I felt very, very passé. The fact that I had held the
stage a long, long time ago was forcibly brought home now.
I did not feel at all in tune with the actor; indeed I almost
disliked him, and I believe that this was mutual. I was sure
that I was putting him off, and suggested this to Richie
Attenborough, who would have none of it and insisted on
me remaining on the set. Film making is a long and tedious
business with endless rehearsal, rearrangement, correction
and repetition—as Richie himself said, 'Over and over and
over again'.

But gradually one could see it all taking shape, and I
almost began to feel myself in the actor's place. The more
familiar his face and figure became, the more I came to
accept him. It was fascinating to watch the director working
it all out, not actually asking me anything but perhaps
glancing my way from time to time so that I was not sure
whether I was being of any use or not. Suffice it to say that I
came to like myself as portrayed, and grew to admire
Anthony Hopkins, as I also came to like the acting of the
extras playing my soldiers. I soon began to feel that they
really were my men. When I met them off the set they often
asked, 'How are we doing? Are we looking like your
chaps? Did you have time to shave? Did they clean their

boots?' As each day passed, the feeling grew—in fact occasionally I nearly checked a man for not saluting.

There were times when the film was going with all stops out when I felt horribly that this had all happened before. What on earth was I doing here?

The premiere in London was a unique experience in itself. I had identified so completely with the company, the producer, the director, the actors, and everyone else concerned that I was on tenterhooks perhaps just as much as any of them. I wondered what my friends were thinking, what the audience thought, how the critics would react, what coverage the press would give and, finally, what did I think myself? There had to be regrets, of course, and these were for omissions and misrepresentations, almost inevitable in a film of this tremendous proportion. The actual real-life parts of Digby Tatham-Warter and Graham Warrack, both of crucial importance in the battle, were slurred so as to become of little account. With the time and space available, one had to accept that there would have to be a certain amount of cannibalization of characters to overcome the problem, but such expedience left a void.

At the end most people were left a little breathless, and perhaps somewhat confused. It was rather long and very noisy, but then war is a very noisy business. The film did not have quite the success that was hoped for, but one feels that it will last and perhaps become more appreciated as time goes by. At any rate it was a most prodigious effort.

CHAPTER 19

Last Thoughts

I had been pleased and proud to have been given the most important task at Arnhem, though I felt that the capture of all three of the town's bridges was a tall order for one battalion. I disliked having my battalion split by the river obstacle because it is always difficult to exercise control in such circumstances. However, it was obviously going to be important to have people on both sides, so I prepared to pass 'C' Company across over the railway bridge on our way into Arnhem.

We had not been told that there was a ferry at Driel, though the capture and subsequent operation of this would have been an ideal task for some of the Royal Engineers. The failure of the planners at all levels to identify and make use of this useful asset is hard to understand.

When I saw the railway bridge blow up, although I knew it was going to make the capture of the south end of the main bridge very difficult, I was relieved to know that I would now have 'C' Company on the north side of the river. I felt that, provided we could take and hold on to the north end, our own ground troops should have a comparatively easy task to take the south.

Freddie Gough's Reconnaissance Squadron had been ordered to seize the main bridge by *coup de main*. Several things went wrong with this attempt, but in any case this unit was not designed to seize and hold. It was trained and equipped to be the eyes and ears of the division. When communications failed to work, General Urquhart felt he had to go forward personally to see the form and was subsequently separated from his headquarters for several vital hours. This was an airborne operation being carried out by specially trained airborne troops: if a *coup de main* for the bridge was needed, then it should most certainly have been done by airborne means. Although the air force planners jibbed at risking large numbers of transport aircraft for the main assaults because of the anti-aircraft threat, they should never have denied the use of the relatively small number of aircraft needed for such a *coup*. There were successful examples as precedents, in particular the capture of Pegasus Bridge in Normandy.

The failure of our wireless communications at all levels was a tremendous disadvantage. There is always a problem with an airborne formation, because there can never be a guarantee that the sets, though carefully netted at the home base, are going to work well in another country, after a hefty bump on landing and when the batteries may have run down a little. The normal ground formation can walk or drive forward with the sets at least tuned in and listening, if not actually working. Anyway, for most of the time during the battle, commanders at all levels were uninformed about what was happening outside their immediate area. It was the resulting thirst for information that caused the G.O.C. and the commander of the 1st Brigade to be stranded with a lone battalion headquarters on the crucial evening of the 17th—the D-Day. Had they been with their own headquarters, designed to enable them to command, other decisions might have been made. At any rate, a fatal order was to emanate from where they were. The 1st and 3rd Parachute Battalions were to halt for the night before continuing their efforts to break into Arnhem in the morning.

Excellent soldiers though the Germans might be, they had one major weakness in that they did not relish fighting by night. They placed great reliance on superior fire-power and used ammunition without stint. Once darkness came the fire effect was greatly reduced, and then was the time to advance upon them, to bypass them, to do what one wanted. These precious hours were wasted: the German soldiers might be resting, but their officers were not, and by the morning all the necessary arrangements would be in hand to thwart our subsequent efforts at manoeuvre.

Nevertheless, in the early hours the two battalions disengaged and moved independently towards our southern route to come to our aid. Major Peter Lewis, with his 'C' Company of the 3rd Battalion, had already managed to slip down the railway line in the darkness and was a most welcome addition to our force by the bridge. But alas, by that Monday morning there was a ring of German infantry and armour besetting us and, despite gallant efforts by the 1st and the 3rd Battalions, joined the next day by the 11th Battalion and the South Staffords, none was able to reach us.

Once the enemy were in position in houses from which they could fire straight down the streets that provided the only practical avenue of approach, there was little chance of success without artillery and tanks which, of course, we did not have. Efforts were made to reach us by moving through the back gardens but these were often walled off, while the enemy had armoured vehicles to bring up ammunition for an increasing number of tanks and self-propelled guns. A fully co-ordinated night attack might just possibly have found a chink, but it was the presence of the much experienced Waffen S.S. Panzer divisions that spelt doom for our venture as it had been planned.

Meanwhile, during most of Monday—D plus 1—the strongest brigade of the division was tied down securing the D.Z. 'Y' (see map, p. 213) for the 4th Brigade, due later that day. This dropping zone was even further away from the objective than D.Z. 'X', which we had already used, so that there was even more dispersion and more time would be lost before either of these brigades could be used to accomplish their aim. The division had been forced to accept the grave disadvantage of D.Z.s out on a limb for the initial stages, but, if it was going to be acceptable for the Poles to drop south of the river near the bridge on D plus 2, it was surely worth taking the risk of putting the 4th Brigade down there on D plus 1. This would have released the whole of the first lift to make for Arnhem on D-Day and if this had been properly handled, even despite the presence of the 2nd S.S. Panzer Corps, they would all have been ensconced in and around the town during that first night, and on both sides of the river. Even if it was then considered too risky to bring the 4th Brigade in on D plus 1, they could have come by night, or indeed dropped with the Poles a little later. At any rate, the whole emphasis would have been on the bridge, the *raison d'être* of our part of 'Market Garden'.

The difficulties that face an airborne formation commander and his staff are formidable, especially when the ground operations are fluid, and it would be miraculous if the planning were perfect. People have grown so accustomed to talk about the failure at Arnhem that they do not notice that it was the delay at Nijmegen and the subsequent failures elsewhere that brought the operation to an end. It is fashionable now to say that such operations could never be mounted again, but who knows? There was a time between the wars when our own General Staff considered that the tank had had its day. While we continue to have an airborne capability, we should have those who know how to use it working with those who may want to. Badly needed is an airborne cell located right beside an army commander, looking ahead with ideas for missions, able to lay on the maps and air photographs, knowing all availabilities of men and supplies, and never to be blinded with excuses from the air forces.

Few, if any, of those who stood at Arnhem Bridge in 1944 can have imagined that their lonely battle would ever become so famous. For some of us it was just another action which we thought would become part of a campaign; for others it was their first and last. I had never seen our men in better shape from the beginning to the bitter end. There was a high degree of professionalism in an atmosphere of calmness. Although one had to raise one's voice to make oneself heard above the din, there was no shouting. People just did their job, had something to eat, a bit of a rest and then back to business. With officers like Freddie Gough and Digby Tatham-Warter about, there was no lack of ribaldry and even tomfoolery (Digby's umbrella was a useful tool). This was Digby's first battle and I remember him asking, 'I would like to know if this is worse or not so bad as the other things you have been in?'

I think I replied, 'Difficult to say. In some ways it is worse and in some ways not. At least we have got food and water. It won't be so good when the ammunition runs out.'

Douglas Crawley's experienced outlook was a great boon. He was ever a man for taking the rough with the smooth. After we were both hit by the same bomb, he alleges that I said, 'There you go again. Always getting wounded. What a silly ass I was to come and talk to you in the middle of a battle.'

And it was wonderful to hear Francis Hoyer-Millar's voice ring out, just as he had had to take up the most unenviable position possible on the ramp of the bridge: 'Well, here we are, for better or for worse.'

Fighting to the last man and the last round may be almost impossible in modern war, although the Japanese were often near to managing it. After the ammunition for anti-tank weapons has gone, there is little to prevent enemy armour from approaching and crushing opposition with its tracks, or from pulverizing positions with its weapons from point-blank range. When the positions contain men who have already been wounded, it may be inhuman and even dishonourable for the yet unwounded to continue resistance when they no longer have the means of killing the enemy. When there were no buildings left to go to, our men dug weapon pits in the back gardens of the ruined houses, but it was difficult to site these with effective fields of fire. Digby Tatham-Warter and other officers were tireless in directing men to new positions as and when they could. They kept control right to the end so that, when the wounded were evacuated and despite the resultant improvement in the enemy's position, our men could go on fighting till they were physically overwhelmed.

'Fear will make even cavalry dig, and without tools', so the old saying goes. But fear is rather a dirty word in the best military circles, and is seldom if ever mentioned, yet, as an emotion experienced by everyone to a greater or lesser degree, it is a most potent factor in war. Many citations for gallantry include the words, 'He knew no fear', when it would be much truer to say 'He showed no fear', for it is the overcoming or the suppression of fear that is so often the crucial achievement in war.

Fear comes and goes so quickly that we soon forget what it was like, but intense fear can paralyse action or judgement and, worst of all, it can be contagious. In the British Army we are inclined to think that our traditions will enable us to overcome fear, but in this respect we confuse tradition with morale, for there is no guarantee that the regiment that fought well at Waterloo is always going to stand firm. High morale comes from confidence, through the leadership that has insisted on discipline, fitness and skills, but all will be in vain if the nation has failed to produce the right weapons for the task in hand.

At one period during the war, the inculcation of hatred for the enemy was a panacea fortunately discarded before the real battles began. Respect for him coupled with a professional determination to beat him comes naturally with actual experience. In battle fear is a constant companion, however brave we may be. We all have to find our own way to overcome it. I tried to make it all seem ridiculous and to insist to myself that I would never again present myself to such dangers if I survived the one I was in. But another voice said, 'There is nowhere else on earth to be but in the midst of 2 Para when there is a battle on.'

Index

Abdulilla, Amir, Regent of Iraq, 1939, 7; death, 1958, 15

A Bridge Too Far: Cornelius Ryan, book & film, xiii, 251–5

Abu George, at Rutba Wells, 1939, 6

Airborne Forces: JF's venture into, xiii; JF's views on the use of, xiv–xviii, 259; *see also* Frost, Maj.-Gen. John; Parachute Brigade; 1st Airborne Division; 1st Air Landing Brigade; 44 Parachute Brigade, T.A.; Glider Pilot Regiment; Indian Airborne Division; 6th Airborne Division; U.S. Airborne Division; U.S. 82nd Airborne Division

Albert Canal, Belgium, 198, 200

Alexander, Ian, P.B., at Tamera, 140

Alexander, Gen., views after Tamera, 168; in Tunisian campaign, 169; in First World War, 170

Algiers, N. Africa in 1942, 66, 80, 88, 103, 118, 120; in 1943, 168, 169, 170; hospitals in, 1943, 170–1

Allfrey, Gen. Charles, 117; at Tamera, 143; after Tamera, 165–6

Allied Forces Headquarters, Algiers, 1943, 118

Alton Priors, Wiltshire, 38, 41

American Airborne Divisions, casualties at Arnhem, xviii; *see also* British and Allied Units

Amesbury, *see* Figheldean

Apeldoorn, Holland, 224

Apulian Aqueduct, Italy, abortive attack on, 29–30

Arnhem; airborne landing at, 1944, xiii, 198–232, 248–51, 251–5 *passim*; summarized, xiv–xviii, 256–60; *see also* Frost, Maj.-Gen. John

Arnim, Gen. von, German commander, 116, 124

Arthur, Gordon, R.A.F., Iraq, 1939, 7

Ashford, Dick, P.B., i/c A Coy 2nd Btn, 67; at Oudna, 82, 83; on retreat from Oudna, 95; killed, 'Happy Valley', 115

Assyrians, *see* Iraq Levies

Atlas Mts, N. Africa, 71

Attenborough, Sir Richard, 252, 254

Attlee, Clement, Deputy P.M., after Bruneval raid, 56

Austrian Units: at Bou Arada, 122; casualties in, 124

Aziz, kennelman of 'Royal Exodus', Iraq, 1939, 8

Barletta, Italy, 190

Barnet, Pat, P.B., 245

Barry, Peter, P.B., 212

Battle of Britain, 1940, 13

B.B.C., in POW camp, Germany, 1945, 240

Béja, N. Africa, 103, 108, 111, 127, 129

Bisley aircraft, 71–2, 73

Bizerta, N. Africa, 66, 68, 107

Blida airfield, Tunisia, 74, 75

Bou Arada, N. Africa, 'Happy Valley', 116–24, 129

Boufarik, N. Africa, 118, 167, 169, 170

Bou Hadjeba, N. Africa, 101

'Bowler Hat', *see* 'Pimples, The'

Briggs, Bernard, P.B., at Arnhem, 222

British and Allied Units:
   Airborne forces, xii–xvi;
   Argyll & Sutherland Highlanders, 128;
   Black Watch, 25, 26;
   Cameron Highlanders, 26;
   Cameronians (Scottish Rifles), xii, xix, 16;
   Coldstream Guards, 104, 106, 135;
   Commandos, 18, 146;
   Derbyshire Yeomanry, 108;
   Durham Light Infantry, 184–5;
   Eighth Army, 66, 107, 153, 184–5, 188, 190, 201;
   5th Army, 190;

Note: Some Generals are so indexed without more detailed distinction of rank.

Stackpole Military History Series

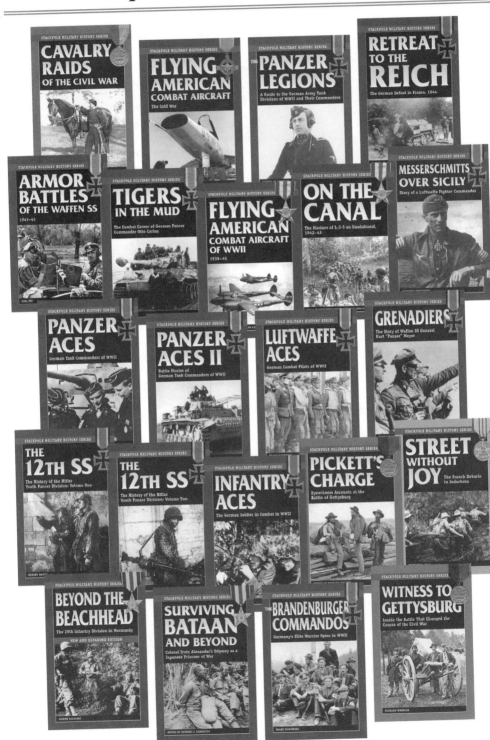

Real battles. Real soldiers. Real stories.

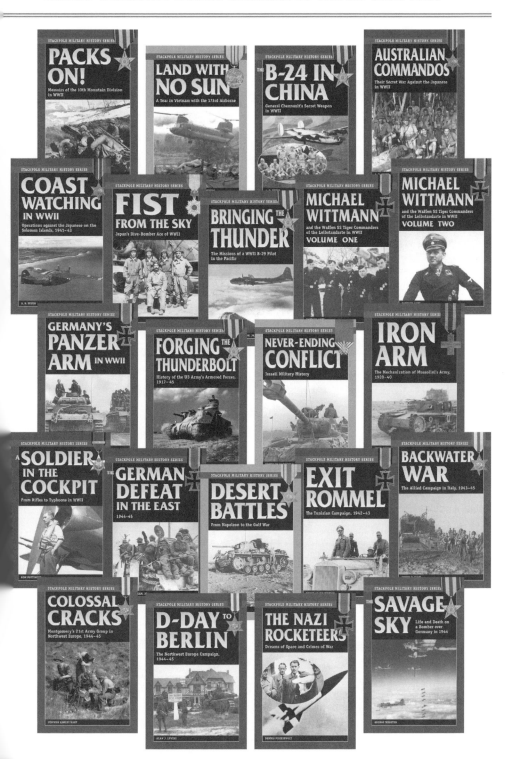

Stackpole Military History Series

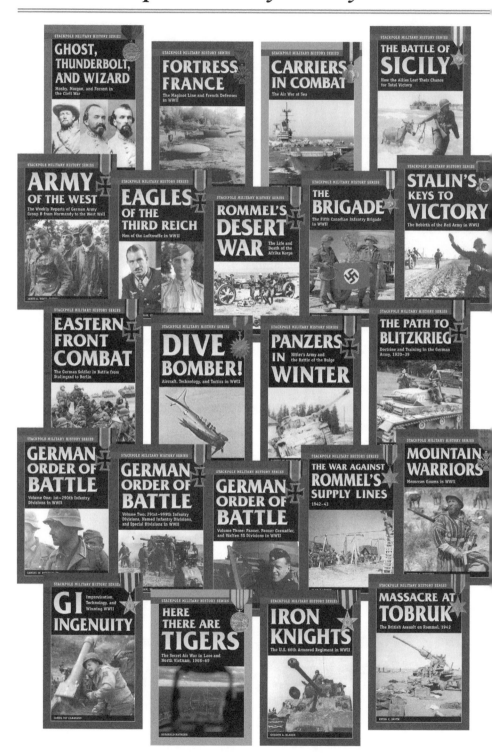

Real battles. Real soldiers. Real stories.

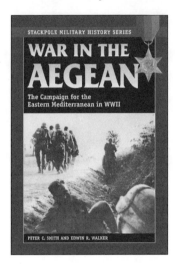

Stackpole Military History Series

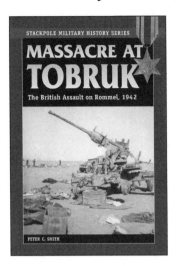

MASSACRE AT TOBRUK
THE BRITISH ASSAULT ON ROMMEL, 1942
Peter C. Smith

By September 1942, Erwin Rommel's Afrika Korps stood
perilously close to breaking through to Cairo and the Nile.
The Desert Fox had captured Tobruk three months earlier
and turned the city into a vital Axis supply port. In a
desperate attempt to halt the Germans and buy time for the
Allies, the British launched a daring amphibious raid on
Tobruk, combining forces from the Royal Marines, Royal
Navy, SAS, Long Range Desert Group, and other secret
units. Boldly conceived and bravely conducted, the assault
nevertheless failed with terrible losses.

$16.95 • Paperback • 6 x 9 • 272 pages • 38 photos, 2 maps

WWW.STACKPOLEBOOKS.COM
1-800-732-3669

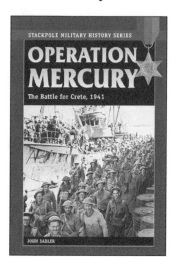

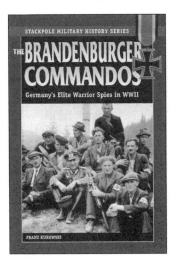

Stackpole Military History Series

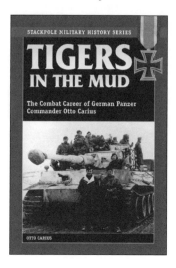

TIGERS IN THE MUD

THE COMBAT CAREER OF GERMAN PANZER
COMMANDER OTTO CARIUS

Otto Carius,
translated by Robert J. Edwards

World War II began with a metallic roar as the
German Blitzkrieg raced across Europe, spearheaded
by the most dreadful weapon of the twentieth century:
the Panzer. Tank commander Otto Carius thrusts the
reader into the thick of battle, replete with the
blood, smoke, mud, and gunpowder so common
to the elite German fighting units.

$19.95 • Paperback • 6 x 9 • 368 pages
51 photos • 48 illustrations • 3 maps

WWW.STACKPOLEBOOKS.COM
1-800-732-3669

Stackpole Military History Series

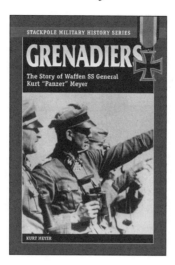

GRENADIERS
THE STORY OF WAFFEN SS GENERAL
KURT "PANZER" MEYER
Kurt Meyer

Known for his bold and aggressive leadership, Kurt
Meyer was one of the most highly decorated German
soldiers of World War II. As commander of various
units, from a motorcycle company to the Hitler Youth
Panzer Division, he saw intense combat across Europe,
from the invasion of Poland in 1939 to the 1944
campaign for Normandy, where he fell into Allied
hands and was charged with war crimes.

$19.95 • Paperback • 6 x 9 • 448 pages • 93 b/w photos

 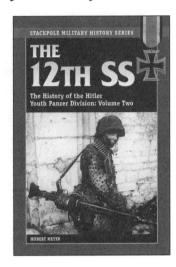

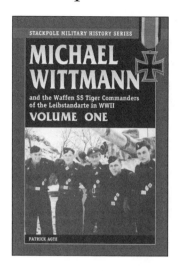 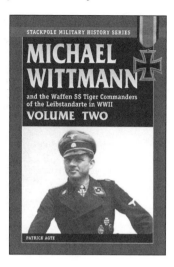

Stackpole Military History Series

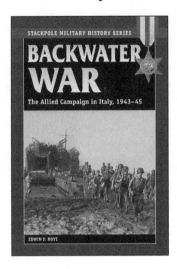

BACKWATER WAR
THE ALLIED CAMPAIGN IN ITALY, 1943–45
Edwin P. Hoyt

Following the fight for Sicily, the battle shifted to Italy in September 1943 with Allied landings at Salerno and Taranto. They pressed inland only to encounter unexpectedly stiff German resistance. Not until June 1944—after landing at Anzio in January and subsequently destroying the monastery at Monte Cassino—did the Allies finally break the German line and capture Rome. By then the invasion of France had overshadowed the Italian campaign, ensuring that its final ten months would indeed be a backwater war.

$16.95 • Paperback • 6 x 9 • 272 pages • 26 b/w photos

WWW.STACKPOLEBOOKS.COM
1-800-732-3669

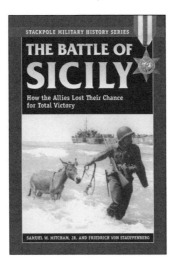

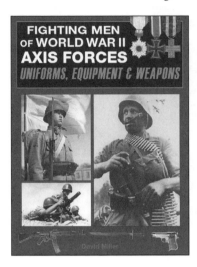
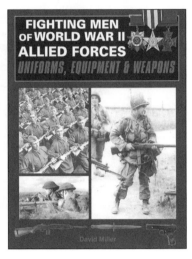